Searching for Home

Margaret G. Hanna

Print ISBNs

Amazon print 9780228625902
BWL Print 9780228625919
Ingram Spark 9780228625926
Barnes & Noble 9780228625933

Copyright 2023 Margaret G. Hanna
Cover by Michelle Lee

All rights reserved. Without limiting the rights under copyright reserved above, no part of this publication may be reproduced, stored in or introduced into a retrieval system, or transmitted, in any form, or by any means (electronic, mechanical, photocopying, recording, or otherwise) without the prior written permission of both the copyright owner and the publisher of this book

Dedication

*To Brave Women Everywhere
who Left the Known For the Unknown*

Acknowledgement

Every writer needs a supportive community. The Airdrie Writers' Group has been exactly that. I so appreciate their comradeship and support in what can be a solitary, and sometimes tear-your-hair-out, endeavour. Thanks especially to Ann Edall-Robson and Judy Dufort.

* * *

A tip of the hat to my Regina-based historian friends, Frank Korvemaker and Margaret Hyrniak. Our coffee-fueled conversations about the joys and challenges of historical research are invigorating and inspiring.

* * *

Thank-you to Jude Pittman of BWL Publishing for her patience as I struggled with Grandma Higham's story. Finally, a big thank-you to the anonymous editor of the Writers' Guild of Alberta and Nancy Bell of BWL Publishing, both of whom worked their magic and turned the manuscript into something worthy of publications. What would we authors do without editors?

Table of Contents

Part 1 7
Chapter One 7
Chapter Two 10
Chapter Three 18
Chapter Four 22
Chapter Five 28
Chapter Six 31
Chapter Seven 41
Chapter Eight 49
Chapter Nine 54
Chapter Ten 65
Chapter Eleven 81
Chapter Twelve 92
Chapter Thirteen 100
Chapter Fourteen 124
Chapter Fifteen 139
Chapter Sixteen 153
Chapter Seventeen 166
Part 2 178
Chapter Eighteen 178
Chapter Nineteen 182
Chapter Twenty 192

Chapter Twenty-One	203
Chapter Twenty-Two	212
Chapter Twenty-Three	216
1937	216
Chapter Twenty-Four	222
Chapter Twenty-Five	228
Chapter Twenty-Six	236
Chapter Twenty-Seven	248
Chapter Twenty-Eight	253
Chapter Twenty-Nine	262
Chapter Thirty	275
Part 3	285
Chapter Thirty-One	285
Chapter Thirty-Two	296
Chapter Thirty-Three	303
Chapter Thirty-Four	309
Historical Notes and Acknowledgements	311
Bibliography	314

Part 1
Sojourn

Searching for Home
Margaret G. Hanna

Chapter One
Beginnings

For the first 40 years of my life, I was from everywhere and I was from nowhere.

I moved, following first my father, then my employer and finally my husband from one continent to another, one city to another, one farm to another. Three times, though, *I* chose to move, to leave behind the known and move forward into the unknown, into either failure or success, although usually it was a bit of both. I don't regret any of those decisions, even though the outcome wasn't always what I expected.

The first time I moved, it was because my parents wanted to leave the farm outside the village of Tinwald, near Christchurch, South Island, New Zealand, and return to England. I was four, almost five years old. It was 1890.

I didn't want to leave. Why would I want to leave my playmates? Why would I want to leave the farm where I had the run of the yard, where I played with puppies, tried to lure wild kittens from their hiding places in the stables and the hedgerows, and found all sorts of treasures – pretty pebbles, bright feathers, a strange-shaped leaf – in the bush around the farm?

I don't know what my younger sister Amelia and my even younger brother – my only brother – George thought, if they thought anything at all. All I cared was that I did not want to leave the only home I knew for some distant unknown place called England.

So I ran away. I ran away from home so I wouldn't have to leave home.

My escape was short-lived. I made the mistake of running through the pasture, scattering the sheep before me, "like the Red Sea parting before the Israelites," Mother said whenever she recounted the story. The flock's frantic bleating alerted my father who was soon in hot pursuit, yelling, "Mary, get back here! Now!" I only ran faster, fearing punishment if I were caught.

But I was caught. I tripped and fell flat on my face. Father grabbed me, turned me over his knee, gave me a sound spanking, and then slung me over his shoulder like a sack of grain. I kicked and pummelled his back with my fists all the way back to the house. "You can't make me leave!" I cried, but they did.

I ran away again, the morning we were to leave Tinwald for Lyttelton, the port at Christchurch, a two-day journey by horse and wagon. They discovered I was missing when Mother yelled at me, "Look after that screaming brother of yours!" I was nowhere to be found. She made Father stop loading the last of our possessions onto the wagon to search. An hour later, they found me, hiding behind one of the haystacks. I received another spanking.

The four-month sea voyage by sailing ship back to Cornwall, England, is a blank space in my memory but I vaguely remember arriving at a gloomy, cold, rain-soaked world of stone buildings crammed together. Once again, according to Mother, I ran away, back to the dock while Father was busy haggling with the inn landlord over the room and the price, and while Mother was trying to shush tired and cranky Amelia and George. Up and down the quay I went, asking the same question of every sailor, "Are you sailing for New Zealand? Can I go with you? That's where I live, I don't live here. Mother and Father can stay here if they want but I'm not going to. I hate this place. I want to go back to New Zealand. Please can I go with you?"

I heard Father call, "Mary!" and I hid behind a stack of crates. He found me and dragged me out. "Don't you ever do that again!" he yelled as he turned me over his knee for yet another spanking. He clapped me under his arm and carried me back to the inn.

"You always were willful," Mother said.

My husband says I still am.

Chapter Two
Feock

My parents had grown up in Cornwall, England, Father in St. Keverne and Mother in Feock. Each arrived in New Zealand under different circumstances. Father had been sent there as a remittance man in 1880 by his father, supposedly for having had "unseemly relations" with one of his father's maids. Or so the rumours said. Mother arrived in New Zealand in 1884 under the immigration program that provided free passage, and better wages than were paid in Cornwall, for experienced tradespeople and domestic servants. They found themselves working on the same farm just outside Tinwald, Father as a horse trainer, Mother as a cook.

They say they fell in love. They were married on January 31, 1885, and I was born barely nine months later. Amelia, the first of my five sisters, was born the following year, and two years thereafter, my brother George.

I don't know what they saw in each other or, more accurately, what Mother saw in Father. They were chalk and cheese.

Father was certainly not his father's son. Dr. George Appleton was a highly respected and influential person in the Land's End region of Cornwall, a man of energy and ambition. He sat on various boards, invested in a luxury hotel, gave sonorous presentations and was instrumental in founding a library. His voice carried weight.

My father was none of that. He was content with being a horse trainer. His biggest ambition was to be a farmer. It was probably just as well he did not study medicine as his father wished. He would have made a terrible physician, not for lack of knowledge – he was a smart, even cunning man – but for lack of sympathy. He saved his sympathy and patience for livestock, especially his horses. He spent hours grooming them and worried whenever one was ailing. It was a different story with people; then he was curt, and that is putting it kindly, unless they were horse people. He talked with those people for hours, or so it seemed, debating the finer points of different horse breeds. Sometimes I think he wished his daughters were fillies instead of people, he might then have been more sympathetic to our desires and hopes. He was different with George, but then George loved horses.

Mother was the one with ambition. Never mind that she was the daughter of a shipwright, that her brothers were fishermen smelling of oysters and the sea and nets, that her mother was illiterate and her sisters, washerwomen. She proudly proclaimed to anyone who would listen, and even to those who didn't want to listen, that her uncle was the famous William "Foreman" Ferris, the designer and builder of the *Rhoda Mary*, the fastest schooner sailing the English coast. She boasted of being related, although she never explained how, to the wealthy Lemon family of Truro who counted tin mining magnates, members of Parliament, philanthropists, and prominent businessmen among their members. She insisted she was a "lady;" she certainly had pretentions of being one and insisted on being treated like one. That attitude rubbed off on her daughters. On me.

Father claimed he was the one who decided we should return to England, but I suspect Mother prodded him into doing so. She had nothing good to say about New Zealand. Whenever Father reminisced about life there, Mother would snort (most unladylike), "Harumph! An uncivilized land fit only for the Natives, and best we give it back to them." Sometimes, she'd admit, "At least it isn't populated by convicts, like *Australia*." She always sneered out "Australia." I think Father would have been quite happy to stay there, training horses, probably even buying a farm there.

We left the only home I had known in September 1890, New Zealand's green and balmy spring, and arrived in Plymouth, Cornwall in December, the depth of

England's cold, damp and dreary winter. Is it any wonder I hated Plymouth? After having had the run of a New Zealand farm, life in a city was constrained and bleak. There were no fields to run in, no garden to grow vegetables and flowers in, no kittens or puppies to play with, no mysterious places to explore. Instead of grass and trees, there were only cobblestone streets and stone and brick buildings. Instead of the smell of horses and sheep enfolded in the warmth of stables and the dank smell of the tussock land, there was only the stench of sewage and manure and garbage in the streets. Instead of the bleatings of sheep and the whisper of wind in the trees, there was only the continual clank and clatter of wagons and carriages, the shouting of hawkers, and the babble of crowds of people pressing against each other and the confines of the buildings around them.

Father rented a small flat in a miserable street and tried to find employment. Mother constantly nagged him to find us a proper house, to which Father replied that he could not afford any house in Plymouth as he was saving to buy a farm. It was an unpleasant time. After a month or so, Mother won the argument and we moved to Feock.

We were three days on the road, three grey, cold, damp, bone-jarring, mud-spattering days by coach, Father riding on top with our meager belongings (he saved a few precious pence that way) and we inside, Mother, her belly prominent with an expected baby, trying in vain to keep Amelia, George, and me from killing each other out of boredom. We were more than bored. We were hungry. Father bought what little food he could afford – boiled eggs and pasties and ale – from the inn each morning, but the basket was emptied long before we reached the next night's inn. Hunger may improve one's appetite, it only worsens one's disposition.

Amelia and I exploded out of the coach when we reached Feock, George stumbling after us on his three-year-old legs and Mother yelling "Come back here, now!" I ran smack into an old man, bent and gnarled from work, from age, from weather, from arthritis. His fearsome appearance was augmented by his equally gnarled black walking stick. This was Grandfather Ferris. I eventually learned he was not as fearsome as he looked, merely old and worn out, with a laugh that boomed across the lane and a lifetime of stories to tell. We sat wide-eyed, clutching each other in terror, as he told tales of raging storms, battles between smugglers and the Royal Navy, ships and men dashed against the rocky Cornish coast, and giant sea monsters that sucked men and ships down into the deep, never to be seen again. He told those stories so vividly – we never questioned the truth of them – that we often relived them in our nightmares.

Grandmother Ferris was another matter. She, too, was old before her time due to years of hard work and too many children, but she was still a force to be reckoned with. Perhaps being encased in a tightly laced corset did that to her. She ruled the house as Grandfather Ferris had once ruled the shipyard. No wonder Mother turned out as she did, a firm adherent to the philosophies of "Spare the rod and spoil the child" and "Children should be seen and not heard." Unfortunately, she did not realize, or chose to ignore, that children learn their ways from their parents, and we learned from her (and Father, too) to speak our minds. Incessantly.

But Grandmother Ferris, like Grandfather, could tell stories. Hers were of fairies and little people and spectres roaming the moors. If Grandfather's stories warned us of the dangers of the sea, then Grandmother's stories warned us of the dangers of sacred places. The fairies and sprites who lived in certain hills or wells, or who protected certain trees, were real to her, and her stories made them real to us. We saw them everywhere, in every fleeting movement, even if it were only a branch blowing in the breeze. We learned to tread lightly and be wary, cautious of offending any invisible being.

We lived with our grandparents for several months until Father rented a cottage nearby on Cross Close. Till then, it was months of living underfoot, nine of us crowded into four rooms, we five in one bedroom, Amelia and

George and I crammed sardines-in-a-can-like into one little pallet while Mother and Father slept in the only bed, such as it was. It was even more crowded when sister Clive was born. Grandparents took the other bedroom and two uncles (Mother's unmarried fishermen brothers) slept on a pallet in a corner of the kitchen. It was a time of too many people living too close together, of scraping and scrimping, of quarrels and accusations, and of the smell of baby pee and spit-up, of wet nappies drying by the hearth, of unwashed bodies, of fish and strong tea and pipe smoke. No wonder Amelia and I escaped as often as we could, George always tottering behind crying at us to wait, to scamper along the streets, to hide in the hedgerows, to wander among the headstones of St. Feock's churchyard, to scavenge for shells and pretty pebbles on Loe Beach. They were days of freedom.

There's something about the smell of fish that brings back memories of Feock. Of Amelia and me roaming the streets unhindered by parental concerns aside from the occasional admonition (yelled at full volume) to "watch George." Of old people smelling of fish and wood and oakum, and telling stories of the sea and ships and wrecks and fairies and ghosts and wraiths on the moors. Of the slap-slap of waves on the shingle at Loe Beach below the village, the rhythmic clang-clang of rigging against masts, the mournful hoot of ships' whistles. Of feeling home.

We had the run of Feock until I started school in 1892. It was preceded by a parental argument that ran for days. Mother fumed, "No daughter of mine is attending a National School, only poor families of no account send their children there." Father retorted, "Fergodsakes, you bloody woman, we are poor, in case you haven't noticed. We cannot afford tuition for a private school. We can barely afford the tuition for the National School."

In the end, Father and the lack of money won out. Mother sulked.

I was unaware of being poor. What child is? But I knew what school was – prison. The room was cold and bleak. The teacher was a spinster, stern and strict, greying hair pulled back tightly from her face, her clothes old-fashioned and threadbare. She stood bolt upright and hit a long cane rhythmically against her hand as she walked back and forth at the front of the room and dictated the rules that would govern our young lives until we escaped. Sit upright! No slouching! Do not shuffle your feet! Be silent! Speak only when spoken to! Stand at attention when you speak! Punishment followed swiftly when we disobeyed. The first infraction brought a slap of the cane across the desk. The next, a slap across the back or the hand. Crying brought more blows. Occasionally, she placed a dunce cap on the offender's head and made him or her stand at the front of the class for hours.

I walked the three miles back home after the first day and announced, "I am not going to school any more!" My refusal to go to school earned me yet another sound spanking and a stern lecture from Father on the need for a basic education, even if I was only a girl. I obeyed, but I didn't change my opinion of school. I had to learn for myself the importance of an education, especially for a girl.

The schoolmistress unwittingly provided my escape, at least in my mind, by teaching us to read. Letters became words, words became sentences, and sentences became stories. Home was devoid of books, but school provided the Bible, the Prayer Book, a history of England and a geography of Cornwall.

The Bible was my favourite. What stories it contained! Stories of passion and heroism. Of Moses defying Pharaoh, Joshua bringing down the walls of Jericho, Elijah confronting Ahab and Jezebel, Jesus hounding the moneychangers out of the temple, Solomon sweeping the Queen of Sheba into his arms, Ruth winning the heart of Boaz and becoming the mother of a dynasty. I tangled those stories up with the ones the old folks told about fairies and ghosts, and created my own tales of pirates and smugglers and gallant soldiers and handsome highwaymen and damsels in distress to entertain my sisters and brother. They'd squirm with excitement, eyes wide open, mouths agape, even when they knew the hero would always save the day and win the heart and hand of the heroine.

Mother won the day when Father tried to take me out of school when I was ten. "She can read and write and do passable needlework, and we can use the money she could earn," he said. Mother put her foot down, hard. "Our daughters will be properly educated even if it is only at a National School. I will not have them live their lives as drudges like my mother did. And I will not have George become a common labourer at the whim of a fickle employer who gives not a fig about his well-being or his family's." The argument raged for days but, in the end, I stayed in school.

Father bought a horse and wagonette shortly after we moved into Cross Close. Twice a week – Wednesday and Saturday – he hauled people, goods and freight the five miles to Truro and back again, in all sorts of weather. He loved it. He was happiest with horses. He was not happy when three more children, all girls, arrived – the twins, Bessie and Maude, born in 1894 and Dorothy in 1895. "Seven children and only one is a son!" He blamed Mother. That caused more arguments.

Our financial situation improved to the point that in 1897, when I was twelve, Mother finally won the battle she had been waging. Amelia, George, Clive and I were enrolled at the not-a-National-School in Perran-ar-worthal, five miles away. "A proper grammar school at last," Mother boasted.

We protested. "Our friends are at this school." "We will have to walk farther." To no avail. The school may have met Mother's ideal of "good education" and "better families", but the discipline was the same. The teaching wasn't much better.

We walked the five miles every morning and every afternoon, the wind blowing fresh off Carrick Roads. Some days took longer than others because there was always something to divert us. We might stop to greet the carters and pat their horses; or watch lambs and calves and foals gambling in the pastures, or draft horses pulling ploughs through the fields, or cows plodding homeward to be milked, a farm boy close behind shushing them onward.

Our attendance there was short-lived, only four months, when Father finally achieved his dream of being a farmer, albeit a tenant farmer, with a ten-year lease of Higher Tregurra, just north of Truro. In the fall of 1897, we left the only home I remembered well, torn away from friends and family, from familiar sights and sounds and smells that had become part of me. I now knew better than to run away even though I felt homeless again.

Chapter Three
Higher Tregurra

George took to farm life like a duck to water. Mother did not. Neither did we girls, Mother made sure of that. "My daughters are ladies, not milk maids!" she declared.

I was starting to think of myself as a "lady" even though I didn't know what that meant if you lived on a farm. Didn't "ladies" live in manors? Dress in white linen? Sit on the terrace sipping tea from delicate bone china cups with their little finger crooked just so while watching a cricket match on the lawn? Swoon and faint in the heat? Marry a handsome and wealthy suitor, scion of an ancient aristocratic family, to live in another manor and breed another crop of "ladies?" Jane Austen said so.

We did not live in a manor, only an old stone house – the stone barn was twice the size of the house. We had no terrace, only an orchard and fields of corn and meadows of hay. We did not dress in white linen but in clothes we sewed ourselves by hand. Our tea cups may have been china but many were chipped with mismatched saucers. The only "Huzzahs" we heard were Father or the labourers shushing the cows to the milking barn. I felt cheated. So much for Jane Austen.

We may not have milked cows or dunged out the barns – George took great delight in doing that – but we still had chores. I looked after the twins and Dorothy while they were babies and toddlers. I helped Mother cook and clean house. I worked in the garden. Only when doing needlework did I feel like a lady, the image that Jane Austen and the Brönte sisters had conjured up in my mind.

I complained to Mother the day she ordered Amelia and me to scrub the hall floor. I drew myself up to full height and yelled, "Ladies don't do menial labour!" Mother gave me The Look – narrow eyes, pursed lips, hands on hips – and said, "Being a lady is a matter of attitude and bearing. Now scrub the floor." It was useless to argue with her, at least while we were children. That changed as we grew older, then we simply left.

Amelia, Clive and I were enrolled in the Truro Practicing School for Girls, a three-mile walk from the farm into Truro. "At least they will learn practical skills for when they're married," Father said. Mother was more concerned that we associated with girls from the "right families," although her beloved and supposedly related Lemon family did not send their daughters there, they attended the more prestigious and costly High School for Girls. We knew nothing of, and cared less about "right families" or even what were "practical skills" for marriage. We were too busy trying to create a place for ourselves among girls we did not know.

Our accent identified us as outsiders. Feock took great pride in being one of the last places where the Cornish tongue was spoken, and even though the last Cornish speaker died decades ago, echoes of it persisted in our grandparents' speech. We had lived there long enough for their distinctive voice to worm its way into ours, in spite of learning Standard English in school. The girls whispered and giggled every time we spoke. Clive was in tears at the end of the first day. "They're always picking on me, calling me names," she sobbed. It took several months before our Feock accent softened. Until then, we were confused and lonely. Amelia and I sobbed into our pillows every night.

Truro was bewildering, strange, huge, noisy and bustling. This was not small, comfortable Feock where we knew everyone and everyone knew us; where the green grocer and chemist knew Father would pay the bill, eventually; where the Ferris name held some sway. No, Truro brought back long-buried images of someplace – Plymouth, I presume, – hazy and indistinct but heart-in-your-throat dark and ominous. We were anonymous, unknown, just another face in the crowd.

Truro never did become home for me. I didn't have friends like in Feock because we lived apart on the farm. Once school was out for the day, there was no reason for us to stay in the school yard and chat with the other girls, we had to go back home to do our chores. My sisters became my friends. They still are, even though, other than Bessie, they live across the Atlantic or, in Amelia's case, on the other side of the world in Australia. I miss them. Letters are no substitute for their presence.

The Practicing School did not have classes in "How to Be a Lady," but it did give us girls an opportunity at a profession – teaching. Each morning, we had our usual classes in literature, geography, arithmetic, the dreaded French (unlike Dorothy, I never was any good at French, and Dorothy gloated when she received much better marks than I did), and the "domestic arts" of cooking, household management and needlework. Each afternoon, we older girls "practiced" what we had learned by teaching the younger girls.

Clive was not happy that I was occasionally her teacher. She complained to Mother: "Mary is bossy!" "She is putting on airs!" "She is not a real teacher." "She thinks she knows everything." I didn't think I was bossy and said so. I still don't think I am bossy, I just speak my mind, that's all.

I finished school in 1902. When I told Father I wanted to attend the Diocesan training college and become a certificated teacher, he scoffed. "Why should I spend money on a girl when you'll just get married? You should be working, earning money, not asking me to spend more on you. You already have a better education than your mother. What more do you want? Make yourself useful, go find employment."

For once, Mother could not persuade him otherwise. She offered a consolation prize of sorts, "Be a governess and teach children in their home."

My turn to scoff. "Never! Governesses are the lowest of the low. No one respects them, not even the scullery maid. They are paid next to nothing. I'd rather be a domestic servant, they're better paid."

The lease on Higher Tregurra ended in 1907. Father sold everything moveable, except his beloved horses, and moved the family to Penzance where he purchased a livery business. By then, I was long gone, working in Helston.

Chapter Four
Escape to Park Brawse

I was 20 the first time I met Grandfather Appleton. When we lived at Feock, we were only 27 miles from The Lizard where he lived but Father refused to visit. "Can't stand the old bastard, and he can't stand me, so what is the point?"

Father's anger had long roots. Grandfather Appleton had sent Father to a boarding school in Helston, which he hated. He had urged Father to follow in his footsteps and become a doctor; he refused. He shipped Father off to New Zealand as a remittance man. Whether or not the rumours for having had "carnal relations" with one of the maids were true, Father proclaimed that being sent to New Zealand "was the only good thing he's ever done for me, not that he ever sent money once I was there."

Shortly after returning to England, Father sent a note off to his father informing him he had returned and intended to take up farming. He laughed as he wrote it, "This will annoy him that his scandalous son has returned, and with a family in tow." No note came back, at least not that we ever saw.

I was 20, old enough to find employment, tired of being the "old" spinster daughter, and growing more weary of the tension between our parents. My only escape was to become engaged as a domestic servant but before I found a suitable position, Amelia came up with a different escape plan. Like me, she was finding our parents' constant bickering tiresome.

"Let's visit Grandfather Appleton," she whispered to me one night as we lay in our bed.

I rolled toward her, "How? We don't have the fare for the omnibus and Father won't give it to us."

Amelia paused, then I heard her snicker. "Mother will get it for us somehow, if only to annoy Father."

I don't know what she told Mother, and I know even less what Mother said to Father, but a week later she handed us a few shillings and pence, "For the fare and lodging and food, and not a word of this to your father. And I've sent a note telling your grandfather to expect you soon." We nodded our assent; we were only too delighted to part of a conspiracy. We whispered our plans to our sisters – but not to George who would certainly tell Father – and they agreed to keep our plan a secret.

The day we left, we announced loudly at the table that we were going into Truro to enquire about employment, and we probably would not return until the evening, all going well. Mother and our sisters received the news with a straight face. Father wished us success. "About time you started earning your keep," was all he said.

The jig was up when we did not return that evening, and Mother bore the brunt of Father's anger but she gave as good as she got, or so Bessie said. "Mother said not to fret, he will get over it eventually," she told me later.

Once on the omnibus, we giggled and laughed like school girls being truants from school. We were on our first adventure, and we intended to make the most of it. The tension drained away, we relaxed and chatted about nothing and everything, and gawked out the window at the scenery passing by.

We were surprised when Uncle Harry, and not Grandfather, met us at the inn. He greeted us warmly, "At last, I meet some of my nieces."

"Where is Grandfather?" we asked. Uncle Harry shook his head. "He is not well, he is dying of cancer, but he is very eager to meet you. It is all he has talked about this last week."

We drove westward towards the sea and the little village of Landewednack. I breathed in the soft sea air as if I was breathing in life itself. The only sounds were the clip-clop of the horse and its jangling harness, the occasional cow lowing in a pasture, and off in the distance the constant low rumble of the sea crashing into the craggy Cornish coast. Tears filled my eyes as memories of our life in Feock ran through my mind. I clasped Amelia's hand. "We are home again." She smiled and nodded.

Park Brawse, Grandfather Appleton's home, sat not far from the sea. Uncle Harry, also a surgeon, and Uncle Tom, who seemed to have no occupation that we could discern, lived there with him. Uncle Harry had warned us of Grandfather's appearance – the cancer was in his jaw which was now malformed – so we took great care not to be outwardly shocked. He, too, greeted us warmly and directed Miss Bray, the servant, to take our things to our room. Amelia whispered to me, "She is no older than you!"

Dinner proceeded well at first. We conversed about the gales that had flooded Yarmouth in January and how reconstruction was still underway; about the footballer Alf Common being paid £1000 (Uncle Harry thought he was worth it, Grandfather thought it outrageous); about the explosion in a colliery in Wales that killed so many (Cornish tin mines have killed just as many, Uncle Tom said); and Emmeline Pankhurst and the suffragettes disrupting a political meeting (how dare women poke their noses into men's business, all three men agreed).

Conversation became awkward when, during dessert, Grandfather asked, "What does your father say about your being here?"

Amelia and I looked at each other. I took a deep breath and squared my shoulders. "I daresay he is very angry."

Uncle Harry glanced at Grandfather. "He doesn't know you are here?"

Amelia laughed. "He does by now."

I broke in. "We told him we were going to Truro to enquire about employment."

Grandfather shook his head. "I see the fruit doesn't fall far from the tree."

I stabbed my spoon towards him. "If we had not, we would not now be here."

Amelia giggled. Uncle Tom laughed so hard he almost choked on his tea. After a brief awkward silence, Grandfather smiled. "Well said, Mary. And I am most delighted you are here. Now, if you will excuse me and your Uncle Harry, I am in need of some medication and then I will retire for the night. But please, make yourself at home."

And we did. For once, we were treated as we imagined ladies should be. We kept our bedroom tidy, but we did not cook, or do the washing up, or wash and iron our clothes, or any of the myriad of chores we did at home. Miss Bray did it all. Amelia and I were free to walk along the coast where we listened to gulls squawking and the ever-present crash and rumble of the English Channel beating against the cliffs. We watched the ships going by, and made up stories about where they were going or returning from, who was on them and what they had seen. We imagined ourselves sailing on one of them to some distant corner of the world. We felt the soft sea air; we smelled grass crushed beneath our boots, freshly turned fields and wild flowers growing in the meadows. We reminisced about our former happy-go-lucky life in Feock and talked about our hopes and dreams for the future. We laughed. We felt the tension drain from our very souls. We slept better than we had in months. We dreaded having to return to Higher Tregurra.

Uncle Harry saved me from that fate. He returned one day from examining some of his patients in Helston, and at dinner he asked me, "Are you still looking for employment." I assured him I was.

"Allow me to present you with an opportunity. Mr. Oxenham, the husband of one of my patients, told me their servant is about to leave for another position, so they are in need of a new servant especially while Mrs. Oxenham is recovering. I immediately recommended you as reliable and capable. I hope I didn't speak out of turn."

I couldn't believe my ears. "No, of course not, Uncle. That is very kind of you. Does Mr. Oxenham wish to interview me?"

"Yes, of course. I will send a note in the post immediately. He did say he would not pursue the matter further until he heard from me."

Thus it was, a week later, I found myself standing in Mr. Oxenham's drapers shop that advertised "Bespoke Dressmaking and Draperies." Customers and clerks bustled about, discussing patterns and sizes and dress lines. I smelled wool, cotton and silk fabric, and heard the tinkle of buttons being counted out, the thump-thump-thump of bolts of fabric being unrolled, and the snip of scissors. From somewhere in the back of the shop came the distinctive clacka-clacka of treadle sewing machines.

A clerk approached me, asking after my business, and when I told him I was here for an interview, he directed me to an office.

Mr. Oxenham rose as I entered and gestured to a chair. "Please, sit down, Miss Appleton. Your uncle spoke very highly of you."

I sat very straight, my hands clasped. I prayed my tapping foot would not betray my anxiousness. "I hope he did not make me out to be a saint."

Mr. Oxenham shook his head. "No, not that I recall, but he said you are very capable and have preliminary training as a teacher." He paused. "Let us go up. My wife wishes to interview you." He smiled. "You see, I may be in charge of this shop, but she is in charge of the house."

Their home was above the shop. Mrs. Oxenham, who seemed quite well enough, if a bit pale, was sitting in the drawing room instructing Janie, the maid, who curtseyed and withdrew as soon as we arrived. Mrs. Oxenham was a pleasant woman but direct and discerning. She questioned me closely on my training and experience, and I must have satisfied her because after an intense half-hour she rang Janie and told her to bring down the children. Amy, aged three, immediately ran to her mother and hid her face in her mother's skirts while little Francis squirmed in the maid's arms until she put him down and he tottered over to his mother. Mrs. Oxenham instructed Amy to curtsey to me. "Miss Appleton will be joining us soon, and you must obey her just as you obey Miss Williams." My heart skipped a beat. I was engaged.

I broke the news to all at Park Brawse. Uncle Harry merely nodded, "I knew she would hire you." Amelia was both happy and sad for me. "Now who will I scheme with?" I laughed. "You have Bessie and Maude and Clive, and I think even little Dorothy is up for a plot or two."

We returned to Higher Tregurra a week later. Mother was pleased I had found employment with a respectable family, "and I'm certain you will find a suitable gentleman there," she added. I rolled my eyes. Father scowled and grumbled, and finally mumbled that he'd have an easier time paying bills with one less daughter to support.

I kissed my sisters good-bye; even George condescended to give me a good-bye kiss. Mother embraced me as if I were leaving for the ends of the earth. Father shook my hand and went back to his haying. With that, I left for Helston on the omnibus.

My dear Mary, As you can see from the postmark, I am back at Park Brawse, Maude is here also. We could no long stomach all the arguing, if Mother's not the one starting a fight, then Father is. Maude can attend school here just as well as in Penzance and we are much happier here as you can well imagine. Alas, Grandfather Appleton continues to decline; Uncle Harry thinks it is only a matter of time until the end. Everyone here sends their love. Amelia

Grandfather Appleton died the following year, in 1906. I requested, and received, leave to attend the funeral. Father was there, much to my surprise. "Couldn't stand the bastard but he was still my father," he growled. Amelia told me later the only reason he attended the funeral was he hoped to inherit some of Grandfather's estate. It was not to be. Uncle Tom received the house and the money in a trust fund. Father stomped home in anger.

Chapter Five
Scandal!

We were naïve. We thought Mother and Father would stay married forever. Hadn't they promised "till death do us part?"

I was not surprised when I heard that Mother had sued for a judicial separation in 1909, but I was shocked. Shocked, because women didn't do that. Not then. Not ladies. Especially ladies. They suffered in silence. They put on a brave face and pretended their husbands were faithful. They ignored clacking tongues, sideways glances and sympathetic sighs. As Mother often said, being a lady was all about attitude.

Not surprised, though, because Mother was a hard person to live with. Her sharp tongue might even have driven him to adultery. She was not one to suffer in silence. She spoke her mind to Father, loudly. She argued with him about everything – his occupation, his income, his drinking, even tracking mud into the house. I remember cowering upstairs, comforting the twins and Dorothy who were crying with fear as the storm raged below, ending only when Father stomped out of the door. When he returned – late – he stumbled up the stairs, mumbling and cursing, and not under his breath either. We could smell the ale.

We don't know how he met "That Woman," but the affair began after they moved to the house on Regent Square in Penzance. Mother became suspicious that something was going on when Father repeatedly had several late-night deliveries to make.

Then the whispers began. Someone had seen Father entering a house on Wellington Terrace, another time at St. James Street or Belgravia Street. Someone had seen him walking with a woman, not his wife, of an evening. Someone had seen him in "compromising circumstances."

She began to spy on them. She saw them on High Street having dinner. She followed them to a house on St. James Street and peered through the window where she saw them, "embracing in a most unseemly and intimate way," she said. Eventually, Mother learned a name: Miss Clara Ryan.

I regret not having been there to witness the confrontation. My sisters said they hadn't cowered like that for years. Mother threw him and his belonging out of the house and screamed that he should never darken the door. That was in the spring of 1909.

Mother became seriously ill that summer, so ill we feared she might die. I begged leave from Mrs. Oxenham to visit. We questioned the doctor closely about her recovery, and among everything else the doctor said, he mentioned Father. "He is very worried for you, Mrs. Appleton, and regrets his actions. He wishes to come back, if you will have him."

"I will if he sends that tart packing." She all but spit out the words. A week later, Father moved back and assured all that Miss Ryan had returned to Nottingham. By then, I had returned to Helston.

The reunion lasted three weeks. A whisper reached Mother that he had been seen dining with Miss Ryan, and she exploded.

My dear Mary, This afternoon, Mother chased Father out for good, and you would not believe the scene. She threw his clothes out in the street. There they were, shirts, trousers, jackets, hats, smalls, everything there for all the world to see. And the language! I didn't know Mother knew such words, but then she does come from a family of shipwrights and sailors. We stood there, gape-mouthed, at the vitriol. We saw curtains pulled aside in several of the neighbours' houses. I don't know if they enjoyed the show, but they certainly had a front-row seat. Dorothy's only comment was, thank heavens we don't have to listen to them fight any more. Mother still holds a grudge, I doubt she will ever forgive him. All our love, Bessie

A month later, Mother filed for a judicial separation. "I'm not giving that bastard the satisfaction of a divorce so he can marry that tart. Let him live in sin till my dying day!"

She was angry beyond words, not just because he had been unfaithful but also because the paper reported the court proceedings in full detail. "Now the entire world knows I have been betrayed," she cried. Ladies do not hang their dirty linen out in public.

She was also angry because now she was living in constricted circumstances. The court had ordered Father to pay alimony of 30 shillings a month, but it covered only essential costs. Mother railed against Father to everyone within earshot, calling him a cheapskate, among other names. She had to let the maid go and took in "guests," boarders by any other name.

I was glad to be not living at home.

Chapter Six
At a Crossroads

I worked for the Oxenhams for seven years. Seven years of living in someone else's home, cooking someone else's meals, washing someone else's linen, looking after someone else's children. They treated me well, they paid me well, but what future did I have? Even if I married, I would still be doing the same work except now it would be his home, his meals, his linen, his children. But marriage to whom? Certainly not Alfred, or was his name Albert? He was the hostler at the Angel Inn, a couple of doors down the street from Mr. Oxenham's shop. He had taken a fancy to me; why, I do not know, I certainly didn't return his admiration. He smelled too much of horses and barns and stale ale for my liking. Too much like Father with too many memories of betrayal. I felt trapped.

England itself trapped me. Heaven help those who tried to rise above their station. People were supposed to "know their place" and stay there. If you were born into the working class, you stayed a working-class person all your life. Otherwise, you were called a social climber and presumptuous, or were accused of "putting on airs."

In short, I had no future, or rather, the future I saw was dismal. My dream of being a teacher had faded long ago. There was nothing to take its place.

We did not realize it at the time, but I think those fantasies Amelia and I dreamed when we stayed with Grandfather – those days of walking along the coast of Land's End, watching the ships sailing by and guessing at their destinations — may have primed us for thinking it was possible to escape this country with all its restrictions and rules and expectations. That there was someplace to escape to where you created your own opportunities, your own future.

July of 1911 provided a temporary distraction from my woes when Clive married Harry Wright, a school master. Mother was overjoyed that one of her daughters had found a suitable husband, but I think she was also relieved that she now had only Bessie and Dorothy to support with her meager alimony and what little she brought in with paying guests. Father attended, of course; he gave away the bride, but then he sat on the far side of the church, and our parents studiously avoided each other after the ceremony. Mother snarled, "At least That Woman had the good sense not to attend."

She was less than amused when George married Carrie Tippett a week later. We thought the world of her, she was a delightful person. Mother was of the opinion George was marrying beneath him (mostly beneath Mother, we concluded) because Miss Tippett's father was merely a tin miner and she merely a parlour maid, most definitely not the class of family Mother had in mind for our prospective spouses. She conveniently forgot she herself had been a cook, albeit in the home of a retired Royal Navy captain, before she had left for New Zealand where she was also simply a cook.

Two days after George's wedding, Amelia announced, "I am going to Australia. I have been hired as a cook in a mining camp in western Australia, and my passage is booked for September." We sat in shocked silence for a moment, teacups frozen in mid-air as we took in Amelia's news.

Mother slammed her teacup down. "Gold fields! Do you know what sort of men scrabble for gold? And what sort of women associate with them? Loose women, yes, loose women, and that is what they will take you for! You will never find a proper husband if you gain a reputation as a loose woman. And Australia of all places. That country is populated with criminals, scum of the earth that we were only too glad to be rid of."

Amelia was not one to back down from a fight. "How dare you forbid me! You went off to New Zealand when you were single. As for finding a suitable husband . . ." – and she sneered the word "husband" – "where will I find one here, I ask you. I refuse to spend the rest of my days with some doddering old fool, no matter how much money or status he has. And besides, people there are no less respectable than here. England hasn't transported anyone there for a century."

"You, you, you . . ." Mother spluttered, then turned and stalked away. Stunned silence filled the room, but only for a moment. Soon we were laughing and talking again, knowing this would be the last time we were all together.

Before I returned to Helston, Amelia and I laughed and cried in equal measure. She promised to write as soon as she arrived in Australia, and she was as good as her word, writing almost every month, as did I. As I feared, I never saw her again.

Amelia's departure for Australia prompted me to consider my own future again. I was 26 years old, a domestic in someone else's household. I did not want that to be my future, but the thought of leaving everything and everyone that I knew was more than I could bear so I put aside the notion of emigrating.

It took a March day featuring leaden skies and drizzling rain to light a fire under me. Four days of rain had put everyone in a foul mood. The nursery was cold and damp in spite of the fire blazing in the fireplace. I pulled the heavy drapes back from the parlour window in a vain attempt to let more light into the room and stared at the drenched street below.

A yell of "Those are mine!" followed by a slap and a yelp broke my reverie. I turned to see Francis, age seven, grab his toy soldiers from his younger brother John and shove him to the floor. John fought back, tears streaming down his face as he tried to grab them back. "I want to play with them, too," he cried.

I pulled them apart. "Quit fighting, you two!" I grabbed Francis by his collar and took him to a chair on the far side of the room. "Sit there! Read this." I gave him a book, then swept up the toys and tossed them in their box. He threw the book on the floor. "No! It's boring. I want to play with my soldiers!"

I strode over to him and shook his shoulder. "No, you may not. Now, tell your brother you're sorry for hitting him." Francis stuck out his lower lip, crossed his arms and kicked his feet against the chair legs. "No! He was playing with my soldiers and he . . ."

I grabbed him by his arm. "In that case, you can go to your room!" I called to Janie, "Here, take Francis to his room." He stuck his tongue out at me as Janie dragged him from the nursery. She looked at me and shrugged before they disappeared.

My head was starting to hurt but there was still John to deal with. He was whining through his sobs, "He hit me! I hate him!" I rolled my eyes – God give me patience, I thought – and heaved a sigh as I tried to console him. "No, you don't hate him, you're just upset." I wiped his tears. "Why don't you play with little Henry?" I asked.

John shook me off. "No. I don't want to. He doesn't play fair. Besides, he's only two. I'm four."

I exhaled long and hard. What am I to do with these cranky children, I thought. I swear I'm never going to have children, and if I do, I'll have a maid to deal with them.

I picked up John. "You're tired. You'll feel better after a nap."

He squirmed in my arms. "Am not! Don't want a nap!"

I held him tighter. "What if I tell you a story?"

He stopped squirming. "Okay. But I want to hear the one about the Royal Navy catching the smugglers. I like how it ends." He rubbed his fist across his dripping nose.

I pulled a handkerchief out of my pocket. "Here, blow your nose. If you know how the story ends, why should I tell it again?"

"Because it's my favourite story, that's why."

As we walked out of the nursery, I called to Janie. "Will you please check Henry? I think his nappy needs changing. Then put him down for his afternoon nap."

As we walked into the boys' bedroom, I saw Francis was already asleep, Winston the Teddy Bear clutched tightly in his arms. I lay John on his bed, covered him with a quilt, then sat down beside him.

"Okay. It all started the night that the Channel was crashing into the rocky headlands of Land's End, a perfect night for the smugglers to land their illicit cargo of French cheese in one of their caves. They had to hurry, they knew gallant Captain Fitzsimmons of Her Majesty's Royal Navy ship was hot on their heels . . ."

John fell asleep long before the gallant Captain captured the smugglers.

I returned to the nursery to find Amy, age ten, sitting quietly on the other side of the nursery, embroidering her sampler. She held up the linen. "I've finished cross-stitching the alphabet. Come see, Miss Appleton."

I took the linen from her and shook my head. "See here, Amy, your crosses are not all the same size. And some of the upper crosses go this way and others go that way. They all have to cross in the same direction. You'll have to redo it."

She put her hands on her hips and pursed her lips. "No! I will not! You're always making me redo it. You're just a mean old witch! I hate you! I HATE you!" She grabbed the sampler out of my hands, threw it on the floor, burst into tears and ran out of the parlour.

I kicked Amy's sampler. I kicked her work basket sending needles and scissors and thimbles and skeins of thread scattering across the floor. I sat down, put my head in my hands and rubbed my pounding forehead. I wished to heaven I was anywhere but here.

I walked over to the window and stared out at the still-drenched street. Leaning my head against the cold pane, eyes closed, I willed the rain thrumming against the window to be the sea crashing against Loe Beach and the wind rattling the slates to be the breeze through the trees around St. Feock's Church. The memory was so comforting. There has to be more to life than this, I thought. There has to be more to my life.

I remembered Amelia's letter that had arrived two days ago.

Dear Mary, Life is certainly rough and tumble and the work is hard, but I am out of Mother's constraints, out of England's constraints. Here, your future is what you make of it, not what is imposed on you. Australia is a huge country barely out of its cradle, still trying to find itself, but what opportunities. Everyone works hard and plays hard, men and women alike. It is so very different from England, I think I understand why Father spoke so fondly of New Zealand. The only thing I miss about England is you and my sisters. All my love Amelia.

That was all it took to set my course. That night, I wrote a letter to an emigration agency, describing my training and my present duties and a desire to find employment in Canada. That country seemed a compromise – far enough away to escape the confines of English society but close enough that I could return for a visit. Never mind that all I knew of Canada was that large red blob at the north end of North America on the old, dusty, tattered Map of the World that hung at the front of the Practicing School classroom, and our geography lessons that talked of beavers and trappers and Red Indians, and, of course, how valiant General Wolf beat the French and secured the country for the growing and glorious British Empire.

The next morning, I stood before Mrs. Oxenham as she sat at her desk, preparing the day's menu. "If I may have a word, Mrs. Oxenham?"

She looked up at me. "Yes, what is it, Appleton? The children. Are they all right?"

"Oh yes, they're fine." I looked down at my hands as I clasped and unclasped them. How do you tell your employer of seven years that you want to leave, especially when she has treated you so well? I took a breath and squared my shoulders.

"I have decided to emigrate to Canada," I blurted out. "I have prepared a letter to an emigration agency, but I need to include a letter of introduction. Would you please be so kind as to write one for me?" There. I'd said it. There was no going back now.

Mrs. Oxenham looked down at her unfinished menu, then capped her fountain pen and folded her hands. "You have made up your mind?"

I nodded. "Yes, ma'am."

She sighed. "I see. The children will miss you. I know how much they like you. Well, you won't be the first young woman to seek her fortune abroad and I doubt you'll be the last. I will talk with Mr. Oxenham this evening. I'm sure he will write the letter you require."

I curtseyed and said, "Thank you, ma'am," before scurrying from the room. The weather outside was still miserable – raining and windy – but in my heart I was already in Canada. Where the sun was shining.

Two days later, Mr. Oxenham gave me the letter. "I wish you well in your new home," he said. I posted my application that same day.

For over a month, I heard nothing and then, in mid-April, the post brought a reply. A Mrs. Waddy, now residing in Helston, was returning to Canada and was in need of a maid to accompany her and her two children. She wanted to interview me, so would I please attend her at 18 Church Street at my earliest convenience? I was surprised and concerned when I read the address; it was Mr. Arthur's boot shop where I had taken many pairs of shoes to be repaired over the years. Would I be working for a mere boot mender's daughter?

I called around the next day. Mr. Arthur looked up from his work bench as the bell tinkled over the door. His cheery smile disguised the fact he had lost his wife of many years only a few months ago.

"Aye, good day to you, Miss Appleton. What shoes have you brought me today?"

"None, Mr. Arthur. I'm here to see your daughter, Mrs. Waddy. She is interviewing me."

"Ah, so you're the one she's hiring. I'll put in a good word for you, lass. She's upstairs, come along, I'll let you in." He ushered me through the workroom to a staircase and called up, "Miss Appleton's here to see you, me girl." He motioned me to go up.

Mrs. Waddy stood at the top of the stairs, holding a crying baby. She seemed a few years older than me but perhaps that was only because she was tired of minding the baby. She motioned me into the parlour. "Please excuse the crying. Nora is teething. I've just put some brandy on her gums so she will quiet down soon."

The room was comfortably, if plainly, furnished. Mrs. Waddy sat on the settee, gently rocking baby Nora. She did not ask me to sit but I was not surprised. If she hired me, she would be my mistress, I merely her servant.

"I read the letter of introduction from your current employer, so I believe you are familiar with the duties I require of you." Baby Nora was now sleeping soundly, so Mrs. Waddy placed her carefully on the settee beside her.

I assured her that they were similar to my present duties. Before I could ask when she wanted me to start, I heard footsteps behind me. A toddler come stumbling into the room. He stopped short when he saw me, then ran over to his mother and clung to her skirts.

"This is Arthur," she said. She turned to him. "Come, sit here beside me. Now, this is Miss Appleton. She is coming with us to Canada. You are to listen to her as you would listen to me. Do you understand?"

Arthur nodded but still sat very close to his mother. I smiled at him. "Good day to you, Master Arthur. Do you like stories? I know many about pirates and smugglers and spirits that roam the moors. Would you like me to tell you some one day?"

He looked up at his mother, then back at me, then turned and hid his face in her skirt.

Mrs. Waddy stroked his hair. "He will be more comfortable with you eventually."

My curiosity got the better of me. "If you please, Mrs. Waddy, I am most curious as to how you married a Canadian."

She narrowed her eyes at me and brushed an invisible speck off her skirt. "He was studying veterinary medicine in Liverpool when the Helston Unionist Club invited him to speak on opportunities in Canadian agriculture. I spoke to him afterwards – I was helping to serve refreshments – and, well, one thing led to another, as they say. He is an agricultural and animal inspector working for the Canadian government. They were considerate enough to give him leave to accompany me to Helston last year to assist me in attending to my ailing mother who, as you may know, passed away a few months ago. Dr. Waddy stayed as long as he could but his duties demanded his return to Canada late last year."

She lifted Arthur onto her lap. "Now, as to our travel, we leave Helston on June 10 for Bristol. You will accompany us to Bristol, of course. Our ship, the *Royal George*, departs on June 12. My husband has booked passage for us, and also the train to Alberta. According to standard practice, you will work for us for two years during which time we will deduct the cost of your passage from your pay."

For a boot-mender's daughter, she has certainly married up, I thought. Perhaps that is why she has such airs.

"What is it like where you live?" I asked.

Mrs. Waddy wrinkled her nose as if she had smelled something off. "The village of Strathmore in Alberta is certainly no Helston. A mere collection of wooden houses and muddy streets on a great expanse of wasteland that produces mostly cattle, although it is reputed to be the best farmland in all the Empire. I don't see why; it hardly rains and the grass is almost always brown. There's not a tree to be seen anywhere except for the few miserable saplings that the foolish inhabitants plant. I doubt they will ever grow to anything larger than a hedgerow."

"Why do you live there if it is such a horrid place?"

She smiled wistfully. "Because I have to follow my husband. The government has posted him there, and as long as he works there, then I have to live there, too."

I promised myself I would never follow any husband – *if* I ever married – to someplace I didn't want to live.

I returned to the Oxenhams in a daze, my heart in my throat, butterflies in my stomach. I was leaving.

I left their employ in mid-May. It was a sad leave-taking, especially for the children. The boys cried: "Who will tell us stories now?" Amy presented me with a cross-stitched bookmark, and she beamed when I complemented her on her fine work. Mrs. Oxenham thanked me for all my service, and both she and her husband wished me well in my new home.

As I walked out the door, I took a deep breath. I had made my decision. The die was cast. There was no going back now.

Chapter Seven
To Canada

I stood on the deck of the *Royal George* as it sailed down the Bristol Channel. Through my tears, I watched England and everything I knew and loved slip by. The ache of leaving felt like a knife to my heart. My stomach clenched. Had I been rash? Would I ever see my sisters and brother again? Perhaps I should have apologized to Mother even though she acted as if I didn't exist. Perhaps it was not possible to leave on better terms with Mother.

I had returned to Penzance to tell Mother, Dorothy and Bessie of my leaving; Maude was still living with Uncle Tom. We were taking tea in the sitting room, and they greeted my news with shocked silence, broken when Mother slammed down her cup so hard the tea slopped out onto the saucer. "Why are you abandoning me? Why are you running away from your responsibility to me?"

Before I knew what I was saying, I yelled back, "Maybe I am running away, just like Father ran away from you." I clapped my hand to my mouth but before I could apologize, Mother stood up, her face red, her entire body shaking, "If you leave, you are never welcome here again, you are no daughter of mine!"

She left the room. We heard her stomp up the stairs and slam a door.

We looked at each other, incredulous. Finally, Dorothy broke the awkward silence "Why did you say that?"

I shook my head. "I don't know, I wish I could take those words back." I started to cry.

Bessie sat beside me and put her arm around me, "We're sorry to see you leave." She smiled that mischievous Bessie grin. "What an adventure you will have. I wish I were coming with you."

Dorothy picked up Mother's cup and saucer. "Never mind Mother, she'll come around. She writes to Amelia, on the sly of course. She is too proud to admit that she has backed down from her disapproval. She'll do the same for you, I just know it. Now tell us all about where you are going."

The next day, I visited Clive and was delighted to learn that she and Harry were expecting their first child. She was sad to hear my news but excited, too. "You must write us about your journey and what Canada is like."

She turned to Harry, "Do you think we will ever travel like that?"

Harry only smiled. "My dear, no one knows what the future will bring." He shook my hand when I left. "You will be just fine, Mary. You are strong-minded enough to meet any obstacle life might throw in your path."

A day later, I visited George and Carrie and their new son, also named George, who had been born only a few weeks earlier. As I cradled baby George, my brother assured me he would look out for Mother. "Don't worry your head about her, she is always thinking of herself before anyone else." We spent a pleasant hour, reminiscing about our life at Higher Tregurra and Truro.

Father arrived just as I was about to leave. "What are you doing here?" I snapped.

"That's a fine way to greet your father, young lady," he replied.

A stinging reply was on the tip of my tongue but before I could speak, George intervened. "Mary's emigrating to Canada, and she's come here to say her goodbyes."

Father raised an eyebrow. "Canada? Now why ever would you want to go to the colonies? They're so uncivilized. What did your mother have to say about this?"

I frowned and crossed my arms. George put his hand on my shoulder. "She was not amused, so Mary said. She all but disowned Mary."

Father snorted a rude chuckle. "I'm not surprised.

Well, good for you Mary. She has to learn she can't always have her way."

I stomped my foot. "I think she's already learned that lesson, thanks to you." I started for the door but Father caught my arm.

"I don't know if going to Canada is a wise decision, but if you come to your senses and want to return to England, I'll send you the fare."

I began to object but Father stopped me. "I am not proposing this out of generosity. I am doing it because of the satisfaction of knowing it will vex your mother."

I shook off his hand. "I doubt I will ever call on you for any kind of assistance." I left and returned to Mother's house, the only place I could stay until I left the following day.

Leave-taking was heart-wrenching. Mother refused to see me off, but my sisters and I hugged and cried in equal measure, promising to write every day. The livery man loaded my black wooden crate – George had made it and he was not much of a carpenter – containing all my possessions and delivered me to the omnibus station. The ride back to Helston seemed long and lonely. A few days later, I boarded the omnibus with Mrs. Waddy and the children, bound for Bristol and the port of Avonmouth.

And now, here I was, on board the *Royal George*, leaving England. Too late for regrets, I told myself. Time to face the future. I turned away from England and faced westward where my future lay.

* * *

The open sea determined my future for the next seven days, which was, in short, to be horribly ill. I may have had seafaring ancestors but they had not bequeathed their seagoing abilities to me. Some days I feared I would die. Other days, I feared I would not die. Mrs. Waddy seemed unaffected, or at least not as badly as I was. She encouraged me to walk on the deck to take the fresh air and ordered the steward to bring me pots of tea or broth or the occasional piece of dry toast that refused to stay in my stomach. Even little Arthur seemed worried, for once or twice he patted my hand.

My stomach settled a little when we sailed into the Gulf of St. Lawrence, off the high seas and into calmer waters. The *Royal George* ceased to pitch and roll, and for the first time I thought I would live. We could not see the shore of the Colony of Newfoundland but we did see an iceberg off in the distance glistening in the sunlight, far enough away so as not to present any danger. I shuddered to think of the many poor unfortunate souls who had perished only two months earlier on the *Titanic*. The words in Maude's last letter came to mind.

My dear Mary, I took my usual walk along the coast yesterday morning and watched a large ship sail westward. I didn't think much of it but then recalled the news that the Titanic was to sail soon. The ship was very far away on the horizon but it was bigger than any ship I had seen and it had four funnels. I am very sure it was the Titanic. To think I might have been the last person to see it before its tragic end. Love, Maude.

We disembarked shortly after noon at the Louise Basin in Quebec City in order to be processed by immigration officials. I stumbled for the first few steps once on shore, quite unaccustomed to walking on ground that did not roll and pitch. Both the immigration officer and the medical examiner were efficient. They examined our travel documents and asked a host of questions: could we read and write, what was our ultimate destination, had we lived in Canada previously and if so for how long, what was our religious affiliation, our first language. I anticipated a lengthy delay, for there were over 900 passengers on board, but by late afternoon, they were done with us. We reboarded the *Royal George* for our final destination, Montreal.

The long summer evening provided enough light to see the villages and farms that dotted both shores of the river. They were so different from English farms. The buildings sat almost directly on the shore, with fields extending in long rows back to the forest behind. Most of the houses were whitewashed with either steeply pitched roofs or mansard roofs. Herds of cattle that looked like English Friesians grazed pastures behind the farm buildings. Each village clustered around a church whose spire reached high into the sky, and from time to time I heard a whisper of a bell tolling over the throbbing of the ship's engines. It was a very pleasant sight to behold, quite unlike the image Mrs. Waddy had painted of Alberta.

We were awakened very early the following morning, the sun barely up, by the ship's crew informing us that we had docked in Montreal and we must depart the ship within the hour.

I had not slept well. I had tossed and turned the whole night while my brain tied itself in knots with regret and anxiety in equal numbers, so I was in no mood to deal with a groggy Arthur who whined and fought to stay in bed. I snapped at him and finally resorted to spanking him when he fought being dressed. In spite of his recalcitrance, within the hour we were trudging down the gangway with the other passengers, the porter close behind us with our trunks. Mrs. Waddy carried Nora, while I, with my left hand, held onto Arthur who was still struggling and whining, and with my right I carried the bag filled with baby Nora's travelling supplies.

I was so preoccupied with Arthur that I barely noticed we were on solid ground or that we were surrounded by crowds of pushing, talking, yelling people until a strangely accented voice caught my attention. "Permettez moi, madame." I looked up from Arthur to see a carriage driver help Mrs. Waddy into his carriage. He turned to Arthur. "Et tu aussi, mon petit," he said as he hoisted Arthur into the carriage. The driver held his hand to me. "M'amselle." With his aid, I took my seat. He took his seat, called something to his horse in a nasally French unlike any I had ever heard in school, and we were off, clip-clopping through the streets of Montreal to Windsor Station where we were to board the Canadian Pacific Railway train to Alberta.

Montreal was not the village of rickety wooden shacks I had expected. It was a prosperous city of business and commerce. My head swiveled from side to side; I gawked, mouth agape like a common tourist, at magnificent brick and stone buildings that would be at home in Truro or Penzance or London itself. And what a hubbub! Even at this early hour, the entire city seemed to be out and about. Crowds hustled along the sidewalks and flowed into the streets, oblivious to the horse-drawn carriages and wagons, lorries, omnibuses and motor cars hurtling pell-mell down the streets. I heard French, English and several other languages. I saw black-robed priests, flocks of nuns, and men wearing black coats and hats. The growl of omnibuses and motor vehicles, the neighing of horses, the creak of wagon and carriage wheels, the shouts of drivers, the honking of horns, all created a deafening cacophony of sound. My head began to ache, it was all so much to take in.

We were delivered to Windsor Station in short order. While Mrs. Waddy paid the driver, I stared up at the hulking sandstone building, several storeys high with an arched arcade in front and people pouring in and out. This was no small-town station; it dwarfed even Penzance's station. I blinked and stared at the porter, the first black man I had ever seen, skin dark as night, who hustled over with a cart and, together with the driver, loaded our trunks onto his cart.

"Come along, Appleton!" Mrs. Waddy's commanding voice startled me out of my astonished state. I gripped Arthur's hand and followed her, she carrying Nora, into Windsor Station. "Sit here and mind the children while I get our tickets," she said to me. To the porter, "Put our suitcases here, boy, then come with me."

I took Nora in my arms and settled Arthur on the bench beside me, then looked around. I was overwhelmed by the scene before me. The station was cavernous; it seemed to stretch on forever under an arching glass roof. Crowds of people poured out of or into numbered doors that led to platforms. Porters scurried back and forth carrying luggage or pushing hand carts piled high with luggage; many were black men of varying hues, all dressed in CPR livery. Were all CPR employees black men, I wondered. The din of people's voices, unintelligible amplified announcements, and the bells, whistles and chugging of locomotives echoed throughout the chamber, creating a wall of sound that caused Arthur to clap his hands over his ears. I gaped at the huge board that listed arrival and departure times for a bewildering number of places. Were there really that many cities in Canada?

The children brought me back to reality. Nora began squirming and whimpering which set Arthur to whining, "Hung'y, hung'y." I wiped drool from Nora's face and tried to shush Arthur but in vain. I was about to give him a quick swat when Mrs. Waddy returned, accompanied by a different porter.

"Our trunks are checked through to Strathmore," she said to me. She turned to the porter. "Carry these suitcases, boy," she ordered.

He touched his cap, "Yes, ma'am. Right this way, ma'am."

He led us to a door marked Platform 8 where we joined the stream of people. Are all these people going to Strathmore, I wondered. Down a flight of stairs we went, along a hall that went under the tracks – we could hear trains rumbling above us – and up stairs onto the crowded platform. The noise was deafening; trains chugged and puffed, smoke billowed out of the stacks, great gusts of steam whooshed out as brakes were released or set, bells clanged, whistles blew; people talked, cried, embraced, waved good-bye. It was Bedlam itself.

The porter led us to our car and handed our suitcases over to the sleeping car attendant who stood ready to help us onto our car. Mrs. Waddy dismissed the porter with a wave of her hand and turned her back on him as if he didn't exist. I wondered if he was used to being treated so dismissively. He touched his cap and turned to leave but not before winking at Arthur.

The sleeping car attendant helped us climb aboard, then picked up our suitcases and led us to our seats in the sleeper car where we collapsed in relief and exhaustion.

"My name is George," the attendant said. "Please call if you need anything. I will make up your beds for the night. If you want your shoes polished, just leave them beside your berth." He turned to Mrs. Waddy. "And ma'am, there is a private room for mothers with babies in the next car." With that, he touched his cap and left to assist other passengers.

Dr. Waddy had reserved an upper and a lower berth for us. I was to share the upper berth with Arthur, Mrs. Waddy the lower berth with Nora. Our tickets included meals in the dining car which was three cars to the rear. I settled Arthur beside me on one of the seats; Mrs. Waddy, holding Nora, took the opposite seat. The conductor outside yelled, "All 'board!" The whistle blew, the bell clanged, and the train jerked two or three times. At 9:40 am, we pulled out of the station and out of Montreal.

I was in Canada, beginning my journey into the unknown. I had made my bed and now I would have to lie in it, come what may. But first, I was about to learn how big that red blob at the north end of North America was.

Chapter Eight

Across Canada

Once I got Arthur settled and Nora fed, the rhythmic clickety-clack and the rocking motion soon put them to sleep. I must have fallen asleep, too, because I awoke with a start when the car attendant announced, "First call for dinner!"

I shook myself awake. "Where are we? What time is it?"

Mrs. Waddy picked up Nora and stood. "We've just left Ottawa. Come along, we should eat. It's been a long time since breakfast."

I took Arthur by the hand. We swayed from side to side with the motion of the train as we walked back toward the dining car. I had never traveled by train so didn't know what to expect, especially in "uncivilized" Canada. What a surprise, then, to see tables covered with white linen tablecloths starched within an inch of their life, and set with linen napkins, china, silverware and glasses. The white-jacketed waiter ushered us to a table, shook out the napkins and placed a menu before Mrs. Waddy and me.

"I'll be back shortly to take your orders," he said, "and we do have special meals for the young gentleman." He winked at Arthur.

The food was excellent, as was the service. I began to feel a little like the lady of my imagination. Arthur sat google-eyed throughout the meal, watching the waiters carry trays of plates and glasses over their heads with one hand, swaying in time with the motion of the train, never spilling a drop. When we walked back to our car, he tried to imitate the waiters but succeeded only in losing his balance and landing in a gentleman's lap. Mrs. Waddy apologized, but the gentleman laughed and said, "Boys will be boys."

I knew Canada was big, and Mrs. Waddy had told me it would take the better part of four days to get to Strathmore. But hearing about it and experiencing it are two different things. Back home, four days by train would take you through several countries on the continent, all the way to Rome. Here, we wouldn't even have crossed all of Canada.

I tossed and turned that first night, carefully so as not to wake Arthur but he slept the sleep of the innocent. Not I. I fretted about my future, conjuring up many frightening possibilities. Then I remembered what Amelia had written.

My dear Mary, Australia is indeed wild and woolly, but no one cares about your family name, only if you are an honest and hard worker. Your future is what you make of it, not what is imposed on you. I have no regrets about leaving England, although I do miss all of you so terribly. Love, Amelia

Perhaps I could do the same in Canada if I set my mind to it.

For the first two days, I saw nothing but interminable dark forest broken only by glimpses of rocks, lakes and rivers. Where was all the farmland and grassland that Mrs. Waddy had described? Who lived in this wilderness? Did the fairies and sprites and other little people of Grandmother Ferris's stories inhabit such places? There must be ghosts, too, like the ghosts of pirates and sailors of the Cornish coast, as Grandfather Ferris had described. Canada must have similar stories of tragedy and treachery, of heroes and villains, of loves lost and won, of mysterious happenings explicable only by recourse to elves or fairies or whatever other spirits lived in these woods. Would I ever learn any? If I didn't know the stories, would I ever feel at home here like I did at Feock or Higher Tregurra?

I did not have much time to wonder about such things. Arthur and little Nora kept me very busy. When I wasn't changing Nora's nappies (disposable paper ones that Mrs. Waddy had packed) or wiping drool off her face, I was running after a bored and restless Arthur who took great delight in charging up and down the aisles. Or, I was mending his trousers, or wiping his tears when he bumped into a seat or trying to settle him down for a nap.

He loved stories, but the stories I had told my sisters of sailors and pirates and smugglers and the Royal Navy were out of place in Canada. Since we were surrounded by trees, why not tell stories about trees? I settled him on my lap.

"Trees talk to each other, did you know that?" He shook his head and pointed at the window. "Tee!"

"Yes, trees, lots of trees, and they do talk, I've heard them. In the morning they say 'Hello, friend. How did you sleep?' and in the evening, 'Good night, friend.' They call to the robins and sparrows, 'Come sing to me'."

Arthur stared at me, wide-eyed, as he toyed with a button on my shirtwaist. "And they tell each other of danger. 'Oh look, here comes that nasty boy who sticks his penknife in us,' and then they swat at him with their branches. 'Shoo, go away, boy!' they yell."

At which point, he wiggled off my lap and ran up and down the aisle again. I sighed, shook my head and got up to retrieve him from yet another couple he was bothering.

And so it went.

The morning of the third day, we woke to see a very flat, well-settled plain with fields laid out in regular squares, not at all like English farms with field of all shapes and sizes. I stared at the huge fields, each seeming as large as an entire English farm. The train passed through several villages of varying sizes but I could see little other than the station and several large, tall buildings that I later learned were grain elevators.

We had barely sat down for breakfast when the conductor strode through announcing "Winnipeg, twenty minutes." The train clickety-clacked across a bridge and someone exclaimed, "Look at the Red River, it's really high this year!" but it looked more muddy brown than red to me. I stared at the houses – small, wooden detached houses sitting on small lots surrounded by picket fences, not the brick and stone terraces I was accustomed to. The industrial area of factories and shops was all too familiar, dirty, gritty, and spewing smoke and smell into the air.

The train rumbled and squealed to a stop at the station. I had hoped to get out and stretch my legs and let Arthur run off some steam but, by the time we finished breakfast, that was impossible. We returned to our seats and watched the new passengers enter our car.

The hubbub on the platform caught my attention. Men hauled wagons loaded with luggage and boxes and mailbags to and from the train. People milled about on the platform, some leaving, and some getting on. Towards the far end of the platform stood several groups of women and girls with head scarves and shawls around their shoulders, and men and boys wearing coats and caps of strange cut, all with their belongings in baskets and carpet bags piled around them. Their dress and belongings looked poor and foreign.

Mrs. Waddy saw me staring at them. "Those are immigrants from Eastern Europe. They swallowed the government and CPR's propaganda about how fertile Western Canada is. They will be sorely disappointed to discover it isn't so." She shook her head. "I don't think it is in Canada's best interest to encourage people of that sort to come here. Canada is part of the British Empire, and we need to keep it British, not dilute it with people who can't speak our language and don't know our customs."

As we pulled out of the station, I caught a glimpse of the commercial section of the city – a broad street flanked by buildings several storeys high – and then we whisked past more small houses on small lots and back onto the flat, flat prairie. Hour after hour, we watched fields, farmsteads, villages and the occasional clump of trees slip by us. Night fell, and we were still rolling through the same landscape, still a day away from our destination.

I decided there was altogether too much Canada.

Sometime during that night, I heard the porter call out, "Next stop, Moose Jaw." Such a peculiar name, I must be dreaming, I thought. In the morning, when we stopped at a place called Medicine Hat, I could no longer contain my curiosity. I asked Mrs. Waddy about the name but she merely shrugged, "I do not know, this country has some strange names."

The conductor overheard my query. "The story is, there was a battle here between a couple of the Indian tribes, I think the local Blackfoot and the Cree from over in Saskatchewan. A medicine man, I don't know if he was Blackfoot or Cree, lost his hat. Hence the name."

Mrs. Waddy laughed. "What ignorance! They think a man mumbling some gibberish can change the course of a battle. Well, the government and the churches are doing their best now to civilize them and teach them some trades. Not soon enough, if you ask me."

For the next two hours, we traveled through rolling grasslands that looked vaguely like the Cornish moors. I could see no farms or fields, although we passed through a few towns. The countryside looked very green but Mrs. Waddy assured me it would be very brown come August when no rain had fallen.

At long last, the words we wanted to hear, "Strathmore, next stop in twenty minutes." We gathered up our things, I retrieved Arthur from passengers two seats down the aisle, and we walked to the door. The train lurched to a stop and we descended, I holding Arthur's hand, Mrs. Waddy carrying Nora, the car attendant carrying our suitcases.

We were home, if home this were to be. I took a breath, remembered Amelia's words, and prepared to make my future.

Chapter Nine
Strathmore

I stood on the platform under a blazing sun and the clearest blue sky I had ever seen. The heat bore down on me, my skin prickled with perspiration. A sudden gust of wind blew a cloud of sharp dust in my face and threatened to remove my hat. I grabbed it with my free hand, and in the process struck myself in the face with my handbag. This was not beginning well.

"Mrs. Waddy, my dear! Welcome home!" A well-dressed gentleman came striding towards us, arms outstretched. He embraced Mrs. Waddy and kissed her! In public! Little Nora cried out, she was not happy about being the filling of their sandwich. Dr. Waddy released his wife with a little laugh and stroked Nora's cheek. "So this is little Nora. Come here, my darling."

Nora was not about to accept the strange man's arms. She wrapped her arms around her mother's neck and whimpered. Mrs. Waddy chided her. "Don't make strange, little Nora, that's your father."

She looked at her husband. "Never you mind, she'll soon have you wrapped around her little finger."

Dr. Waddy turned to me. "And you must be Miss Appleton. Welcome to Strathmore."

I curtseyed. "Thank you, Dr. Waddy. I hope I shall be of satisfactory service to you."

"Appleton has been of great service on the trip across Canada, although," – Mrs. Waddy smirked – "she was of no service on the voyage. I was afraid she would expire of *mal de mer*, she was that ill."

I nodded. "That is true. At one point, I even prayed I would expire."

Dr. Waddy spied Arthur; he squatted and held out his arms to the boy who was hiding behind me. "Arthur, how you have grown! Do you remember me?"

Arthur grabbed my skirt and buried his face in it. Dr. Waddy sighed. "I'm not surprised he doesn't remember me. When I left to return to Canada, Arthur wasn't much older than Nora is now."

He stood up and took Mrs. Waddy's hand. She smiled at him. "Don't you worry, dear. He will soon get over playing strange and then he will pester you ceaselessly."

"Are these your trunks, Mrs. Waddy?" A workman was pointing to two trunks and my ugly black box.

She nodded, "Yes, Mr. Boles, please deliver them to our house as soon as possible. We have had a long journey." With that, we walked to the Waddy residence.

I got a good look at Strathmore as we walked the several blocks to the Waddy residence. I gazed around in disbelief.

Strathmore was no Helston. It looked as if it had been slapped up only last month. The businesses along High Street were wooden buildings – the bank was the only brick building – strung along rough, rutted dusty streets that, I soon learned, covered you in dust when dry and sucked you down into mud when wet. The boardwalks were few and far between and existed only where an enterprising businessman had built one on his own initiative in front of his business. The town was busy, people were everywhere as were saddle horses, horse-drawn conveyances of all sorts and even a few motor cars, all kicking up dust that blew everywhere in the wind, especially into my eyes. I saw no trees worthy of the name, just little leafy sticks that would barely stop a breeze or cast the slightest bit of shade. The strong smell of cattle and horses and barns was everywhere. I wrinkled my nose against it.

We turned into a residential area and walked past houses both large and small, some well-tended, others barren of anything save whatever grass was brave enough to grow. I sighed in relief when I saw the Waddys' home, a large, well-tended house with a verandah running across the front. Dr. Waddy opened the door and ushered us into a central hall with stairs to the first floor directly ahead.

Dr. Waddy's next words confused me. "Your bedroom is at the back of the second floor."

The second floor? I thought this house had only two floors. Was there another one I had not seen from the outside? He noticed my confusion and laughed.

"Forgive me, Miss Appleton, I forgot you're used to English terms. Here, the main floor, the one we're on right now, is the first floor. Upstairs is the second floor. I suffered a similar confusion when I went to England for my training, everything seemed topsy-turvy. Don't worry, you'll get used to it."

My heart fell as I walked through the house. It had none of the modern conveniences I had enjoyed in Helston and Penzance. I might as well be back at Higher Tregurra with its onerous and unpleasant tasks I thought I had left behind. Coal oil lamps instead of electric lights; I would have to relearn how to trim wicks and clean the chimneys. A hand pump at a large enamel sink in the kitchen instead of faucets and running water; I would have to heat water on the stove.

I saw no fireplaces in any of the rooms. "How do you heat the house?" I asked Dr. Waddy.

"Ah, yes, English houses, I remember them well," he replied. "Fireplaces are no match for Canadian winters. Here, we use a furnace that heats the entire house. It's in the basement. You'll see it soon enough."

I shook my head and tried to imagine a "furnace."

Upstairs consisted of four bedrooms and the bathroom, or what was meant to pass for a bathroom. Instead of a sink and faucets, a large china basin and an equally large china jug sat on a washstand with a pail beside it in which the wash water was dumped. Emptying that pail would be another of my daily tasks. I looked for a bathtub, in vain. Instead, I saw a large tin tub leaning against one wall. I would have to haul pails of hot water upstairs to fill it and then haul pails of dirty water downstairs. I looked for the WC, also in vain. Instead, I found elaborately decorated ceramic potties under each bed. Their beauty belied their nasty contents. I grimaced at the thought of emptying them each morning into the privy that stood in the back yard and then cleaning them.

I found my bedroom, the smallest of the four at the rear of the house, and plunked down on the bed, its springs complaining with my slight weight. I was back in the Dark Ages. Father was right, I thought. This place is uncivilized.

Our trunks arrived within the hour. The men hauled them up to the bedrooms and I began to unpack my black box. I put everything into the chiffonier except my two most valuable possessions, my little Bible received "For Early Attendance and Religious Instruction" when I graduated from the Practicing School, and the photograph of Mother, Maude and Dorothy standing in front of the house on Regent Square. As I set them on top of the chiffonier, my heart broke. I was so homesick, my very bones ached, and I burst into tears and cried like a baby. I plopped down on the bed and rocked back and forth and cried until I had no tears left in me to cry.

I heard Mrs. Waddy call for me, and I answered, "I'll be down shortly." I found a handkerchief and wiped my eyes and blew my nose. I went into the bathroom and splashed water on my face, tucked in a stray strand of hair, adjusted one of the combs and smoothed my skirt, and then went downstairs to commence my duties.

Thus began my life in Canada as a domestic servant. Mrs. Waddy had not grown up with servants so she did not understand the unspoken contract between mistress and servant. She was haughty and demanding, quite unlike Mrs. Oxenham. As far as Mrs. Waddy was concerned, I was part of the household but not of the household, more like a piece of furniture that was always at her beck and call. I ate in the kitchen with the children. I ran errands, dusted, swept, washed, ironed, carted, hauled and toiled in the garden (I didn't mind that). I wiped children's noses, mended their clothes and sewed them new ones as they grew out of their old ones. I was teacher, comforter, mediator, advisor, all rolled into one underpaid person. When my day was done, which was always late, I retired to my little bedroom and fell into a deep sleep. Morning always came too soon.

Dr. Waddy, on the other hand, treated me with respect and dignity – he always called me Miss Appleton – but then he had grown up with servants, his father being a prominent surgeon in Toronto, the master of a large house and grounds. He understood that a well-treated servant is a happy servant, one who will stay with the family through thick and thin.

On my second day at Strathmore, I encountered both the furnace and the garden. Mrs. Waddy asked me to fetch some jam from the cold room in the basement. I walked down the stairs, my hand brushing the cold concrete wall, and stepped onto an equally cold concrete floor. In the middle of the room stood an enormous round metal contraption with tubes octopussing out from the top, going off in all directions and heading into the floor above. I opened its small door and smelled long-dead ashes and smoke. Would cleaning the furnace also be part of my duties, I wondered.

The furnace might have been interesting but the garden was disappointing. I stood on the back step to survey the yard and sighed in dismay. How unlike our garden at Higher Tregurra with its flower beds and apple orchard. What was supposed to be a garden had gone to weeds. The hedge was badly in need of trimming. Dr. Waddy was definitely not a gardener, nor it seemed was Mrs. Waddy; she was more interested in Strathmore's social scene. Over the next two weeks, I pulled weeds and dug out invading grass to reveal a few daisies, some cosmos, several bachelor buttons and a clump of iris ready to bloom, all struggling toward the sun. It was too late to plant any vegetables, the best I could do was nurture what had survived in spite of being abandoned. Next spring, this will be a proper garden, I promised. Perhaps even a little bit of England.

The third day, I encountered Canadian money. Mrs. Waddy gave me a purse of coins and sent me to purchase some groceries at Mr. Simmons' store: canned beans, eggs, cheese, baking powder, tea and bread. I piled the purchases on his counter and waited while he added up the total. He stuck the pencil behind his ear. "That will be $2.45, Miss Appleton."

I opened the purse to see a bewildering assortment of unfamiliar coins. No shillings and pence here. I dumped them out on the counter and began to sort through them. Mr. Simmons smiled. "Ah, you're new to Canada, Miss Appleton. Here, let me show you." He proceeded to give me a lesson in Canadian currency. "Thank-you," I said with great relief.

"Never you mind, Miss Appleton, you'll soon get the hang of it."

Money wasn't the only thing that was different.

The food, for example. No pilchards. Mr. Simmons suggested canned sardines, but they were only headless fishy bits that neither looked nor tasted like pilchards. No one, other than Mrs. Waddy, had heard of hevva cake or fairings. No Cornish cheeses, only a hard orange cheese that claimed to be Cheddar but wasn't. Here, biscuits were called cookies, and what they called biscuits were a pale and tasteless imitation of a saffron bun but with neither saffron nor currants. No self-rising flour, so I had to learn how much baking powder or baking soda to use. Lots of beef but not a joint of mutton to be had for any amount of money.

No sound of the sea, only the wind that blew constantly, some days harder than others, sucking moisture out of every living thing, even the earth itself, turning my skin to sandpaper. It set the eaves to rattling, the dust to blowing; it put nerves on edge and rendered us all cranky and mean-spirited. The sun beat down mercilessly and the heat was unbearable, although the evenings often cooled down so we could sleep reasonably well. As for rain, some days the clouds teased us with a few drops that did nothing other than make the dust stick to the windows. Other times it came down in torrents that threatened to wash everything away.

In spite of the horrid weather and the bleak surroundings, the residents of Strathmore, all 350 or so of them, seemed to thrive in this country. They were full of optimism and enthusiasm; they saw the future as glorious, never-ending growth. It had been that way since the CPR established the station in 1881, and the residents saw no reason why it should not be thus in the future. I wasn't so sure.

Just south of Strathmore was the CPR's extensive demonstration farm where immigrant farmers learned how to overcome the challenges of farming in Alberta. This was where Dr. Waddy spent some of his time when he wasn't inspecting shipments of cattle and other livestock either arriving at or leaving Strathmore.

Dr. Waddy loved his work. He said there was nothing more satisfying than declaring a herd of livestock to be healthy. We could always tell how his day went by how he came home. If it had been a good day, he came in whistling and smiling; he'd toss his hat onto the hat rack, give Mrs. Waddy a kiss and hug the children, then go into his office to write his reports. If not a good day; a day when he had to tell a farmer his prized cow was diseased and had to be put down, a day when the farmer railed against government interference in his farming, Dr. Waddy would come home glum, slap his hat on the hat rack and walk stone-faced to his office and shut the door against the world.

Sunday, after I had prepared breakfast and done the washing up, was my day. Weather permitting, I walked through the gardens and greenhouses of the CPR's demonstration farm. It was such an oasis, filled with thousands of trees and extensive flower gardens. The greenhouses held a marvelous variety of vegetables to supply the CPR trains and hotels. I inhaled the blossoms' heady perfume, remembering the flowers that Mother had coaxed into glorious bloom at Higher Tregurra.

On my first visit in early July, I spied hollyhocks, and memories flooded back. Those same flowers had stood in ranks along the lane to our house in Feock. My sisters and I called them our "Coldlane Guards" and stood at attention to salute them. Their lovey shades of pinks and yellows and creams filled a corner of our garden at Higher Tregurra. My sisters and I picked the flowers, dipped them in melted paraffin wax and made "Ladies" – the fully opened blooms became the skirt; the partly opened flower, the bodice; and the bud, the head. We stood our Ladies beside our beds till the paraffin melted and the blooms withered and died.

I walked over and stroked the broad leathery leaves. The flowering stalks, not yet in bloom, already stood taller than I. What I would give to have a garden of my own rather than tend to someone else's.

"They will make a grand display when they bloom in a few weeks."

I was so lost in my memories I had not heard the man walk up behind me. I jumped at his voice and turned around. He doffed his cap. "Sorry, ma'am, I didn't mean to startle you." He extended his hand. "I'm Mr. Hughes, the head gardener."

I shook his hand. "Miss Appleton. I am newly arrived, this is my first time visiting the gardens. They are beautiful." I paused. "Would you allow me to collect some hollyhock seeds once they are done blooming? They're my favourite flower, you see, and there are none growing in our garden."

He nodded. "You are most certainly welcome to take as much seed as you desire." He doffed his hat again. "I must be on my rounds. Please to make your acquaintance, Miss Appleton. I hope to see you here again."

I smiled. Next summer, hollyhocks would grow in Dr. Waddy's garden. In *my* garden. In my mind, they were already blooming.

My other Sunday occupation was to read letters from home and to write replies. Those letters were a mixed blessing. They brought news of home but they also renewed the ache in my heart. More than once, I poured out my longing and misery in letters, only to tear them up and write something less tragic. I did not want them to know how lost I felt.

My dear Mary, We are all well although Mother still refuses to speak your name. Clive and Harry were here for supper last week, they are already planning the nursery. Clive said she would write you, have you received her letter? The roses are in full bloom, a spectacular display. Their sweet heady aroma fills the air. How I wish you were here to enjoy them with us. With all our love, Bessie and Dorothy

Dearest Bessie and Dorothy, I miss those roses almost as much as I miss your happy chatter. How I wish I could be there to smell them with you. The CPR has many rose bushes even though it is a struggle to keep them through Alberta winters, so Mr. Hughes, the head gardener, told me. He promised to show me how they bed them down with mounds of straw come October. However, there is a wild rose bush that grows across the prairies in abundance, producing a multitude of single pink blooms with a delicate smell. They make a delightful scene especially now that the country is drying up and turning brown. Love, Mary.

Dear Mary, Weather today at Landewednack is blustery, the wind lashes against the windows fit to break them. No walk on the coast today unless I want to join the smugglers' ghosts of your many stories. Uncle Tom is the same as always, and helping Miss Bray care for him brings me a great deal of satisfaction. Perhaps I shall become a nurse one day. Uncle Harry is busy with his doctoring. He sends his love and asks you to write if you have the time. All my love, Maude.

My dearest Maude, Strathmore is nowhere near the sea but it has equally terrible storms. This Tuesday past started a dreadfully hot oppressive day and ended with a terrifying bang. Black clouds boiled up from the west, covering the sky, turning day to dusk. The air chilled, and with a blaze of lightning and a crash of thunder, the clouds unleased a torrent of wind-driven rain. That was not the worst of it. Hail, the size of peas and larger, pelted down, shredding leaves, hammering against the walls and windows with a deafening noise. Arthur was terrified and would not be comforted till it ended and the sun came out. We walked out to survey the damage. He was heartbroken to see a sparrow killed by the hail. "Birdie die?" he asked. I helped him dig a little grave in the garden and he stuck a broken branch into the ground to mark the grave. My love to all. I think of you constantly. Tell Uncle Harry I will write soon. Love, Mary.

Dear So-Far-Away Mary, Mother has her knickers in a twist about Dorothy. She has dreams of becoming a teacher now that she has graduated from the Practicing School but Mother insists she marry Charles at Number 20. You remember him, you once called him an anemic string-bean. Mother thinks he's perfect because he has a bright future as a clerk at the Bank of England, but Dorothy thinks he is a total cad and not worth the space he takes up. We have a new set of "guests," from America this time, who do nothing but complain how backward England is. However, "guests" are necessary if Mother is to have sufficient money for our daily living expenses. Some days I envy you. All our love, Bessie.

Dear Bessie and Dorothy, Please accept this Canadian dollar but please do not tell Mother about this. She would probably tear it up, if I know her. I don't know what it is worth in shillings and pence, but it should help a little with your expenses. I don't need much money, just enough to buy stationery and a few fripperies from time to time, and a little to put in the bank for when I leave the Waddys at the end of my service. Love, Mary.

Dr. Waddy came home in early August, brandishing an official-looking letter. "We're moving to Regina. I've been appointed Inspector in the Health of Animals Branch beginning September 1. The best news is my salary is increased!"

Mrs. Waddy threw her arms around her husband. "How wonderful, dear. Imagine! A city with electricity and running water and a social scene that offers more than baseball games and rodeos."

All I could imagine was the packing to be done. Dr. Waddy went to Regina to find a house to rent and returned well-pleased with himself. "It's only two blocks from the office and downtown," he declared. "I've already talked with Mr. Boles and the CPR about shipping everything to Regina."

The rest of August went by in a flurry. In amongst all the sorting and packing, Nora started toddling about the house, and with every few steps she lost her balance, plopped down on her toosh and started to bawl. I was constantly assuring Arthur that we would not lose his precious teddy bear. I wrote one last letter to my sisters and brother giving them my new address: 2075 Hamilton Street.

We spent our last night at the King Edward Hotel before leaving for Regina on the afternoon train. I wasn't sorry to leave Strathmore but I had been willing to accept it as my home, at least until I had paid back my voyage and was in a position to decide my future. I clung to the hope that Regina would hold more prospects.

At least no sea voyage was involved this time.

Chapter Ten
Regina

We arrived in Regina at 5:30 am on Friday, September 30. We were all tired, having sat up the entire night because Dr. Waddy had reserved only coach seats.Ized Dr. Waddy carried a very groggy and grumpy Arthur, I carried Nora, and the porter carried our few bags off the train. Even at that early hour, the station was filled with people coming and going. Dr. Waddy hired a car to take us to a nearby hotel where we took two rooms for a few hours to rest. I put the children into bed, then lay down on mine without undressing. I slept fitfully until finally falling into a deep sleep.

I was awakened by Arthur poking my arm. "I hungry," he wailed. I could hear Dr. and Mrs. Waddy moving about in the adjoining room. I washed my face, changed Nora's nappy, combed Arthur's tousled hair and straightened his shirt, and went down to the dining room for breakfast.

Our walk to our new home took us along the east side of a park in the centre of the city. We stopped and stared at what we saw. We had read about the cyclone that had ploughed through the heart of Regina earlier that summer, but those reports did nothing to prepare us for the destruction that lay before us.

The buildings on the west side of the park were in ruins, although workmen had long cleared away the rubble. The roof of First Baptist Church was gone, the upper half of Metropolitan Methodist Church was gone, and what must have been a magnificent stained-glass window in Knox Presbyterian Church was now a gaping hole. The north wall of the YWCA was ripped away. The public library was nothing but a vacant lot. To the south, towards the Legislative Buildings, the continual sound of sawing and hammering filled the air as workers rushed to rebuild the houses the cyclone had demolished. The city had mourned their dead and their losses, now they were rebuilding and renewing. Tragedy had done nothing to diminish their optimism about the future. It was an attitude I was to encounter everywhere in this country, even in the darkest times.

Our new home was in a pleasant residential area of large houses with front gardens surrounded by picket fences. Dr. Waddy unlocked the door and we trooped in, weary from traveling. The CPR had yet to deliver our furniture, but we were home and happy to be here.

I wandered through the house, inspecting it. What a joy to see it was electrified; light fixtures hung in every room, even the kitchen. No more filling coal oil lamps, trimming wicks and cleaning chimneys. The kitchen, my domain, was dominated by an enormous McClary range, and attended by a substantial icebox, a large worktable, an enameled sink with hot and cold running water, and a pantry off to one side for baking.

The basement housed not just the furnace, hot water heater and cold room, but also a wringer washer. Joy of joys! I no longer ran the risk of scraping knuckles on a washboard. Let Nora soil her nappies! Let Arthur get grass stains on his trousers! Let Dr. Waddy come home with manure on his coveralls! Washday would no longer be the chore it had been in Strathmore.

Upstairs consisted of four bedrooms and a bathroom. A *modern* bathroom, with an enameled tub and enameled sink, both with hot and cold faucets. No more hauling pails of hot water upstairs for the bath. No more hauling pails of cold dirty bath water downstairs. Best of all, a proper WC sat in its own little room. No more dumping out stinky potties. I was in heaven!

As for the back yard and garden, there wasn't much to see other than dying grass and a shed. Perhaps people who rented didn't want to invest time and energy in a garden and flowers when they didn't know if they would stay long enough to enjoy the fruits of their labour. I wondered how long we would live here.

City services included more than electricity and Mr. Thomas Crapper's conveniences. The mailman delivered twice a day, the milk man every morning except Sunday, and the ice man twice a week. The house had a telephone in Dr. Waddy's office and he had sole use of it until Mrs. Waddy discovered she could ring up the grocer and have groceries delivered. That lightened my work somewhat.

As before, Sundays after breakfast were my day, and all autumn, as in Strathmore, I walked through one or other of the city parks, weather permitting. The city had taken care to transform parts of this bleak and barren prairie into an oasis. Victoria Park was in the centre of the city, Central Park only a few blocks south, and a few blocks farther south was Wascana Park with the magnificent Legislative Buildings on the south side of a small lake created when they damned the little creek.

My walks through Wascana Park were especially pleasant. Families, couples and single people like me came to enjoy this oasis of green. I smiled at children squealing with delight as they fed ducks and geese or chased each other about. They brought to mind my carefree childhood in Feock. I watched young couples walk arm-in-arm, and wondered if I would ever do the same with a handsome young man. I was envious of families eating picnics; would I ever share a picnic with my children, I wondered. The beautiful shades of yellow and orange of the autumn leaves and the water lap-lapping against the shore created a very pastoral scene. It was hard to believe that the park had been a centre of death and destruction when the cyclone ripped into the city.

I made the acquaintance of an English girl on one of those Sundays. I was sitting in Victoria Park, enjoying the warm autumn sun, when she walked by and stopped. "Excuse me, Miss, for being so forward, but you live at the Waddy residence, don't you?"

I raised my eyebrows, "Yes, why do you ask?"

She smiled, "I work for the Longworthys at the end of the block, I've seen you walk by a few times, I presume on errands." She pointed to the bench, "May I join you?"

I motioned for her to sit, "Yes, please, it will be nice to have someone to talk to, especially someone from Devon."

She started. "How did you know?"

I smiled. "I recognized your accent. I am from Cornwall."

As it turned out, Isabelle was from Paignton, a shop owner's daughter. She, like I, had wanted to be a teacher but her father, like mine, saw no reason to waste money educating a daughter. She came to Canada three years ago, still with the dream of being a teacher. "I have saved enough money to attend Normal School in the spring," she proclaimed. Over the winter, we spent many pleasant Sunday afternoons at a nearby tea shop. Even after she started her training, we met for a walk and tea.

One sunny afternoon, as we sat in Victoria Park, I asked Isabelle if she had been in Regina when the cyclone hit. She paused, twisted her hands together and took a deep breath. "Oh, yes, it was like the end of the world." She bit her lip and glanced down at her lap.

"We'd heard thunder for a long time, getting louder with every moment, and suddenly Mr. Longworthy came running into the house, shouting, 'Everyone into the basement.' We hid under the stairs and listened to the banging and crashing, the wind roaring like '40 million shrieking devils,' the *Leader* described it. I swear I felt the house shudder. Mr. Longworthy was praying for deliverance, Mrs. Longworthy was sobbing and their daughter was screeching 'We're doomed, we're going to die!' I'm not ashamed to admit I was shaking in my shoes, praying just as fervently as Mr. Longworthy. And then there was silence. We walked upstairs, relieved to see our house was intact. But when we went outside . . ."

She paused, took another breath. "It was horrible what we saw. Devastation everywhere. Beautiful buildings thrown down as if they were made of kindling. Knots of people standing around, stunned, as we were. We could hear people calling, crying out for help. And then people just started digging, throwing bricks and timbers aside to rescue those still living." Her shoulders shuddered. Tears streamed down her face. "So many didn't."

I dug a handkerchief out of my handbag and gave it to her. "I'm sorry. I didn't mean to distress you."

She wiped her eyes and blew her nose. "It's all right, Mary." She turned to me. "Maybe I needed to talk to someone about it. Maybe now the nightmares will cease."

We sat in silence for a moment, a silence broken only by the laughter of children and the chatter of couples walking through the park. Isabelle patted my hand. "Enough of cyclones. Let's go have tea and talk about happy things."

Until I met Isabelle, I had felt alone but now I had a friend, or at least an acquaintance, from a similar social class and the same part of England. She reminded me a little of Bessie and Amelia, full of piss and vinegar, and a bit rebellious although, unlike Bessie, she did not smoke, thank heavens. I enjoyed our times together but they made me realize how much I missed my sisters. I couldn't even remember their voices and if it weren't for their photographs I feared they would disappear completely from my memory. Worst of all, I felt homeless; all that I knew in England was fading away but nothing here felt like home.

I was not the first to experience that sense of homelessness. One crisp October Sunday, as we strolled through Wascana Park, I asked Isabelle, "Do you feel at home here?"

She cocked her head. "Hmm, ye – es." She paused, then nodded emphatically. "Yes, I do. Now. Not at first, though. I felt like the Israelites in Babylon – a stranger in a strange land. But now Regina feels like home. I still miss my sister and brothers, but I have friends, like you, and I have a future here that I would never have in Devon. Don't worry, Mary. You'll feel at home here, too, after a year or two."

I took her hand. "Thank you. Now, no more talk of homesickness."

***

In early October, Dr. Waddy strode into the house, beaming, and slapped the *Regina Leader* on the table. "The Duke and Duchess of Connaught are coming to Regina on October 12. The city is declaring it a holiday."

Royalty coming here? My heart skipped a beat. My parents may have argued about almost everything but they were of one mind about the monarchy. They had mourned the death of Queen Victoria in full style by drawing our window blinds and dressing us in black. They managed to wedge us in amongst the crowd standing at the back of Truro Cathedral for one of the many memorial services held across the British Empire. Mother sobbed as if she had lost her nearest and dearest friend. The following year, they toasted King Edward VII's coronation, Father with whiskey, Mother with a pot of strong Twinings English Breakfast tea. Mother repeated the mourning when the King died in 1910 and the celebrating when King George V was crowned; I assume Father did the same. They made us memorize the names of all of Queen Victoria's sons and daughters, and whom they had married, making European royalty one giant family. And now, the Duke of Connaught, son of the late Queen and uncle of the King, was coming to Regina.

On the appointed day, the sun shone but did little to dull the sharp wind that tried but could not chill our enthusiasm. We stood amongst the throngs on Victoria Avenue, mufflers wrapped around our necks, shoulders hunched up around our ears, stamping our feet, blowing on our reddening fingers, flinching each time the guns at Wascana Park boomed out the Royal Salute. A cheer rippled through the crowd – "Here they come!" – and we craned our necks to see. Dr. Waddy lifted Arthur onto his shoulders. Mrs. Waddy motioned me to hold Nora up high and wave her little hand.

And then, there they were, the Duke and Duchess in their open carriage, waving grandly, preceded and followed by a troop of mounted Royal North-West Mounted Police in their brilliant red jackets. We cheered, we clapped, we waved our flags. A woman next to us fainted with delirium. And then it was over. They were gone. Off to City Hall and the speeches and festivities. We walked home. But I had seen Royalty. Of one thing I was sure – I would not have seen them if I were still in England. I wrote my sisters and, oh, they were so jealous!

At the end of October, I received wonderful news from Clive.

My dear sister and now Auntie Mary, Yes, you are once again an auntie. I was delivered of a beautiful baby girl on October 7, three days before your own birthday. We have named her Peggy, not Margaret, just Peggy. I am certain that Harry in his heart of hearts was hoping for a son but now that Peggy is here he is smitten with her and I fear I am no longer the love of his life. Of course we are all smitten with her, especially Mother. She cannot get enough of her first granddaughter and I fear Peggy will be spoiled rotten before the year is out. With much love, Clive.

I found a beautiful little bonnet and some booties for Peggy at R.H. Williams' department store. When I told the clerk they were for my new niece, she smiled. "You've made a lovely choice," and she wrapped them carefully in white tissue paper and put them in a sturdy box.

Dear Clive and Harry, I am so chuffed at your news, how I wish I could be there to kiss my new niece so please kiss her for me. This gift comes with all my love. Mary (Auntie and sister)

I shed a tear as I put them in the post; I so wished I could deliver them in person.

Mrs. Waddy was also expecting, the new arrival due in the spring. Dr. Waddy was thrilled. Arthur, who was now three, was not sure he wanted another sister but a brother would be perfectly acceptable. Nora, who had just celebrated her first birthday, was too young to realize what was happening.

I was introduced to a prairie ritual in mid-October. Three workmen arrived shortly after breakfast to remove the window screens and replace them with storm windows. I stood gape-mouthed, hardly daring to breath, as I watched one climb up the ladder to remove the screen from a second-storey window, hand it through the open window to the man inside and then maneuver the storm window out and hang it on the frame. I was fully prepared to see him and window come tumbling down in a tangled, bloody mess. Arthur tried to climb up the ladder after him, but I caught him before he was out of reach.

"Up! Up!," he wailed as I dragged him inside. When the workmen left, one said, "We'll be back next spring to put the screens on."

The following week, the Royal Coal Company shoveled a load of coal into the basement. A black grimy dust filtered through the entire house, bringing back too many memories of cleaning the house at Higher Tregurra after coal was delivered. I scolded the men, "Dr. Waddy purchased your coal only because you say it is free of dust! So what is this on the floors and tables?"

They shrugged, "We are just the delivery men, Miss," and left me standing in the kitchen with mop and bucket to clean up the mess.

* * *

My acquaintance with prairie winters began in early November when the first snow fell. Not much but enough to cover the ground and get tracked into the house. Dr. Waddy arranged for a boy to clean off the walk early in the morning, for which he was paid five cents. He earned every penny, and my everlasting thanks, as the snow piled up.

I feared I would freeze to death that first winter. The house was cold and drafty, no matter how much coal Dr. Waddy shoveled into the furnace. The parlour fireplace sent as much heat up the chimney as it sent into the room. The kitchen was the only warm room in the house, thanks to the McClary stove. At night, the house snapped and creaked; I feared I would wake to find all the nails sprung out and the house fallen apart. Come morning, I scraped frost off my bedroom window to see only a frozen world.

The sun blazed brightly enough but did little to moderate the frigid air outside. My breath froze on my muffler and my fingers reddened and tingled in my gloves. Snow squeaked underfoot. Dr. Waddy might exclaim about the beauty of hoar frost covered trees but I saw only never-ending bitter cold.

That first Christmas was painfully lonely. The city sparkled with lights and window displays, quite unlike the dark sadness that filled my mind and heart. Everything we did, everything I saw, reminded me of England, of home, of my family. Mother scolding, "No, don't hang the streamers there." "George, the star is crooked." "No, Dorothy, we will not light the candles now, wait till Christmas Eve." "Mary, the tea is cold." "Bessie, for heaven's sake, put out that awful cigarette!" Father uncorking the whiskey bottle and glug-glugging some into his glass. The pudding steaming and the goose roasting. Carolers singing "In the Bleak Midwinter" and "God Rest Ye Merry, Gentlemen" and "Here We Come a-Wassailing."

I wrapped some small gifts for my family – handkerchiefs I had embroidered, a lace collar, a silk scarf, a pair of gloves for George, a bonnet and jacket I had knit for Peggy – and put them in the post. I mailed my heart with them. I knew Amelia's gift probably wouldn't arrive in Australia until Easter but she would understand.

Dr. Waddy dragged in a spindly evergreen tree the Saturday before Christmas and we spent the afternoon decorating it and the parlour. Mrs. Waddy hung stockings for Arthur and Nora on the fireplace mantle. Arthur grabbed his stocking and peered inside. "No p'esent!" He held it up to his father. "No p'esent, Daddy!" He pouted when his mother said, "You'll have to wait till Christmas Day."

I was in the kitchen early Christmas morning, stuffing the goose and putting the pudding on to steam, when they came down. Arthur ran over to his stocking, "Santa b'ing p'esents, Mommy!" followed by the sound of paper being ripped off and Arthur exclaiming, "A t'uck! Daddy, look! A t'uck!" He was less impressed with the nuts and orange in the toe of his stocking.

Nora found a rattle in her stocking and after a few brief rattle-rattle-rattles she threw it on the floor and tried to grab Arthur's truck. I was called in to break up the squabble that ensued.

Arthur spent the morning pushing his truck everywhere, including the kitchen where he was quite underfoot until his father took him by the arm, "Miss Appleton has quite enough to do without worrying about you." Mrs. Waddy embroidered, Dr. Waddy read and smoked his pipe, and I cooked.

The smells soon filled the house. Arthur wandered in, "I hung'y, gookie, please."

I whispered to him, "Don't tell your mother," and gave him a shortbread cookie. "What do you say?" I asked. "Ta, Miss App'ton." He sat at the table and ate the cookie, leaving crumbs on the floor.

I served dinner in the early afternoon and ate mine, as usual, in the kitchen. Dr. Waddy complemented me on the goose and chestnut stuffing. When I had finished clearing the table, he said, "Will you join us in the parlour for the gifts?"

Mrs. Waddy drew the drapes to darken the room while Dr. Waddy lit the candles on the tree. Arthur's eyes opened wide, "O-o-oh!" Nora tottered toward the tree and I grabbed her before she did any damage. Dr. Waddy handed out the gifts, then snuffed out the candles. "Don't want the house to burn down on Christmas Day!" he declared.

My gift from the Waddys was a large box of beautiful stationery embossed with my name. When I thanked them, Mrs. Waddy said, "I knew that would be useful. You are always writing so many letters." That night, I used the first of the many sheets to write home.

The New Year came in with a blizzard. For two days, the wind howled and the snow flew so thick we could hardly see across the street. The third day dawned bright and clear and very cold. Every window was frosted with amazing patterns. Snow drifts blocked walkways and streets. The air sparkled and two brilliant spots – sundogs, Dr. Waddy told me – flanked the sun. The mercury refused to leave the bottom of the thermometer.

Dorothy's March letter did not help my mood.

Dearest Mary, Spring is well on its way. The daffodils were especially glorious this year although they are now finished, and the trees are budding out. Mother is already fussing over her roses, ordering me to prune them even though my attempt last year was a royal cock-up, or so she said. Love, Dorothy.

Dear Dorothy and Bessie, I am so jealous. Winter still has a firm grip on this country. Today is overcast, blustery and cold. The wind is whipping the snow around, people are wrapped up in mufflers and heavy coats. Not a blade of grass or leaf or anything green to be seen anywhere, only snow, snow, snow in piles and drifts. Isabelle hates spring, she says the melting snow reveals all the horse droppings and other garbage that the snow hid all winter. Sometimes, I wonder why people live here. Love Mary.

* * *

May tempered both the weather and my mood. Elm trees put on a green haze then burst into leaf. Tulips in the neighbour's yard pushed up and set buds. Grass turned from dead brown to spritely green. The seeds that I had planted a couple of weeks before were now pushing up through the ground. Perhaps this country isn't so bad after all, I thought.

I started to count the months I still had to work for Mrs. Waddy who was beginning to try my patience sorely. She seemed to think being married to a veterinary doctor erased her humble beginnings, but not in my opinion. Occasionally, she condescended to enter the kitchen to give me my orders, but usually she summoned me into the parlour to set forth my day's tasks. She was even more insufferable now that she had made the acquaintance of Mrs. George Forsyth, who lived across the street from us.

Mrs. Forsyth was the Vice-President of the Young Women's Christian Association, and she and her husband were prominent members of St. Paul's Cathedral which was where Mrs. Waddy had met her. It was a continual litany of "Mrs. Forsyth this," and "Mrs. Forsyth that." Mrs. Waddy preened on the few occasions that "my *dear* friend, Mrs. Forsyth" asked her to tea, and she always returned with additional demands because "Mrs. Forsyth does it that way."

Things came to a head late one May afternoon. Mrs. Waddy had badgered me all morning. "This needs doing!" "That needs doing!" "I need this done immediately!" I was in the parlour, sweeping the ashes out of the fireplace, and spilled some on the floor just as she walked in. "Appleton, what a mess you've made. Mrs. Forsyth's maid keeps her house much cleaner."

I stood up, dustpan in one hand, whisk in the other, and faced her. "Then perhaps you should hire Mrs. Forsyth's maid!" I stomped into the kitchen, threw the ashes in the bin and sat at the table. I was shaking so much I could not even pour myself a cup of tea, cold though it might be. I longed for Strathmore with no Mrs. Forsyth.

That evening, I heard Mrs. Waddy say to her husband, "We should dismiss Appleton. She is too impertinent. You should have heard her talk back to me this afternoon."

"But the children love her. She's so good with them. I'll have a word with her, if that will put your mind at ease."

I was not dismissed.

* * *

In early May, Mrs. Waddy went into labour.

I was in the midst of spring cleaning, polishing the furniture in fact, when I heard her cry out. She was doubled over, her hand on her stomach, and standing in a pool of water

"Call Dr. Waddy," she cried out between groans and moans.

I had not used the telephone before but I had watched Dr. Waddy so I knew the procedure. I lifted the earpiece, turned the crank a few times, and when Operator answered I told her to ring the Health of Animals Branch. Eventually, I was put through to Dr. Waddy. After several breathless exclamations of "Oh my goodness!" and "Are you sure?" and "Is she all right?" he said he would be home forthwith and I was to call the hospital to ensure they were waiting for her. He arrived within a few minutes – by then I had retrieved Mrs. Waddy's night case – and he hustled her out the door and into a waiting taxicab, flinging "Please look after the children, I don't know when I will be back!" over his shoulder.

"Mommy sick?" Arthur asked.

"No, your mother is just going to have the new baby. She will be fine. Now come, let me tell you a story."

I sat Nora on my lap and Arthur beside me on the chesterfield to begin a tale of pirates and how the glorious Royal Navy defeated them in battle. Nora squirmed and whined until I let her down. She ran around but bumped into the table and began to cry. I snatched up Nora, grabbed Arthur's hand and took them up to their rooms for their afternoon nap.

Dr. Waddy didn't return until the early hours of the morning. I met him on the landing. "A baby boy born an hour ago, mother and baby both fine," he said. It was May 13.

Mrs. Waddy came home two weeks later, very thankful to have had the attention of a doctor and well-trained nurses to assist in the birthing. "Imagine what crackpot doctor might have attended me in Strathmore," she complained. A month later, he was christened John Colson Waddy at St. Paul's Anglican Church. I created a christening gown for him, embellished with pin tucks and embroidery, worthy of the Prince of Wales, in my opinion.

Arthur was overjoyed to have a brother but he was sorely disappointed when Mrs. Waddy had only a tiny baby to show him. "He play with me?" he asked. He sulked when he heard he would have to wait a long time.

Spring turned into summer. We settled into a routine, or as much of a routine as was possible with a newborn baby, an almost-two-year-old girl who was quickly learning how to wield her "No!" and a three-year-old boy who had more energy than all the adults in the house.

The routine was thrown into chaos when Dr. Waddy came home one afternoon in early July. He all but slammed his hat onto the hat rack and sat down heavily in his chair. "I've been transferred!"

"What! Again?" Mrs. Waddy put down her embroidery. "Where?"

Yes, where indeed, I wondered. I was feeding Arthur and Nora in the kitchen, so I moved my chair such I could see into the parlour while still keeping an eye on the children.

Dr. Waddy leaned forward, his forearms on his legs. "North Portal in southeastern Saskatchewan, on the border with America. Mr. Tamblyn calls it a promotion, lots of responsibility, says my salary will increase." He reached over to the side table, picked up his pipe, filled and lit it. He leaned back and blew out a cloud of smoke.

Mrs. Waddy coughed and swatted the smoke away with her hand. "When?"

"First of August."

"That's only three weeks away! How can we be ready to move in three weeks? And what about my club? And the YWCA rummage sale? Mrs. Forsyth put me in charge of it. And the theatre? We have tickets to the theatre starting in September." Her voice broke. She turned away and dabbed a handkerchief at her eyes.

She turned back to face Dr. Waddy. "You could resign and go into private practice like Mr. Tamblyn. Then we could stay here. I don't want to leave. I have friends here now."

I, too, don't want to leave, I thought. I have friends here, too. And my flowers. I will never see my flowers bloom. I heard a clatter behind me and turned to find that Nora had thrown her spoon and plate on the floor. I sighed as I cleaned up the mess.

For the next three weeks, the house was in turmoil while we packed boxes and trunks. The CPR agent came to assess the cost of shipping everything to North Portal. We informed all the delivery people. I wrote home with the news and our new address. Isabelle and I had one last visit, a sad one filled with good-byes and promises to write.

Two days before we left Regina, I stood in the back yard and looked at the flowers, at *my* flowers. The bachelor buttons and delphiniums were blooming, and the lilies were about to bloom. All that time spent weeding and watering in the belief that we would live in Regina, at least until my service to the Waddys had ended. Now, here we were, once again, leaving, and for what kind of place? I was so frustrated I was sorely tempted to take the hoe and chop everything down. If I couldn't enjoy the flowers, well, then neither would anyone else. But I didn't. I sighed, turned on my heel and walked into the house, promising myself I would never plant another garden. Something deep inside me told me that was a vacant promise.

That same day, I received a letter from Amelia.

Dearest Mary, I have escaped the barbarism of western Australia and am now living in civilization, Sydney. I had enough of my employer. He took it into his head that because I worked under him, I should also sleep under him. I was having none of that and told him so in very plain language. He grabbed my arm and began to call me names. Bad mistake on his part because I was stirring soup. I smacked his face with the spoon, splashing hot soup all over him. He yelped and tried to hit me but I wielded that spoon like a Roman sword and beat him about the head and ears. You're fired, he yelled at me. I quit, I yelled back and threw the spoon onto the floor and flounced out of the kitchen back to my room and threw all my belongings into my trunk. I sailed for Sydney two days later. It's a proper city, not some thrown-up rough and tumble camp. I met a nice young man on the trip, Albert Sanders is his name. He's from Bristol. Love, Amelia.

On July 30, the CPR drayman collected everything and we moved into a hotel. The next day, we took the morning train to Moose Jaw. We had almost six hours to wait before catching the train to North Portal so we walked up Main Street and looked in some of the shops. Arthur was delighted when we found a park where he could run around. We had dinner at the Royal George Hotel, across the street from the CPR station, and Mrs. Waddy reminded her husband the hotel had the same name as the ship we sailed in from England. At 4:30 pm, we boarded the train to North Portal and arrived there just before midnight.

The Grandview Hotel was expecting us, although perhaps not two very cranky children and one sleeping baby. We stayed there for two nights until the CPR had delivered our goods and we then moved into our new house.

Chapter Eleven
North Portal

My dear Amelia, I am so envious of you, having gone from barbarism to civilization. I have gone in exactly the opposite direction, from civilization to barbarism. You should see this place. I am beginning to wish I had never left England even if it meant marrying the hostler at the Angel Inn. I so miss my sisters and brother, at times my heart breaks with loneliness. Do you feel like that, too? All my love, Mary.

I thought Strathmore was a dump but it was the epitome of civilization compared to North Portal. According to Dr. Waddy, it was a border town of some import, but I called it a sorry excuse for a town. The hotels were the only two buildings of any substance. The Grandview offered only a saggy bedstead, a chipped and dirty sink, and a rug that has seen better days. The WC was down the hall, and I guessed its last cleaning was some time last century. At least there were no bedbugs or lice.

Dirt wasn't all the Grandview offered. A noisy fight broke out our first night and terrified the children. Dr. Waddy asked Mr. Hetherington, the proprietor, to keep better order but he might as well have been asking the prairie wind to stop blowing for all the good it did. We were so glad to leave that establishment. Mr. Hetherington made some of his income from renting rooms, but he made a killing, as they say, from the beer parlour. And what a noisy, rough-and-ready lot they were that frequented the place. Some were locals – ranchers, farmers and coal miners – but most came from North Dakota where prohibition reigned, and they made the most of their visits.

Almost every day – morning, afternoon, evening; it didn't matter when – fights began over the slightest excuse, and more often as not they spilled out into the street. Both hotels kept the Royal North-West Mounted Police very busy, breaking up fights and tossing the combatants in jail to sober up.

The CPR railway divided the town in two. On the west side were the immigration buildings and what passed for the business section of town with the CPR station, shops selling groceries, clothing, sweets and hardware, a bakery, a bank, a blacksmithy, a lumber yard, two livery stables and the Union Hotel. They all looked as if they had been slapped up just last week. Further to the west were the Government's quarantine barns and stockyards. The pungent barnyard smell and the sound of bawling cattle and neighing horses, not to mention grunting pigs and baaing sheep, was constant, day and night, summer and winter. Most of the houses were on the east side of the tracks, as was the Grandview, only a few steps from the border. Distance did not spare them from the pervasive aroma, thanks to the almost constant west wind.

Our house was on the west side, close to the quarantine station and the smell. At least it had a diesel power plant in the basement for electric lights. I noted with dismay there was no running water, only a hand pump by the kitchen sink, and no bathroom other than the little house out back and the dreaded chemical toilet upstairs. Mrs. Waddy didn't think much better of it than I did. We curled our lips and wrinkled our noses as we walked from room to room. It was sorely in need of a good cleaning. It took me almost a week of sweeping, scrubbing, dusting, shaking out rugs and washing drapes to make the house livable. I found evidence of mice so Dr. Waddy bought some traps and I spent days trapping the critters. I caught a finger while setting one of the traps and it was sore for several days thereafter.

Dr. Waddy was kept very busy, for several trains a day came through the village, bound to and from Chicago and Seattle via Minneapolis-St. Paul. Upwards of 200 passengers arrived on each train, mostly immigrant settlers whose possessions, including livestock, were contained in the many boxcars that made up the train. All livestock had to be quarantined, which annoyed the owners to the point of being abusive to both the vets and the immigration officers. Dr. Waddy seemed to be as much occupied with paperwork – recording which animals were owned by which people and were going to which destination – as he was with inspecting the animals themselves. Come winter, the cold and snow didn't help him in his work. He often came home chilled to the bone, and he would stand by the cook stove and drink several cups of tea, often fortified with whiskey, to warm himself.

That Thanksgiving, my second one in Canada, I could only grumble while everyone else gathered around the table laden with food to give thanks for health, wealth and happiness. What do I have to be thankful for, stuck in this hole, washing up dust and mud tracked in from the street, listening to Mrs. Waddy complain how "Mrs. Forsyth wouldn't put up with this." My mood lightened when I realized in less than a year, I would have paid back my passage and I would be free to leave.

After having enjoyed the bounty of Regina, North Portal's shops were a disappointment, offering only limited goods, and those at exorbitant prices. One day as I was posting a letter home, I saw a thick catalogue from the T.E. Eaton Company beside the wicket. I flipped through the pages, amazed at what it offered.

"You can buy anything you want from them, Miss. If it isn't in their catalogue, it doesn't exist," the postmaster said. "You can even buy a house, if you're so inclined."

I scoffed, but a neighbour who was picking up his mail said, "He's right, Miss. I know someone near Estevan who bought one, a big two-storey house with a verandah. Came with everything except the workmen to assemble it." The two of them laughed. Eventually, I decided to give Mr. Eaton's catalogue the benefit of the doubt and ordered some things. I was not disappointed.

Summer turned to autumn turned to winter. Now instead of mopping up dust and mud I was mopping up snow and mud. How could a four-year-old boy with such little feet track in so much mud? Dr. Waddy tracked in manure from the barns, no matter how careful he was to scrape off his wellies. The mop and pail got a good workout almost every day as did the scrub board (and my knuckles), getting the mud and manure off trousers and coats.

December approached, and Mrs. Waddy and I made good use of Mr. Eaton's catalogue to order Christmas gifts for everyone. I baked cookies and puddings and fruit cake. We decorated the house and a spindly evergreen tree and piled gifts around it. Nora was now old enough to know about Santa Claus, giving us two children anxious about what he would leave in their stockings. In no time, Christmas was upon us, a day of gifts and feasting and relaxing for the Waddys, a long day of cooking and cleaning up for me. And then it was over and we were into a new year.

The letters from my sisters were usually full of news and gossip but one I received from Bessie early in 1914 was filled more with worry than gossip.

Dearest Mary, Mother is more anxious than ever about finances because, once Maude and I turn 21, Father will not have to pay for doctors, should we be ill. The 30 shillings a month he pays plus what we receive from our "guests" barely covers our necessities. I may have to go into service as you did. Some days I dream of going to Canada but I can't even afford the fare to Lands End, so Canada is out of the question. Love, Bessie.

Oh, how I wished Bessie could come to Canada! It would be so wonderful to have her near me, but, like her, I could not afford the fare. I was depressed for days until I remembered Father's offer to pay my way back to England if I should ever decide to return. A devious thought sprang to mind. What if? No, that would be deceitful. But he had deceived Mother so maybe he deserved a bit of his own medicine. And I would so love to have Bessie here.

I wrestled with my conscience for a couple of weeks. And lost. If I could not go back to England, I could at least bring a bit of England – Bessie – to me. That evening, I composed a remorseful letter.

My dearest Father, Canada is not the fountain of opportunity that I expected, and the people are indeed backwards and ignorant, as you predicted. If you have heard otherwise from my sisters, it is only because I did not want my letters to give them grief over my situation here. Once I am free of my obligations to the Waddy family, I desire nothing more than to return to England. Alas, in spite of saving what I can from my pay, I lack the funds to do so.

Thus, I am asking a great favour of you. Would you please consider the longing of your oldest daughter to return to England, and forward me sufficient funds to pay my passage home, as you once promised? I have no means of discerning what sum that might be but it must cover both train fare on the Canadian Pacific Railway as well as passage by ship. Perhaps one of the emigration agencies in Penzance might advise you. I will always be indebted to you for your kindness. As always, your loving daughter, Mary.

That same night, I wrote to Bessie. *I have a plan but I dare not divulge it for fear it may come to naught. If all goes well, I will be able to send you the fare to Canada.*

Did I feel guilty? Perhaps a little bit. But I was helping Bessie and that was more important. I waited. Time crept by.

Father's reply arrived at the end of March. I trembled as I opened the envelope. I pulled out the letter and found three crisp new £10 notes enclosed. He must have obtained them from the bank for I had never seen him with anything more than shillings and the occasional tattered one pound note in his pocket.

Dear Mary, How unlike your mother you are to realize the error of your ways. I always knew you were a sensible woman. Business has been exceptionally brisk this month. In addition to my regular customers, I was hired to attend at three funerals and was well paid for my efforts. I have therefore included £30 which should more than cover the cost of your tickets. Regards as always, Father.

I could hardly believe my luck. I danced with glee. So what if Father would be furious when he learned of my deception? Let him disown me. I didn't care. After what he had done to Mother, deserting her for that Nottingham tart, this would be only just retribution. Plus, he had defied his own father, so sauce for the goose and all that.

That evening I informed Dr. and Mrs. Waddy that I was intending to bring my sister over, and asked if she could live here while she looked for employment.

They looked at each other, eyebrows raised. Dr. Waddy set down his pipe, "She will have to pay room and board."

Mrs. Waddy took up her knitting, "I am sure one of the hotels could use another maid," she sniffed.

I thanked them and ran upstairs to write Bessie with all the details.

Dearest Bessie, My devious ruse worked! I've enclosed the £30 that Father sent under the illusion it was to pay my fare back to England. Little did he know the truth. Book your passage to Montreal, hire a carriage there to take you to Windsor Station where you will buy a ticket to Moose Jaw. There, take the Soo Line train to North Portal. Get a berth if you can afford it, otherwise you will have to endure the settler car. There is plenty of work here, the hotels are always looking for housecleaners. Please let me know when you will arrive. I can hardly wait to see you. Give my love to my sisters and brother. Love, Mary

I folded the £10 notes inside the letter and the next morning posted it.

And waited.

Bessie's letter arrived the end of April.

My dear Mary, What a devious scamp you are! I told Maude and Dorothy of your scheme, and we all had a great laugh. I have booked second class passage on Mr. Cunard's ship, the Ascania. She leaves Southampton on June 11 and arrives in Canada on June 21. I hope to be with you within the week. My sisters are envious of my coming adventure. Mother, as usual, flew into a fit. She accuses us of abandoning her in her advancing years, never mind that Maude and Dorothy are still with her, and Clive and Harry and George and Carrie all live nearby. I have not told Father, and our sisters have promised not to inform him until I am safely on Canadian soil. I can only imagine the rage he will fly into; I pity whoever it is who has that unenviable task. I can hardly wait to see you. All my love, Bessie.

I have never been so impatient for a particular day to arrive, not even Christmas when I was a child, or the bell ringing to signal the end of school. The wait was interminable even though I was kept very busy. A four-year-old boy whose greatest joy was to run around the house and yard, tearing the knees in every pair of trousers and acquiring every scrape and bruise possible; a little girl in the throes of the terrible twos, who was constantly running to me crying that her big brother was picking on her; and a baby screaming with colic; this on top of all my other duties, and it seemed I had no time to think for myself. Except at night, in the few brief minutes between when I crawled into bed and when I fell asleep, that was when I imagined what it would be like to have Bessie with me.

On June 22, I received a telegram: SAFELY ARRIVED MTL TODAY STOP ARRIVE MJ JUNE 24 NP JUNE 25 STOP. Only three more days.

On the designated day, I all but ran to the station. I paced back and forth on the platform, I peered down the track, I checked my pocket watch at least a dozen times, and then I heard, off in the distance, a Woooo-Woooo-Woo-Woooo as the train approached the last crossing. There it came, huffing and puffing great clouds of smoke into the air, the bell ringing, steam belching out from the wheels, brakes screeching, the deafening noise setting the platform to vibrating. I could barely breath with anticipation.

I saw the conductor step out of the passenger car, hold his hand up to help someone descend, and there she was, cigarette in hand as always. I lost all composure. I waved and called out, "Bessie!" and ran towards her, arms outstretched. She saw me, waved, jumped off the last step, tossed her cigarette aside and ran towards me. Her hat went flying. We embraced, we cried, we laughed, we danced around each other like schoolgirls, and then we did it all over again.

I stooped to pick up her hat. "I am so glad to see you. Welcome to North Portal."

She plopped it back on her head. "I am so glad to be here. You didn't tell me this country is so big!"

"Yes, I did!" And we laughed again.

She fumbled in her handbag and pulled out a package of cigarettes and a box of matches. I grimaced. "Do you still engage in that disgusting habit?"

She grinned. "Yes, mostly because it annoys Mother. Now, let's go home. I need a nap. I had to sit up all night in the station waiting to catch this train at the infernal hour of 4:00 o'clock this morning!" She blew out a cloud of smoke. "I had several propositions to keep me amused, though none of them worth following through on."

"Bessie!"

She laughed. "Just teasing you, dear sister."

I took her arm. "Now tell me all the news from home."

A blast of the train whistle and a yell, "Miss, is this your trunk?" interrupted us, and we ran to collect her belongings. I told the baggage man to deliver them to the Waddy household.

"Not much has changed since I wrote you. Oh, Amelia is married, did you get her letter? I can not imagine what sort of man would marry her, given her quick tongue. Quiet and retiring she is most definitely not. Dorothy said she would tell Father after I left, said she would take great delight in stabbing him in the pocketbook. Oh, there are rumours of war, things are stirring on the continent but I don't know if it will come to that."

Then she grinned. "I think I can one-up you when it comes to being deceitful."

"What have you done?"

"Well, the booking agent was not at all keen to sell me passage when he learned I was only 20, so I told him I would be living with my sister. He asked, 'Is she married or single?' I decided to air on the side of caution so I said, 'married'."

"But I am not!"

Bessie threw back her head and laughed. "No, but he didn't know that. Neither did the immigration officer in Quebec City. I watched him scrawl 'going to married sister' on the passenger manifest."

I shook my head. "Bessie, you haven't changed one bit. And thank heavens for that."

She sniffed the air and looked around at the village as we walked. "How long do we have to stay in this rat hole of a place?"

"Only a couple of months more, then I will have paid back my passage and I am free to go. I have inquired about work, and the Union Hotel says they can use another cleaning lady. And believe me, their cleanliness is far from godliness." I motioned to the house before us. "Here we are. I will introduce you to Dr. and Mrs. Waddy."

Two days later, we witnessed our first North Portal Dominion Day celebration, followed three days later by the Americans' Independence Day. What a change from my two previous Dominion Day celebrations. Nothing had happened in Strathmore due to heavy rains, although many went into Calgary on the mistaken assumption it might be drier there. It wasn't, and they came home soaked to the skin. Regina's celebration last year was energetic but dignified. We spent the day at Wascana Park along with the throngs, watching the regatta and partaking of a picnic. I overheard several say how disappointed they were that there were no fireworks.

The people of North Portal (and North Dakota) certainly trotted out the fireworks, of all kinds. The celebrations were loud and raucous involving, at least on the part of the men, a lot of drinking accompanied by a lot of fighting well into the night. We witnessed foot races (Dr. Waddy demurred from entering) and baseball games and horse races (the latter accompanied by heavy betting and more drinking). The children had three-legged races and wheelbarrow races, and a peanut scramble that resulted in more than one skinned knee and ripped trousers and one little girl running to her mother crying, "The big boys wouldn't let me get any peanuts!" whereupon the mother took a couple of boys by their ears and made them share their peanuts. At supper time, everyone spread blankets in the school yard and opened up their picnic baskets. The men churned ice cream, such a treat. Come darkness, the town set off fireworks, not to be confused with the "fireworks" happening inside and outside the two hotels, and their loud banging set several little children to covering their ears and crying with terror. At the end of the day, Bessie said, "I do believe I have just witnessed the wild west of penny novels."

    I paid the last of my passage that month, after which I informed Dr. and Mrs. Waddy that I would leave at the end of August. They thanked me for my service and wished me well in finding new employment. Later that day, after supper, I overheard Mrs. Waddy complain that they would be hard pressed to find a Canadian girl who knew her place as a domestic, "Canadian girls think they are too good for service," she said. I didn't tell her what I was thinking: I am sure you will be only too willing to instruct her as to her 'proper place.'

    One night, as we were getting ready for bed, Bessie asked, "Since you won't be working for the Waddys much longer, what will you do? Where will we go? Any ideas?"

    "Bessie, I am not staying in this place a day longer than I have to. As for where, either Regina or Moose Jaw would be good places to find work. Both have lots of shops and fine homes so we should not have much trouble finding work."

    Bessie giggled. "And they have amenities. Don't forget that."

    I threw back the bedcovers and crawled into bed. "Amenities, yes indeed. Electricity. Running water. A proper WC. Everything we don't have here."

Bessie crawled in beside me. "So where will we start? Moose Jaw or Regina?"

I yawned. "The Soo Line goes only as far as Moose Jaw so let's start there. We can always go to Regina if necessary. Good night, Bessie."

*　*　*

The morning of September 2, we boarded the 5:30 am train to Moose Jaw. Everyone aboard the train was talking of nothing but the war just started in Europe. We overheard one young man say, "Let's sign up, it'll be a cracker of a jaunt, don't you think?" His friend agreed.

I don't know what happened to the Waddys. We never wrote. They weren't friends, just employers. But I am grateful to them. Because of them, I came to Canada and my life became what it is. Otherwise, who knows what would have happened to me if I had stayed in England. Perhaps I would have married the hostler at the Angel Inn and would now be listening to him drone on about the cost of horseshoe nails. Heaven forbid!

Chapter Twelve
Moose Jaw, Briefly

We stood in the middle of the huge, crowded CPR station in Moose Jaw, echoing with the sounds of people and trains coming and going. I looked back and forth, trying to think of something, anything, when a middle-aged woman approached us. "Are you looking for accommodation?"

When I nodded, she continued, "I'm Mrs. Rutherford, the traveller's aid for the Young Women's Christian Association. Our rooms are safe for young women and the charge is very reasonable. Are you interested?"

An angel in disguise! "Yes, thank you, that would be wonderful. We are new in town and don't know our way around. What about our trunks?"

Mrs. Rutherford smiled, "Follow me." She led us to the baggage department where we pointed out our trunks and Mrs. Rutherford told the man where to deliver them. Then, we walked to the YWCA which was only a few blocks away.

Mrs. Rutherford ushered us into the lobby. "Miss Currie, these two young ladies have just arrived on the Soo Line and are in need of accommodation."

Miss Currie reminded me of no one so much as my school mistress in Feock. Middle-aged, grey hair pulled tightly back into a chignon, a black jacket fastened over a plain white high-necked shirtwaist, and steel-rimmed spectacles that she looked over as often as through. She was peering over them now, seeming to assess our character. I felt like a six-year-old standing before her waiting to be admonished.

Her voice was nothing like the old school mistress's. She even smiled as she spoke. "I have a room but you will have to share the bed. Shall I put you down for a week? The price is 50 cents a night, payable in advance, plus a deposit of 50 cents for the key. As for meals, we have a cafeteria there" – she indicated the direction with a nod of her head – "and the prices are more reasonable than in any of the reputable cafes in town."

I dug into my handbag and counted out $4.00 in coins. Miss Currie opened a large register book and handed me a pen. "Please sign here, the both of you." She looked at our signatures, "Hmm, sisters, I see. And from England. I presume you are looking for employment?"

"I've been working in Canada for two years now, but my sister is newly arrived," I said. "And yes, we are both looking for work, either as a domestic servant or a shop clerk."

Miss Currie handed me the key. "Families are always looking for help. I'm sure you will have no trouble." She pointed towards the stairs. "Your room is number 12, upstairs and to your left."

The room was plainly furnished but clean. Bessie ran her finger along the top of the chiffonier and held it up. "Look, no dust. I couldn't say the same for the Union Hotel, even after I'd given the rooms a good cleaning."

We ate a light meal at the cafeteria and then set off to explore the city. Main Street was chock-a-block with trolley cars, carriages, wagons, buggies and motor cars. People crowded the sidewalks and charged willy-nilly across the busy streets, mindless of the traffic. Many of the young men were in uniform and in high spirits as if they were off on a grand adventure to give the Huns and the Serbs a sound thrashing before coming home for Christmas. The garishly ornamented façade of the Rex Theatre offered entertainments both high and low, while further down the street the Presbyterian and Methodist churches offered sober Christian antidotes to such frivolities.

We walked to the park I remembered from the journey of a year ago, and compared to the cacophony of Main Street, the peace and calm were refreshing. After inspecting the new library – "This city is indeed civilized," Bessie exclaimed – we walked back to Main Street and stopped at a café for a much-needed cup of tea. I noticed a milliner's shop across the street. "We both like hats. Let's go talk to the shop owner. Perhaps he will hire one of us."

"And we can buy ourselves new hats while we're at it."

I shook my head. "We have to be careful with our money."

Bessie crossed her arms. "You are the serious one, aren't you? Come on. They can't be that dear. We should at least take a look. That doesn't cost anything."

The proprietor, Miss Margery Plested, wasn't in need of another clerk, but we did strike up a long conversation about hats and fashions. We agreed the new shorter, ankle-length skirt was much more practical. "Who knows, perhaps one day hems will be at our knees," Bessie said.

"What a shocking idea!" Miss Plested exclaimed. We giggled at the outrageous notion. As we left, Miss Plested said, "Please come again, I enjoyed our visit. And perhaps next time, I can sell you a hat."

That night, I tossed and turned for a long time. For the first time in my life, I was the one in charge and the thought frightened me. Bessie was under the impression that I knew my way around, having been in Canada for two years, but the truth was, I didn't. Dr. Waddy had always taken care of accommodation, transportation, even employment. My mind was filled with "What if this?" and "What if that?" I had several years of experience as a domestic servant but Bessie had none. Who would hire her? What if we didn't find work? What if we had to work in different cities? Perhaps I should have used Father's money to return to England. I finally fell into a sleep filled with disturbing dreams of being impoverished and transient.

All that week, we searched. We enquired at shops. We answered "Domestics Wanted" adverts in the paper. I was invited to an interview only to discover the husband's English was so accented I could hardly understand him and the wife spoke none at all. They had a toddler, a babe-in-arms and a third one on the way. I declined their offer. I felt bad, they needed the help but what help would I be if I could not understand them, or they me. Shop owners were not interested in hiring Bessie for no reason that we could determine, perhaps because she was still unfamiliar with Canadian money.

By week's end, I was thoroughly despondent, but Bessie was chipper. "Next week we'll find work, I'm sure of it," she said, scraping some strawberry jam onto her toast.

"Let us hope so," I said.

Sunday, we decided to attend St. John's Anglican Church. Following the service, we mingled with a few of the parishioners when, suddenly, we heard behind us a man's voice. "Is that an English accent I hear?"

We turned to see a tall, tanned young man with the bushiest eyebrows I had ever seen. He, too, had an English accent although not Cornish.

"And if it is? What might that be to you?" I asked.

He doffed his hat. "Caleb Higham, formerly of Bodicote, Oxfordshire, lately of Belbeck, Saskatchewan. And where might you be from, if I may be so bold as to ask?"

Bessie and I exchanged wary glances. Should we trust this stranger? Finally, Bessie said, "Since you are so bold as to ask, we will be just as bold to reply. We are formerly of Penzance, Cornwall, lately of North Portal, Saskatchewan, if it be all the same to you. Which I'm sure it isn't."

We turned to walk away. He caught us up.

"Just a minute. I didn't mean to offend. I haven't heard an English accent in a year or so, and your voices sounded like music to my ears compared to the flat Canadian voice or, worse still, an American accent."

"You must be hard pressed for music if you think that of our voices," I said.

"Allow me to buy you a cup of tea, at the very least. I don't have to be back to the farm until this afternoon."

I opened my mouth, about to decline his offer, when the vicar arrived. "Ah, Mr. Higham, thank you for lending your fine tenor voice to our choir again this morning."

He turned to us. "I see you have made Mr. Higham's acquaintance. However, I have not had the pleasure. I am Mr. Wells Johnson, the vicar of St. John's. And you are . . ?"

"I am Miss Appleton," I said.

"As am I," Bessie added.

"Very pleased to make your acquaintance. I hope we will see you at St. John's regularly," the Rev. Wells Johnson said.

"As do I," Mr. Higham added. He was smiling.

"That may be, or perhaps not. It all depends on what our future holds," Bessie said.

"Now, as for that cup of tea I offered . . ." Mr. Higham began.

"I don't think so, not today. We have business to attend to," I snapped.

Mr. Higham frowned and nodded. "Then good day to you, Miss Appleton times two."

We watched him walk away then turn the corner in the direction of the station. I sniffed, "Impudent scoundrel, who does he think he is?"

Bessie giggled. "Did you notice he always looked at you when he spoke? I think he likes you."

I glared at her. "I doubt it. Let's find us some lunch."

We were almost out the door Monday morning when Miss Currie called to us. "Have you found work yet?"

We shook our heads, "No, alas."

She waved us over to the counter. "Have you looked for work on farms? Harvest is in full swing and wives are always wanting help with cooking for all those men." She adjusted her glasses. "Now that things are falling apart in Europe, there will be even more positions wanting, what with all the young men going off to war."

She sighed. "Why they want to go to war is beyond my comprehension. My brother went off to South Africa to fight the Boers and came back not himself. And it wasn't just the missing leg. He was moody, jumpy, even mean at times, not like he was before. Then one day, he blew his head off with the shotgun. It was horrid, tore the family apart. I tell you, war is a nasty business but those young men think they are heading off to a picnic. They will learn differently once they get there."

She peered over her glasses. "My apologies, I did not mean to impose my family's sorrow on you. I wish you well in your search."

We had no experience with war, though we'd heard about the Boer War. We could only imagine what her brother had gone through. We thanked her for her suggestions and left to buy yet another newspaper. We ignored the news of the war – the Germans were closing in on Paris, the Russians were closing in on Germany, and over 5000 men were killed or missing – and turned immediately to our favourite section, "Domestics Wanted." Most were the same as had been posted the past several days. I pointed to an advert.

"Here's a new one. 'Good girl for general housework on farm,' and there's a phone number."

Bessie peered over my shoulder. "I wonder if they need two good girls." I wondered the same.

The operator in the telephone office recognized us immediately from our previous visits. We gave her the phone number. "Hmm, a long-distance number. It will cost you more per minute. You can use that booth and I will ring you through."

The phone at the other end rang three times in quick succession, paused, then three more times. A woman answered. I asked if the position was still available. "Yes," she said, "What experience do you have?" I told her. She replied, "Have you worked for a farm family before?" I told her that my father had been a tenant farmer, and I had worked as a domestic for about nine years now in both

England and Canada, and that I had letters of introduction from both employers if she would like to see them.

She paused. "A Saskatchewan farm is different, they're larger here, you know."

I said, yes, I knew that, and added, "Cooking won't be any different, though. A frying pan is still a frying pan, no matter what country it's used in."

She laughed. "You will have to do for now, we need someone immediately I am expecting a child soon and you are the first to reply. We pay $4.00 a week during harvest and $10.00 a month thereafter. Are you in Moose Jaw now?"

When I said, yes, she replied, "I think you've missed the morning train but you can catch the afternoon one, I think it leaves about 4:00 pm. We live outside of Belbeck, do you know where that is?" No, I told her, so she told me which train to catch. "My husband, Will Grigg, will meet you at the station. And what is your name?"

I told her and then I blurted out, "My sister is also looking for employment. Do you have need of two helpers?"

"No, we don't. Oh, just a minute." She must have put her hand over the mouthpiece because all I heard was muffled talk. After a minute, she came back. "My sister says that Mrs. Smail down the road could use some help. They're an older couple, getting on and not quite as able as they used to be. I will call them and see if they are interested. Where can I reach you?"

My heart skipped a beat. Oh please, let them need Bessie, I thought. "We are staying at the YWCA."

"Good, I will call there and leave a message for you. Don't forget, you have to take the 4:00 train to Belbeck." I said, yes, I would remember, and thanked her for her time.

Bessie cornered me before I had barely put back the receiver. "What did she say?"

I took a deep breath. "One of her neighbours might need some help. She is calling them and will leave a message for us at the YWCA." We walked back to the operator and paid for the call.

"But what if they don't? Then what?"

I rubbed my forehead. "I don't know. I think . . ." I paused. "If they don't need you, then I will tell Mrs. Grigg I can't work for her. I am not going to leave you alone here. I feel responsible for you. After all, it's because of me that you are here."

"No, you won't. You will take that position, regardless. Remember, I wanted to come to Canada, so I am just as responsible as you." She took my hand. "Let's go have a cup of tea. That will calm you down."

I pretended it did, but my mind was busy tying itself in knots, imaging what we would do – what *I* would do – if Mrs. Smail did not want to hire Bessie. I snapped out of my worrying when she tapped my hand. "You haven't heard a word I've just said, have you? Stop worrying. Everything will work out fine."

I added a drop more milk to the tea. "I hope you are right."

She was. Miss Currie called Bessie over when we walked into the YWCA. "Mrs. Grigg left a message for you, Miss Appleton the Younger. Mrs. Smail will hire you and Mr. Grigg will drop you off at their home." She smiled at me. "I was delighted to hear you will be working for Mr. and Mrs. Grigg. I know them from church, they are fine people and you will be very happy working for them. Now, you had best get packing. I will call the dray man to pick up your trunks immediately."

By 3:30, we had tickets in hand, our trunks were tagged and on the baggage cart, and we were standing on the platform, waiting for our train to be announced. I was so relieved. We both had work. We would be living close together. What more could we ask for?

Chapter Thirteen
Belbeck

Belbeck didn't amount to much, two grain elevators, a tiny CPR station, a general store that also served as post office and hotel, although why anyone would stop here who did not live here was beyond me, and three or four houses. We descended from the train and saw two men standing on the platform, one with his hand on the baggage cart. As he pulled the cart over to the baggage car, he pointed to us, and the other man, dressed in dusty clothes, walked our way.

"Miss Appleton and Miss Appleton, I presume?" he asked. "Welcome, I'm Will Grigg. You've come just in time. My wife . . ." He was interrupted by the baggage man who came up with our trunks. "Excuse me, ladies, while I help Frank get your trunks on the buggy."

Once they were loaded, Mr. Grigg helped us up and we were off. He turned to Bessie, "You're having supper with us. Mr. and Mrs. Smail are coming afterwards to pick you up."

For having been two years in Canada, I had never really seen the countryside except as we whizzed by in a train and even then, it was mostly at night, too dark to see. The 45-minute ride down the narrow dirt road gave me a good opportunity to see what I had missed. Canadian fields were much larger and laid out in regular squares, not various shapes and sizes, all higgledy-piggledy and separated by hedgerows like in Cornwall. However, harvest time in Canada looked the same – a constant stream of motion and sound. Men yelled. Horses nickered and whinnied. Horse-drawn binders whirred and clattered round some of the fields, cutting standing grain and spitting sheaves out the back; men followed behind, gathering the sheaves and standing them into stooks. I remember George coming back after a day of stooking, scratching, his arms prickled red by the stalks. Those men, mere lads by the look of them, would be doing the same by day's end. Elsewhere, huge stationary engines roared and belched smoke, attached to equally huge threshing machines with men on both sides heaving sheaves off the hay ricks into its maw. Everywhere, hay ricks were in motion, ones loaded with sheaves going to the threshing machine and empty ones going back to the field for more sheaves.

It was anything but a quiet ride.

A horse-drawn wagon approached as we clip-clopped down the road. Mr. Grigg yelled "Whoa." So did the other driver as he breasted us.

"Alfred, how're you doing?"

"I'm off to the elevator. And who be these fine young ladies you're out and about with?"

Mr. Grigg nodded to me. "Excuse my manners. Alfred, this is Mary Appleton, she's the new help. And her sister, Bessie. She'll be working for the Smails." He nodded in Alfred's direction. "This is my brother, Alfred. He lives a couple of miles east of us."

Alfred touched his hat. "Pleased to meet you, ladies. Well, I'd better be off, I won't be getting paid for this wheat sitting here talking with you." He cracked the reins and went off. We continued clip-clopping down the road.

"It's nice having family so close," I said after a bit.

He nodded. "I agree. I've another brother, John. He lives six miles west of us. Don't see him as often as Alfred but we manage."

After a few minutes, I said, "You were about to say something about your wife as we were leaving the station."

Mr. Grigg was silent for a space. He looked straight ahead as he spoke. "We are expecting another child very soon but my wife has not been well this time. The doctors are worried. So am I." He snapped the reins for no apparent reason. "Her sister is living with us, she has been a great comfort, and her parents will arrive in a couple of weeks once the baby is born. But in the meantime, we are in desperate need of help, especially since harvest is going full tilt."

"I am sorry to hear about your wife, Mr. Grigg. I am glad I can be of service."

We chatted the rest of the way about family and where I'd been in Canada and his family back in Ontario. Soon, we turned into a lane leading into a farmstead consisting of a large three-storey house with a garden behind it, a huge barn and numerous outbuildings, all surrounded by three rows of trees. A young woman about my age was taking laundry off the clothesline. She put the last sheet in the basket, picked it up and came over to meet us as we climbed down.

She pushed a strand of hair back off her face. "Which one you is our Miss Appleton?"

I adjusted my hat that had become askew. "I am. You must be Mrs. Grigg's sister." I nodded towards Bessie, "This is my sister."

She motioned us to follow her into the house. "I'm so glad you are here, these men and the children run me ragged. And please, call me Emeline, I hope you don't mind if I call you Mary. We don't stand much on formality here."

I was not entirely comfortable calling her by her Christian name, but if she insisted . . . I held the door open for her. "How many children are there?"

"Three, all girls, and you are about to be overrun by them."

I heard someone behind us call, "Just a minute, hold the door open. We have our hands full with this ugly black box."

I whirled around. "Mr. Higham!" I exclaimed.

"Well, I'll be damned, if it isn't Miss Appleton of Cornwall!"

Mr. Grigg almost dropped his end of the box. "Do you know each other?"

"We met yesterday at St. John's." Mr. Higham grinned. "Would you believe it, Will? She declined my offer to take her to tea."

Mr. Grigg nodded at me. "Wise woman, Mary. You have to be careful with this man. He's a devil of a ladies' man."

"Ah, so you do have a first name," Mr. Higham said as the two struggled by.

I saw Bessie smirking. "What!" I snapped.

"Oh, nothing."

I turned to Emeline. "Does Mr. Higham live here?"

"Cale? Oh yes, he's one of the hired hands. A good worker, too, but Will is right, he is a joker. Now, come along, Rhoda, my sister, is resting but she will be down for supper."

There's a fine kettle of fish, having to work at the same farm as him, I thought.

The three girls were adorable. Florence held up all fingers of her left hand and pronounced, "I t'ree!" She held up her doll. "This Miss Piggly."

Emeline shrugged. "I don't know where she came up with that name."

Pearl tugged at my hand. "I am in Grade One and I know all my numbers and letters."

"Aren't you a smart girl," I replied.

"I'm smarter," crowed Gertie. "I'm eight and in Grade Three. I can read and write. Pearl can't do that."

"Can, too," Pearl retorted.

"Now, now girls. Let Miss Appleton get settled," Emeline said. She turned to me. "Come along, I'll show you your room."

As we walked up the stairs, Emeline said, "I hope you don't mind, you'll have to sleep with me. My parents will be in the bedroom where you would normally sleep." I assured her that would be fine. I unpacked my belongings quickly and scurried back down to the kitchen where supper preparations were almost finished. I began to clear the dining room table before setting it. Emeline saw me. "No, Mary, we're eating in the kitchen."

I stood there, a stack of plates in my hands. "All of us?"

Emeline was taken aback. "Of course, all of us. What did you expect?"

I carried the plates back into the kitchen. "It's just that, well, I always ate in the kitchen while my employers ate in the dining room. I assumed it was the same here."

Emeline took the plates from me and began setting them around the table. "Heavens, Mary, don't be ridiculous. You are part of the family so you eat with us."

I felt rather awkward at first when we sat down for supper, all ten of us, family and hired hands alike: Will and Rhoda, who was definitely in a delicate condition, Emeline, and the three girls, Cale, Guy the other hired hand, and Bessie and me. We talked and laughed and shared stories. Florence and Pearl seemed particularly fond of Cale who made faces that set them giggling.

Mr. and Mrs. Smail came by after supper. They were a pleasant elderly couple who lived only a half-mile down the road, "next door neighbours," Mr. Smail said. They took to Bessie right away. Mrs. Smail patted Bessie's hand, "Dear girl, we are so pleased to have you with us." Bessie whispered to me, "What a relief! I was half expecting a dragon of a lady like our mother."

The Griggs were so different from the Oxenhams and the Waddys. They welcomed me in as part of the family. I was Mary, only the girls called me Miss Appleton; I decided they had been well brought up. No one put on airs. We worked side-by-side. Emeline was as likely to be up to her elbows in dishwater or bread dough or laundry as I was. Will worked side-by-side with Cale and Guy at all the farm chores, be it milking, dunning out the barns, repairing machinery or feeding livestock. They were who they were, hard-working, proud, independent and friendly people.

Bessie had the same experience with Mr. and Mrs. Smail. "I may as well be her granddaughter," she said to me one day. "We're as likely to spend the afternoon gossiping over a cup of tea as doing any work."

Those three weeks of harvest were the hardest I had ever worked. From well before dawn to 11:00 at night, it was go, go, go, with barely time to take a cup of tea or wolf down a slice of bread. The men didn't work any less. They had the usual farm chores in addition to all the long hours and extra work that went with harvest such as maintaining machinery. Will was adamant about keeping machinery in good repair. He once said, "I saw a man get killed when the drive belt snapped. That's not happening on my farm." We had a brief break when it rained hard for a day, but other than that, it was non-stop work.

Barely a week after I joined the Griggs, tragedy struck. We were at breakfast when Rhoda suddenly cried out and doubled over. "The baby," she gasped.

Will jumped up so fast he knocked over his chair. "Mary, fetch Rhoda's bag, I'll call Alfred, he said he'd drive us to the hospital. Emeline, call your parents!"

Ten minutes later, Will helped Rhoda into Alfred's car and they drove off to Moose Jaw. Emeline was trying to console Florence who was crying, "Mommy! Mommy!"

I held Pearl's hand. She looked up at me, "Mommy sick?" I squeezed her hand. "No, she's not sick. She's going to have her baby. She will be home in a week or two with a new baby brother or sister for you."

Gertie was very quiet but later I found her in her bedroom, sobbing her heart out. "I'm so worried about her. What if she doesn't come home?"

I put my arm around her. "She will come home, never you fear."

Will called that night; Emeline answered. When she hung up, she leaned her head against the telephone for a moment before sitting down at the table. She was close to tears. Her voice choked. The news was not good. "The baby still hasn't come. Will is staying in Moose Jaw with friends. I told him my parents are arriving in two days." I held her hand, I didn't know what else to do.

Will came home two days later, accompanied by Mr. and Mrs. Hudson. Mrs. Hudson was in tears, Will and Mr. Hudson stone-faced. Will collapsed on a chair, his head in his hands. "She has lost a lot of blood. The doctors are doing what they can, but . . ."

"The baby? What about the baby?" Emeline asked.

Mrs. Hudson embraced her. "It's a girl, she's fine. I wish I could say the same about Rhoda."

Emeline broke into tears. "Oh, my dear sister!"

Over the next week, Will called the hospital each day. Each day the news was the same, Rhoda was no better. We paced. We ate in silence. We did our work but there was no joy in it. We slept fitfully.

The phone rang late one night after we were all in bed. I heard Will charge down the stairs. We ran down to see Will leaning his head against the wall, the receiver in his hand. He was crying. "She's gone. The doctor said she just, they couldn't . . ."

We stood there, stunned. Mrs. Hudson and Emeline began to weep. "How will we tell the children?"

"Tell us what?" Gertie stood in the doorway. "What has happened?"

Emeline swept Gertie into her arms. "Oh, my dear motherless child."

Gertie let out a wail like I had never heard before, but then neither have I seen a child loose a mother. Tears ran down my cheeks. We sat in the parlour, trying to console each other. An unspoken question hung over us all: how do we look after a motherless baby?

Alfred took Will and Mr. and Mrs. Hudson into Moose Jaw the next day to make funeral arrangements and bring home the baby. Emeline spent the day consoling the girls and writing to friends and family. I readied the house, drawing down all the blinds and closing the drapes and putting away everything that seemed frivolous. They returned late that afternoon, bearing the new baby named Mabel, the only bright light in this sad time. Gertie and Pearl fussed over their new little sister but Florence wasn't so happy because she was no longer the baby of the family.

The funeral was held at Zion Methodist Church and Rhoda was laid to rest in Moose Jaw Cemetery. I did not attend, I stayed at the farm and looked after Mabel and prepared the lunch for when they returned. Sadness hung over the family for a long time thereafter.

* * *

Autumn work continued in spite of everything. Emeline, Mrs. Hudson and I were busy with canning and preserving. There were potatoes and carrots and turnips to dig and bury in sand boxes in the basement, cabbages to pick and turn into sauerkraut or hang from the ceiling in the cold room. We slaughtered several chickens and canned them. Mr. Hudson, slowed as he was with arthritis, helped with farm work. The work of ploughing up the garden for the winter was left to the men, Caleb in particular, for he was fussy about the garden. And of course, there were the girls to mind, especially Florence who demanded a story at every opportunity.

It was one of those crisp clear autumn days, the sun bright, the air invigorating, the gentle breeze refreshing. The poplars were bare, they had long ago strewn their golden leaves all around. A couple of cheeky magpies scolded from the safety of the caragana hedge. I was in the flower bed, cutting back the hollyhocks and delphiniums when I heard Caleb singing while driving the horse and plough up and down the garden. He was so focused on the ploughing and his singing that he didn't see me. He did have a fine tenor voice, and he was in full voice, singing "When Father Papered the Parlour." It was a very funny music hall song, and I couldn't help but laugh. He heard me and whoa-ed the horse.

"Miss Appleton, is that you?"

I straightened up. "Indeed it is. I'm putting the flowers to bed for the winter."

He walked over to where I was working. "If I'd known I had an audience, I would have chosen a more suitable song to serenade you with." He looked at the pile of stalks at my feet. "I've been off flowers ever since my kid brother, Len, won first prize for his flower arrangement at the Bodicote fair. Give me taters and neeps to mind any day."

I threw more stalks into the growing pile. "Flowers need as much tending as taters and neeps, Mr. Higham."

"Please, call me Cale, everyone else does."

"Very well, Cale." I shook my finger at him. "You may call me Mary, just don't you go shortening it to 'Mare'."

He laughed. "I wouldn't dream of it, especially while you're wielding that nasty pair of shears. Well, I'd better get back to ploughing the garden." He whistled as he walked back to the horse and called "Gee-up." He started singing, this time "All the Girls are After Me."

Ha! Cheeky sort. This is one girl who isn't, I thought.

My dear Mary, Well, aren't you the secretive one. Bessie writes you have a suitor. Why haven't you told us? To think you had to go all the way to Canada to meet a suitable English bachelor. I have met mine. I was serving refreshments at a dance, a fund-raiser for the war effort, when this dashing young man in a Devon Regiment uniform asked me to dance. Old Mrs. Evansham told me to go on, so I did, and one dance led to another. His name is Private Harold Kerswell, he's a mechanic in the tank corp. He asked if he could write me, having a special girl waiting for him was good for morale. Maybe he was taking the mickey, but I said yes. I actually received a letter from him yesterday. Now it's your turn to tell us all about your special man. Love, Dorothy.

My dear Dorothy, Don't believe a word Bessie says. I do not have a suitor. If she is referring to Caleb, she is so wrong. He thinks too well of himself. I might be more inclined to like him better if he didn't drink so much. He spends almost every Saturday night drinking with his mates and comes home three sheets to the wind. When he's drunk he gets in fights and then comes home with a bloody nose and bruises. Mrs. Hudson, Emeline and I take great delight in banging the crockery come Sunday morning, just to hear him, bleary-eyed, holding his head, wincing at every noise, groan and beg for mercy. Mrs. Hudson scolds him, "Drink is the devil's instrument" as she slams down the tea pot. So no, he is no suitor of mine. Love to all, Mary.

I was almost as annoyed at Bessie for thinking Cale was a suitor as I was at Cale for being so arrogant. I couldn't stand the man. He claimed Cornwall was a backward place beyond the pale. I told him I came from a sophisticated city of several thousand people whereas he came from some back-of-beyond village that no one had ever heard of. I told him he was only a farmer's son whereas I was the daughter of a businessman. He'd retort, "Yes, one who abandoned his wife for a hussy," and then the fight was on. I don't know why I defended my father but I wasn't about to let Cale get away with insulting him.

He called me a Cornish bal-maiden – a girl who worked in the tin mines breaking up rock – when one of my batches of bread was less than perfect. I called him nowt but a lazy ag-lab – an agricultural laborer – and if he didn't like my bread then he could just go hungry.

One morning, he called me a miserable old cow when I admonished him for being hung over. Oh, that was the wrong thing to call me! I dressed him down good, then slapped his plate of bacon and eggs down so hard they splattered over the table and onto his shirt. Pearl looked wide-eyed at Cale. "Why did you call Miss Appleton an old cow?"

Will glared at her. "Never you mind, Pearl, eat your porridge."

"But Daddy . . ."

"Eat your porridge, I said."

Pearl pouted. I gave Cale a particularly frosty reception for the rest of the day.

We argued about everything, the war, prohibition, women getting the vote, you name it. I never hesitated to tell him that his opinion was off the mark. "Whatever happened to 'Gentle Mary, meek and mild'?" he asked once when he got the worst of an argument.

No, Cale was no suitor of mine.

* * *

This Christmas was, for me, a happy one. Bessie was here and the Griggs had taken me into their bosom, so to speak. Christmas Eve, we all climbed into the cutter, snuggled down under horse blankets, and drove to Alfred's place. It was a cold clear night, the stars so bright I thought I could touch them. The only sounds were the hissing of the runners on the snow and the rhythmic jingle of the harness bells. Cale managed to sit beside me and put his arm around me, "to keep you warm," he said. I tried to wiggle away but wasn't too successful. On the return trip, we were treated to a glorious display of Northern Lights dancing across the sky. We serenaded the countryside with *Jingle Bells*, Cale singing better than most others.

The house was packed on Christmas Day. Will's brothers Alfred and John and their families arrived, arms full of food and gifts, and soon the house seemed about to explode from the press of people and the volume of sound. Cale and Guy brought in a table from the bunk house and placed it at the end of the dining room table. Another smaller table was set for the children. The kitchen table was piled high with food. The house was filled with aromas of turkey and gravy and squash and pudding, the sound of potatoes and turnips and carrots bubbling on the stove, the table laden with buns and salads and pickles, all setting our mouths to watering and the children to asking, "When is dinner? I'm hungry." We all were.

Somehow, we all squeezed in around the tables. We ate and talked and laughed, but under it all was a current of sadness because Rhoda was no longer with us. Later, when I took my gifts upstairs I heard the sound of someone sobbing. I walked quietly down the hall to the girls' room and saw Emeline with her arms around Gertie who was crying her eyes out. I left as quietly as I had come.

We cleared the table and brought in the mince pies and hard sauce, the plum pudding and the cookies. I told of the time Father poured too much brandy on the pudding and when he lit it, the flames leaped up and singed his beard, after which he was always clean-shaven. Cale laughed. "If that had happened to my father, his bushy eyebrows would have set the whole house on fire!" Will told of the time Christmas dinner was rudely interrupted by a neighbour announcing Will's cows had broken through the pasture fence and were in his yard.

When we could not eat another crumb, we cleared the table and did the washing up while the men repaired to the parlour and the children ran outside to run off their energy and the meal. At last, we gathered in the parlour to exchange gifts. I was surprised to receive a gift from Cale, a beautiful pair of white kid gloves. I stared open-mouthed at them and then at him, sitting across the room. He grinned and held up the sturdy work gloves I had given him.

"Just what I needed," he yelled across the room. He got up and walked over to me. "Do I get a kiss in thanks?"

"What cheek!" Mrs. Hudson huffed. Cale winked.

I blushed but, much to my surprise, I also smiled. "No, I will not give you a kiss, but I will give you my thanks. They are beautiful."

I told Bessie about them next day when I visited her. She laughed and nudged me. "I knew it. He is sweet on you. Just you wait. Next, he will be asking you to marry him."

I retorted, "I doubt it. Even if he did, I'd say no."

Bessie smirked. "Sure, Mary."

My dear Mary, Harold sent me a Christmas card and the sweetest letter ever. I really like him. We've met up a couple of times since the dance. I am so glad he doesn't drive one of those tanks, they're just rolling coffins in my opinion. Bessie writes you are quite besotted with Cale in spite of your continued denials. Maude is back home, fidgeting. She wants to do something for the war effort but is undecided how or what. Mother seems to be softening her opinion of you. I found her reading your last letter, I don't think she knew I was watching. All our love, Dorothy.

My dear Dorothy, I don't know what Bessie is going on about. Perhaps you should ask her about <u>her</u> beau, one Willie Lamb by name. I confronted her last week when she teased me about Cale, and she actually blushed and said,

"Oh, he's just a friend." It was my turn to say, "Sure, Bessie!" They met at a dance at Tuxford, a town north of here. He's a first cousin once removed of one of our neighbours. I hope Willie is up to the challenge of courting Bessie, she is no shrinking violet. My love to all, even Mother, Mary.

* * *

Cale rarely talked about his life in England, but over the winter, I learned a little. His father farmed near Bodicote, just south of Banbury in Oxfordshire, and was a well-respected man in the area. He described his mother as a force to be reckoned with. "She had to be, since her father was more often drunk and vicious than sober and working," he said. He had an older brother John, "a bit of a weird duck" who would probably find some way to stay out of the war; a younger brother Len, a blacksmith apprentice, "also an apprentice publican and loving it," Cale said, and several sisters.

He'd been a long-distance runner. "I even won the Earl of Jersey's cup one year," he boasted. Then he laughed. "And a cruet set! Now what was I to do with a cruet set? I gave it to Ma and she proudly displays it on the sideboard." He had worked for the CPR for a few months after arriving in Canada, "but only because I couldn't afford a farm and the CPR paid good money." When I asked why he left the CPR, he shrugged. "It seemed the time."

Eventually, I had to admit, but only to myself, that he could be a decent chap, when he wasn't being arrogant. He was hard-working; Will said he was one of the best hands he had ever hired – up early and late to bed. There was nothing he wouldn't do or try. Emeline said Cale never hesitated to give her a hand doing some of the more onerous chores around the house such as putting the drapes back up once they were washed. And, she went on, he was great with the girls.

The girls loved him. He would swoop Florence up onto his shoulders and run around the house or yard, Florence squealing with delight, Emeline calling, "Be careful!" At the table, he often set the girls to giggling by wiggling his ears or nose. He walked on his hands, and more than once Emeline or Mrs. Hudson had to stop Pearl or Florence from trying the same. Gertie said she was too old for such things.

He was also ambitious, as I learned one night. We were sitting in the parlour after supper when the men got to talking about farming, how crop yields and grain prices had been down last year and what the prospects were for this year. Will turned to Cale. "Are you still sure you want to be a farmer? Maybe you should go back to working for the CPR. You'd get a steady wage there."

Cale shook his head and started rolling a cigarette. "If I wanted to be a brakeman for the rest of my life, I'd still be working for the CPR." He paused to lick and seal the cigarette and sweep the loose bits of tobacco strewn across the table back into the can. "As soon as I save up enough money, I'll buy a farm, even it is only a small one. I don't intent to be a hired hand for the rest of my life, much as I like working for you, Will."

He stuck the cigarette in his mouth, then looked at me and grinned. "Although, now that I think of it, being a hired hand here does have some benefits." Everyone laughed.

I sat up straight and crossed my arms. "Ha! Very funny!"

Emeline patted my arm. "He was just joking, Mary."

Cale raised an eyebrow at me and cocked his head. "Maybe." He struck a match, lit his cigarette and blew out a cloud of smoke. "But I wasn't joking about being a farmer."

* * *

I was ironing one March morning when Cale came into the house, a blood-soaked handkerchief wrapped around his hand. "Cale, whatever have you done?"

"I caught my fingers in some machinery. Nothing a bandage or two can't fix."

"Let me see." I put the sad iron back on the stove and grabbed a tea towel while he unwrapped his hand. He had a nasty cut across the back of three fingers, and I wrapped the towel around them tightly.

"Hold that. I'll find some gauze and cotton." I fetched them from the pantry cupboard, then took Cale over to the sink and unwrapped the towel. The cut was now only oozing.

"Take a breath." I started to dab on the iodine. Cale jerked his hand back from the sting.

"Hold still or you'll start it all to bleeding again," I snapped.

"Yes, Sister Mary." He kept his hand still as I wrapped layers of gauze around each finger and taped it in place.

"Are you sure you want to be a farmer? Keep this up and you may have fewer fingers than you were born with."

"It will take more than a cut or two to make me change my mind. I came to Canada to be my own boss and I intend to be that no matter how many fingers I have."

I turned to put the gauze and iodine away. "Yes, your own boss except for the grain buyers and the bankers and the CPR and machinery dealers."

"Well, what about you? Did you come to Canada just to be someone else's servant for the rest of your life?"

"I don't know what else to do."

He grinned that annoying grin of his. "You could always get married."

"Being married won't change much. I'll still be a kitchen maid, just in my own kitchen."

"I doubt that. You'll rule whatever house you live in." He flexed his wrapped fingers, then looked at me, one bushy eyebrow cocked. "So then, you are thinking of marriage. Do you have anyone in mind?"

"If I did, you would be the last one to know. Don't you have chores to do? I have to finish this ironing, so don't distract me anymore lest I scorch the shirt."

"Yes, Sister Mary," he said and left, whistling.

I returned to the ironing. Why would I want to marry a farmer, especially Cale? Yes, he was a decent chap, hard-working and ambitious, but I'd had a taste of farm life at Higher Tregurra. I didn't like it, Father and George and the hands always tracking in mud and manure, the constant smell of barnyard, the teasing from girls at school that I stank of hogs and cows. I had to deal with more mud and manure when working for Dr. Waddy. And here too, working for the Griggs. No, I'd rather marry a rich businessman, live in the city, maybe even have a domestic servant of my own. Yes, that was the life for me. I was not about to become a farmer's wife. Especially, Cale's.

* * *

April came on, warm and sunny one day, cold and miserable the next. The last snow drifts in the trees finally gave up and melted away. When Will and Cale weren't fussing about soil moisture, they were cleaning grain and examining the seeder. Cale also got to fussing about planting potatoes and turnips.

"Dark of the moon is coming on, so we'd best get those potatoes cut," he said one day in late April

"What's the moon got to do with planting potatoes?" I asked. I was drying the last of the dinner dishes.

He raised his eyebrows. "Don't you know? Anything that grows underground has to be planted in the dark of the moon."

Two days later, I helped him haul up the last of the potatoes from the cellar. We sat together on the porch, several pails of potatoes at our feet, cutting them into thirds or quarters and dropping them into other pails. It was a relaxing afternoon. The sun shone on the porch, taking the chill off the air.

We chatted as we worked. He told me about his racing adventures and his friends in the Banbury Harriers Club, especially his friend Sam Greenway. "We were always trying to outrun each other," he said. I, in turn, told him how Bessie and Dorothy were always flouting convention, especially with their smoking.

He laughed. "Isn't that just like Bessie, always ready to provoke a reaction." He turned to me, a sly smile on his face. "As are you."

"Oh, come on. I'm not nearly as bad as Bessie. I'm the older sister, I have to set a good example."

Cale hooted and threw a potato in my lap. "You! A good example? Well, now that I think about it, you are an example, although of what, I wouldn't care to say. After all, you got your sister here under false pretenses."

I threw the potato back at him. "Mr. Higham, you are terrible!" We both laughed and resumed cutting potatoes.

The next thing I knew, we reached for the same potato. Our hands touched for just a moment. Cale cleared his throat and reached for a different potato. I was confused, not by his reaction but by mine. I hadn't minded at all.

I told Bessie about this the following Sunday. She laughed and clapped her hands. "I knew it! You're in love! When's the wedding?" She was obviously enjoying my discomfort.

"Wedding? There is no wedding. For one thing, no one's asked me."

"He will, and soon, I bet. Cale doesn't strike me as the sort to dither about when the mood strikes him."

I sniffed. "Hrmmph! We'll see." But what if Bessie was right, I wondered.

* * *

How do these things happen? You start off snarling at each other, then you like each other, and the next thing you know, you're thinking about marriage.

Cale proposed on Victoria Day.

It was a beautiful warm sunny day. It had rained a couple of days before, leaving everything green and fresh. Seeding was almost finished. Everyone gathered at the Belbeck school for the celebrations: races and games including the inevitable peanut scramble for the children, and ball games and horse races for the adults. Cale and Will teamed up for the adults' wheelbarrow race but that came to an end when Will let go of Cale's right leg and they both tumbled to the ground. Bessie and I doubled over laughing.

Come evening, everybody spread blankets and opened up their picnic baskets. Just in case someone hadn't brought enough food, several ladies brought "dainties," a name that confused me until I learned it referred to squares and cookies and cakes cut into small pieces. Cale churned one of the several ice cream makers.

We moved into the school when everyone had finished eating. The men cleared the desks to one side, and a local band of guitars, fiddle and piano struck up. Cale and I danced several times before he said, "It's warm in here. Let's go outside for a bit."

Bessie saw us leave; she had been dancing with Willie. She grinned at me and mouthed, "Say yes." I ignored her.

We weren't the only ones getting a breath of fresh air that fine evening. A few couples were walking about taking the air, and some men were standing in knots talking about the crop prospects. Several children played tag, yelling and laughing all the while. We heard the band strike up a polka. Meadowlarks and robins were singing, and I could hear a kildeer cry. In the midst of our chatting about nothing much, Cale said, "Indeed, just the perfect setting."

"What do you mean?"

"Well . . ." He paused. He looked off into the distance. He scuffed one shoe against the grass.

"The perfect setting to ask if you will marry me?"

For a moment, I thought I had misheard. I laughed. "Will I what?" That probably wasn't what he expected because he looked glum. I caught myself and apologized. "You caught me off-guard. I wasn't expecting a proposal of marriage."

"Was it that much of a surprise?"

"Mmm, maybe, maybe not." I must have seen it coming but had chosen to ignore it, perhaps because I couldn't imagine anyone wanting to marry me at my age, after all I was, well, of an age, as they say. I smiled and took his hand. "Since you have asked, here is my answer. Yes, I will marry you."

Cale gave a whoop that turned heads. He grabbed me round my waist and twirled me around and then, right in front of everyone, he kissed me!

"Mr. Higham, I do declare, Mrs. Hudson is right. You are a cheeky sort."

He grinned. "Which is exactly why you're marrying me, isn't it? Come on, Mary. Fess up!"

I said nothing, only smiled and took his hand. "Let's tell the others." When we did, Bessie threw her arms around me and crowed, "I knew it! Didn't I tell you?"

Emeline hugged me, too. "I'm so happy for you, but now I will have to find a new helper. I don't know where I will find someone as good, or companionable, as you."

Will shook Cale's hand. "Congratulations Caleb, She's a good woman." Then he clapped Cale on the back. "But are you sure you're up to living with her? She can be one terrifying lady, you know." He winked at me as he spoke.

Cale laughed. "I waited until she was in the right mood." I poked him in the ribs.

"However, Will, this means I won't be working for you much longer. Once seeding is finished, I'll need some time to go looking for work and a place to live in Moose Jaw."

"We'll be sorry to lose you, Cale. You're a good worker," Will said.

The next morning, Emeline and I were doing the washing up after breakfast when she said, "Why the big sigh, Mary?"

"Did I sigh?" I was silent as I dried the last of the plates. "I was thinking of my family in England. They won't be able to attend."

Emeline wrung out the dish cloth, then turned to me. "You don't realize how much you are a part of our family, more like a sister to me than a housemaid. I know we're not your family, but just the same . . ." She paused.

"Will and I would love to give you a proper prairie wedding, lots of guests, lots of food, a big party. We talked about it last night."

"But we can't afford that," I objected.

"Bosh! Prairie weddings don't take a lot of money, just a lot of neighbours, and I know none of them will object to sitting in a church for a half-hour or bringing piles of food for the party afterward. You've made a name for yourself around here, you and Cale both. You can't possibly expect us to ignore such an important day."

I hugged Emeline and wiped a tear from my eye. "That would be wonderful. Thank you."

"Now don't you bother your head about any of the details, except what dress to wear to stun your betrothed with. And don't worry about the food, everyone will bring something."

"Yes, including whiskey," harumphed Mrs. Hudson who had just walked into the kitchen.

I was curious. "How many people do you think will attend?"

"As many as will come," she replied, which left me none the wiser.

Dear Mary, What wonderful news! We are all so happy for you, even Mother in her own grudging way. She muttered, "Well, it seems she's chosen well." Now for my news. I am working as a clerk at the Royal Navy Auxiliary Hospital in Truro, keeping inventories of bandages and such, and pushing the tea cart around. I am in awe of the nursing sisters, they tend the wounded with such grace and kindness. Mary, it's enough to break your heart, those poor soldiers broken in body and mind. How they will ever recover is beyond me. Which reminds me, Dorothy's Harold has some sort of chest ailment, she's very worried about him. She writes him every other day. I would not be surprised if they marry soon. All my love, Maude.

***

A month later, I stood beside Cale, promising to love, honour and obey till death would us part. Rev. Wells Johnson had raised his eyebrows when we met with him to arrange a date. "You were very abrupt with Mr. Higham when I introduced you to him."

I gave the vicar a piece of my mind. "It's your business to wed us, not to question my change of heart." Rev. Wills sat back in his chair, surprised. I added, "Mr. Higham has proved himself to be a gentleman and is well capable of supporting a family."

Cale laughed. "I persuaded her with my charm." He waggled his eyebrows at me.

I shook my head and smiled. Mrs. Hudson was right – he was a cheeky sort. We settled on June 30 as the wedding date, at 11:30 in the morning.

I spent a day in Moose Jaw with Margery, she of the millinery shop, combing through every ladies wear store for a wedding frock. All were elaborately embellished with lace and beads, with long flowing trains and gossamer veils, and cost far more than I could afford.

Over a mid-afternoon cup of tea, I said, "I could make one for a fraction of the price." Thus decided, we went to Joyner's department store where I selected yards of white cotton muslin and lace.

Margery vanished for a moment. "I'll be right back," she said. She returned just as I was paying the bill. "Here's your 'something blue'." She handed me a large pale blue fabric rose. "I'm sure you will find a place for it on your lovely frock."

My eyes widened in surprise, then I smiled. "How kind of you. I'm sure I will use it but only if . . ." and I emphasized *if* ". . . you consent to be one of my witnesses."

Margery gasped then laughed and embraced me. "Of course, Mary. I would be delighted. Oh dear, now I will have to find a dress."

What with all my other duties, it took almost two weeks to design and sew the frock, especially the collar that I embroidered and pleated. I did not make a train – that was an ostentation I could do without – and I used Margery's flower to hide the belt clasp.

Cale was busy on his own quest in the city for work and a house. Eventually, he was hired as a driver for Farmers' Dairy and he rented a house on Chestnut Avenue. "It's small but affordable, and not a chestnut tree to be seen anywhere," he said. We spent a long Saturday in the city buying furniture, including a Singer sewing machine, to be delivered once we took possession of the house on July 2.

June 30 was a hot, steamy day; thankfully St. John's was cool inside. Bessie and Margery were our witnesses, and Will, Emeline, Mr. and Mrs. Hudson and the girls, and Mrs. and Mrs. Smail attended the ceremony. Cale looked quite dashing in his suit, the same one he had worn the day we met, although he fidgeted all through the ceremony. He told me afterwards, "I could have done with a lot fewer words, especially when the Reverend went on at great length about the sacred institution of marriage and how it was not something to be entered into lightly. Obviously, he doesn't know you very well!" I poked him in the ribs, again.

At last, Cale put the wedding ring on my finger, and Rev. Wells Johnson pronounced us "man and wife." I no longer had to fear being someone's old spinster aunt.

After the service, we walked over to Weeks and Pugh's photography studio on High Street to have our wedding portrait taken. We ordered several copies to send back to our families in England and Australia.

Will drove us back to the farm in his Model T. As we rode along Main Street, Cale pointed to all the flags and bunting hung in anticipation of tomorrow's Dominion Day celebrations. "Why, how important we must be! The city is decorated everywhere just for us!" And he laughed.

It seemed as if half the country was at the Griggs for the reception. Emeline and several of the neighbouring farm wives put out enough food to feed all of Moose Jaw, or so it seemed. Cold roast beef, cold chicken, potato salad, deviled eggs, piles of buns and bread – there was no end to it. The women drank tea, the kids drank lemonade, and I am certain the men were drinking beer and whiskey. The house was crowded, and those who couldn't fit in the house sat around outside.

Eventually, Will called everyone to attention and proposed a toast in which he interspersed wishes for our future happiness with humorous bits of advice.

"Remember, Mary," he raised his glass in my direction, "you should always let your husband have the last word."

I harumphed.

Will turned to Cale. "And Cale, your last words should always be, 'Yes, dear'."

Everyone laughed, even I. Bessie nudged me with her elbow. "Don't let him forget it!"

Some of Cale's mates hollered, "Don't forget who's boss!" and "Ball and chain, Cale, ball and chain."

It was well into the evening when Will took us back to Moose Jaw. Someone had strung a couple of old shoes and some tin cans on the back of the car and attached a sign saying "Just Maried," obviously written by someone who had failed elementary spelling. We were showered with rice and confetti and good wishes as we got into the car, and with a few loud back-firings, we rattled our way down the road and into Moose Jaw.

We made quite a sight and sound as we drove down Main Street, what with the few cans that had not fallen off on the dirt road banging and clanging behind us. Many people were out walking, enjoying the warm summer evening and they stared at us as we drove by. Some waved to us. One man yelled, "Good luck, poor sod!" and his wife elbowed him.

We pulled up in front of the Royal George Hotel. Cale helped me out of the car while Will grabbed our suitcases and put them on the sidewalk. "I'll bring your gifts in a couple of days after you've moved into your house." He yanked off the last of the cans and removed the misspelled sign. "Don't need those anymore." With that, he left us.

The Royal George had a reputation of being the best hotel in the city. "This is all the honeymoon I can afford," Cale said. I watched him write "Mrs. and Mrs. C. Higham" in the registry. We walked up the stairs to our room. Cale unlocked the door and offered to carry me over the threshold but I declined. "I can walk. I'm not a cripple." Instead, he ushered me in with a flourish of his hat and a bow.

He set our suitcases on the bureau and put his arm around my waist. "Well, Mrs. Higham?"

I shook my head. "It will take me a while to get used to my new name."

Cale kissed me. "How long will it take for you to get used to that?"

I giggled. "Not very long, I think."

As I lay in Cale's arms, I mused about what strange turns my life had taken so far – growing up in England, coming to Canada with Mrs. Waddy, and now married to a hopeful farmer. What else would my future hold, I wondered. Before I could wonder any longer, Cale kissed me. Again.

We spent the rest of the night getting used to each other.

Chapter Fourteen
Moose Jaw, Again

July 1, 1915 was Dominion Day, a day of parades and patriotism. In spite of the raging war, in spite of the dead and maimed, people were celebrating. Main Street was festooned with Union Jacks. Red, white and blue bunting hung everywhere. Every shop window featured a flag, or exhortations to pray for men serving overseas or to buy a war bond, or simply showed a helmet lying on some bunting.

We stood among the crowds and watched the parade. The mayor and councillors rode by in their cars, and one patriotic float after another rolled down the street interspersed with brass bands playing their best rousing marches. People cheered loudly as troops of young soldiers marched by, staring straight ahead in best military form. Cale muttered, "They're just kids, fergodsakes."

Not all cheered, though. A woman of about my mother's age bravely waved her flag as the soldiers passed, then turned with tears in her eyes to bury her head in her husband's shoulder. He wrapped his arms around her and said something to her. They must have a son serving overseas, or worse, perhaps he is already missing or dead, I thought. There must be many other mothers, fathers and families amongst those throngs, not just here but also back in England, who have the same mix of emotions.

I must have sighed because Cale looked at me, then put his arm around me. "Let's walk through the park."

Crescent Park was a calm in the midst of all that bedlam, and I soon regained my composure. We weren't the only people taking refuge amongst the trees and flower beds. Little children, their mothers close at hand, giggled and laughed and squealed as they fed breadcrumbs to ducks and geese in the creek. We heard the thwack of racquets and cheers at the tennis courts on the far side of the park. We smelled flowers in bloom and heard leaves rustle in the breeze, the same breeze that cooled our faces. We admired the new public library, a magnificent building worthy of any city in England, that the city fathers boasted was built without financial assistance from Mr. Carnegie who had judged the plans much too ostentatious for a city of Moose Jaw's size.

We stayed at the Royal George a second night, and the following day, we moved into our new home at the corner of Chestnut and Hall. It was a modest storey-and-a-half, small in comparison with the other two-storey houses along the street. A concrete path led across unkempt grass to an open verandah and the front door which opened directly into the parlour. I walked across the hardwood floor and into the kitchen, complete with a large porcelain sink with faucets promising hot and cold running water. The back porch also had a small sink. The stairs up to the second floor (and also those going down to the basement) led off the kitchen.

While Cale went down to inspect the basement, I went up. The two bedrooms with their steeply pitched ceilings were small but adequate. I clapped my hands in joy when I entered the bathroom. Hot and cold running water for the sink and enameled clawfoot bathtub, and a proper flush toilet! No more commodes, no chemical toilet and no smell. I smiled as I thought of Gertie holding her nose and crying, "It stinks!" whenever Cale or Will took out the very full pail from the chemical commode.

I walked out the back door to inspect the back yard. I shook my head in dismay. A patch of grass in desperate need of mowing and rain, a vegetable garden so overgrown with weeds it was impossible to see what vegetables or flowers might be growing there, a lilac bush that should have been dead-headed a month ago, and, at the far end, a shed in need of painting. But, joy of joys, along the side fence separating our house from the neighbour's was a line of hollyhocks, buds already formed. Remembering what we had done as children, I stood at attention and saluted the row of "Coldlane Guards."

"What are you doing?" I jumped at Cale's voice; he had sneaked up behind me.

"Oh, nothing, just looking at the yard. It's in need of some tending."

Cale peered to either side of the house. "I saw you salute." He grinned. "Are you planning to run away with a handsome soldier?"

I took his hand. "Now, why would I do that when I already have a handsome milkman at my beck and call?"

He put his arm around my waist. "And what are you becking and calling me to do now, Mrs. Higham?"

I smiled. "Perhaps if we went inside, you would find out."

We had no chance. A hammering on the front door interrupted us. Cale opened it to let in the men delivering our furniture: a davenport and easy chair for the parlour, a table and four chairs for the kitchen, and a bed and chiffonier. We were barely done with them when other delivery men arrived with our boxes of dishes and pots and pans. We'd just seen the back of them when more men arrived struggling to bring in the cook stove and ice box. The ice man came, the coal man came, the milk man came.

In the midst of this pandemonium, Will and Emmeline and the girls arrived with our gifts. I decided it was time for a break from all the chaos, especially since I had just found the tea kettle and tea pot. Emmeline and I managed to get the kitchen into some semblance of order while Cale and Will arranged the furniture. We sat down to enjoy tea and the cake that Emmeline had brought along with a couple of loaves of freshly made bread, butter and strawberry jam.

We were exhausted when we fell into bed late that night, although we did have enough energy for some "becking and calling" in our new bed.

We had a few more days to put the house in order before Cale started work at the dairy. That first Monday morning came all too soon, 4:00 am, in fact. As I got up, Cale said, "Go back to bed. I can make my own breakfast."

"What kind of wife do you take me for?" I retorted as I shrugged into my housecoat; there'd be time for a proper wash and dressing later on. I sent him off with a good breakfast and then turned to face the day.

The house was quiet. No hired hands stomping in, no little girls to tend or entertain, no Emeline to talk to, no Mrs. Hudson tut-tutting over some perceived indiscretion. I was all alone. I had never had a house all to myself.

I busied myself with the breakfast dishes, then turned to put away items that still hadn't found a home. I grabbed the shears and went into the yard to start setting the garden in order.

Our neighbours were a mixed lot, some Canadian-born, some English born and some foreigners. Most were working class, a couple of them were traveling salesmen. I knew them to say hello if they passed by while I was outside tending the flowers or the garden but I never made an effort to know them more than that.

Cale visited them more than I did, especially the man who worked for a rival dairy and another who was a foreigner working for the CPR. "What do you and that foreigner talk about?" I asked him one day.

He shrugged. "Life on the rails, mostly. He reminds me of one of the men I knew then, from the same country I think, they have the same accent. He had the dirtiest job of all, crawling inside the locomotives to grease them, but he was happy. He once told me that back in his home country, nothing was possible but here in Canada everything was possible, maybe even his son becoming mayor of Regina."

"I doubt very much that a foreigner could become mayor of any city, this is a British country after all."

Cale shrugged. "As he said, anything is possible."

* * *

My dear Mary, Even here in Australia we are not safe from this war. Young men are joining up and the terrible news from Europe does nothing to discourage them. The Aussie boys are nothing but cannon fodder at Gallipoli, I've lost track of the numbers killed and maimed there and still they keep at it. They say we're fighting for God, King and Country, but I say hogwash, it's lies, all lies. I hate this war already and there's no sign of it stopping. Albert is talking of enlisting. I tell him I'm not letting a husband of mine go off and get himself killed, but I may as well be talking to the doorpost. Before I forget, congratulations on your wedding. Wish I could meet Caleb, he sounds like a good catch. Love, Amelia.

Dearest Mary, How fortunate you are being so far away. Sometimes I wish I wasn't working at the hospital where I see it all close up. The wounded keep coming, horribly maimed, minus hands, arms, legs, even parts of their faces blown away, their eyes hollow, their minds still on the battlefield or wandering in some fearful place. Their screams and cries and moans fill the air. The nursing sisters scurry back and forth doing what they can but they can do little other than hold their hands, or change their bandages, or give them blissful sleep with morphine. How long will this horror, this senseless slaughter continue? Must England use up all its young men? I despair of ever seeing peace again. Love, Maude.

Dear Mary, Thank you for your kind letter. Yes, please call us Mam and Dad, after all you have wed our son so are now like a daughter to us. We are all fine here, Len and John have not been called up yet, both are busy. Len still has his temporary licence for the Wheatsheaf Inn in Adderbury, he says it is easier than blacksmithing. John is the nearest to us, he and Hettie have a new daughter, Mary, a lovely wee bundle. I worry how Dad will manage the farm if John is called up, his heart is not what it was when he was young, and it is now so hard to find men to work on the farm, they are all fighting or training to fight. We hear such horrors of the trenches, it's enough to make your hair stand on end. There's nowt in France and Belgium but rats and rain and mud and dead bodies torn apart and bullets and bombs flying everywhere. But we fight to keep the

Germans out, so everyone is doing what they can. Tell Cale to write some time, his hand isn't broken. Love, your new Mam and Dad Higham.

My dear Dorothy, Your news of Harold is worrying but at least he's not stuck in one of those terrible trenches, fearing for his life. He should mend soon now that he's in the hospital. Thank heavens George has not been called up yet but I worry that day may come soon enough and what will poor Carrie do then? Each day, the Moose Jaw Times carries the list of killed, wounded and missing, and it sometimes runs to two columns. Two houses on our street have black bunting on their doors so it is striking close to home. We stopped by to give our condolences but I fear nothing can console you when you've lost a son. Everyone carries on, though, knitting socks or rolling bandages, or doing whatever we can although I wonder what good it all is. The world seems intent on blowing itself apart. All my love, Mary.

* * *

Two lesser battles – prohibition and women's suffrage – were waged on the home front. Both walked hand-in-hand into our home.

It began when Mrs. Cochrane, a neighbour, came knocking, a sheaf of papers in her hand. I had barely opened the door when she started railing against the government for not protecting women and families from the effects of drunkenness.

"I am a member of the Women's Christian Temperance Union and we are circulating *another* petition for the government to give women the right to vote. Only when *we women* have the vote will we be able to bring in prohibition." She held a pen out to me. "I do hope you will join us in this endeavour."

Memories flooded my mind as I listened to Mrs. Cochrane. Emmeline Pankhurst and her army of militant women trying to invade Westminster, being thrown in jail and going on hunger strikes. Mother railing against their tactics: "No proper lady would descend to such depths." Father declaring it all nonsense: "What do women know about politics and voting? Keep them home where they belong." My sisters and I debating the rightness of women's suffrage: Maude and Clive saying things were fine as they were; Bessie, Amelia, Dorothy and I arguing it was about time for things to change.

Mrs. Cochrane was still standing there, pen poised for me to sign. I shook my head. "I don't understand. Are you presenting a petition for women's suffrage or for prohibition?"

"Forgive me, Mrs. Higham, perhaps I am confounding the two issues. This is a petition for women's suffrage. You may have observed that our politicians, all of whom are *men*, have been too cowardly or perhaps too much in the pocket of the liquor trade to enact total prohibition. However, we women are the ones who suffer the consequences of drunken behaviour. *Therefore*, once we obtain the vote, we can pressure the government to hold a referendum and, by virtue of the power of voting, *we women* can ensure that prohibition becomes a reality. Do you not agree?"

I thought of the many times Emeline, Mrs. Hudson and I had scolded Cale when he was hung over, with as much effect as scolding a brick wall. And how Cale ranted in early July when the government ordered hotels to close their beer parlours by 7:00 pm. How he sometimes came home after work, especially Saturdays, smelling of beer and sporting a cut lip and bruised knuckles. If signing this petition was the first step to having a sober husband, then . .

I took Mrs. Cochrane's pen. "Where do I sign?"

She handed me a page and pointed, "Right here."

I added my name to the list. She thanked me and continued down the block, knocking at each and every door. She may not have been Miss Pankhurst but she was persistent.

Cale shrugged when I told him I had signed the petition. "Just so long as you vote Liberal," he said.

I crossed my arms. "*If* the government gives women the vote, and *if* it then holds a referendum on prohibition, I fully intend to vote for prohibition."

That got his attention. "Why in god's name did you do such a bloody fool thing?"

"It's not such a fool thing, as you call it. You'll thank me when you no longer suffer from hangovers."

"How am I supposed to relax at the end of a hard day's work? Tell me that! And here's my brother, Len, in charge of the Wheatsheaf Inn, doling out ales and bitters to his heart's content and I won't get so much as a sip!" He grabbed the tobacco tin and papers, and began rolling a cigarette, spilling tobacco all over the table.

"How about a nice cup of tea?" I waggled the tea pot at him before setting it down on the table, rather hard. "Besides, I don't want you coming home drunk when there's a baby in the house."

He stopped in mid-roll, mouth agape, eyes wide open. "What?"

"I'm expecting. At least, I think I am."

He sat, stunned, for just a moment, then leaped up from the table. He grabbed me by the waist and whirled me about the room. "Put me down, I'm getting dizzy," I told him.

"When is the baby due?" he asked.

"May, I think."

He rubbed his hands together. "I hope it's a boy to help me on my farm."

"Cale, stop dreaming. We don't know if it is a boy, and you don't have a farm. I will be glad enough that the baby is healthy and I survive."

The grin left Cale's face. "Yes, of course." The memory of poor Rhoda was still strong.

* * *

Winter set in. I was prepared for snow and cold, but I wasn't prepared for the maladies that accompanied pregnancy. Morning sickness was bad enough but then my legs and feet swelled up. Bessie commented on them one Sunday afternoon in January when she was visiting.

"Perhaps I could live with you and help around the house."

"I don't need a nursemaid. I'll be fine."

Bessie was not to be put off. "Mary don't be so stubborn. You can use the help, especially after the baby is born. Look on it as recompense for all the times you looked after me when I was a baby." Finally, she announced that she was coming to live with us and that was that!

Cale looked up from reading the *Moose Jaw Times*; he was reading the "Farms for Sale" adverts. "Just a minute, don't I get a say in this?"

We looked at him like he was a stray cat trying to wander into the house. "No!" we said simultaneously, then we looked at each other and burst into laughter. Cale didn't think it was funny.

Bessie turned to Cale. "Would you mind? If I find work, I can help out with expenses."

Cale struck a match, lit the cigarette and offered it to Bessie. "First, let's see how Mary does the next couple of months. If she decides she needs help, then you are welcome. Now, pour me some tea, my cup is empty."

"Pour it yourself," Bessie and I said in unison. We laughed again. I poured Cale another cup.

Bessie came to stay in March. I enjoyed having her so near, and I needed the help.

* * *

Cale started planning the vegetable garden in early May. I told him, "I won't be of much help. I can hardly bend over to tie my shoes. You'll have to plant the flower seeds, too."

He shook his head. "Don't worry about that. Your turn will come when all those vegetables have to be harvested."

He finally decided he would plant the potatoes in mid-May when the moon was in its dark phase. He spent the preceding Sunday digging and hoeing until he had a sizable garden, then he was off to buy potatoes and other seeds. I made sure to give him a list of the flower seeds I wanted.

Alas for Cale's plans, I, or rather our coming baby, threw a spanner in the works. That afternoon, the day that he had planned to plant potatoes, he came home to find me doubled up with labour pains. Bessie was standing at the door, my little case in her hand. "Where have you been? What's taken you so long to get home? The baby's on the way. You've got to get Mary to the hospital."

I hadn't seen him move that fast since being called in for supper at the Griggs. He ran across the street to ask the neighbour, who had an automobile, to drive us to the hospital. I moaned and groaned all the way there while Cale fussed at the neighbour to drive faster. He shot back, "This Tin Lizzie is going as fast as she can."

Cale was ordered to wait while I was taken into delivery. What seemed like an eternity later, just as dawn was breaking on May 14, our baby – a girl – was born. After a lengthy discussion, we caller her Marjorie Amelia.

Cale was less than enthused about the "Amelia" part. "I thought she disowned you. Why would you want to name our daughter after her?"

"It's a tradition, family names are always passed down to children. If it's any consolation, you can name our first son Caleb." That seemed to satisfy him.

As soon as I could, I wrote letters to everyone in England, both my family and Cale's. Cale rarely wrote; he said I was the official letter-writer in the family.

The return letter from Cale's mother, Annie, brought mixed news.

Dear Mary, we are so happy that you have given us another granddaughter. She'll be a blessing to you. Here, the war is going on with no end in sight, men dying across the Channel like so many flies. My husband can't do farm work like he used because of his heart, and it worries me so. He's gone before the military review board this past month and asked that our John be exempted from service. We were terribly worried when he got his joining up summons, Class A he was, which means right fit to go get himself blown up, just what every young man here is yearning to do. If the King and the Kaiser were down in those trenches, the war would be over tomorrow, I tell you. But the review board listened and gave John six months stay but if we need him after that, my husband has to go before the review board again. John's wife is much relieved, she was so worried that she'd be left on her own and with a baby girl not even a year old. There are many widows like that now, and we fear there will be many more before this war is over. Give our love to Cale. I know he doesn't write but tell him it won't break his arm to do so once in a while. All our love, Mam and Dad Higham

Even Mother wrote.

Dearest Mary, how thankful we are that you have been safely delivered of a child. I do wish that you had written me directly with the news. I resent that you saw fit to write to your sisters and brother but not me. I am pleased that you chose to give my name to your daughter. She will be a blessing to you and your husband. We are all sick of the war here. Young men are still being called up. Thank the good Lord that George is not all that well at least he is spared the indignity of rotting in a trench in France. All the grandchildren here are thriving and are a delight to my heart. Perhaps when this cursed war is finished and men have come to their senses, you will consider returning to England so that I may have the privilege of holding another grandchild to my bosom. Mother.

Cale exclaimed, "Well, the old dragon lady finally gave in. I guess all it takes is to give her name to our daughter."

I replied, "She didn't call you by name, that's her revenge for not having approved you before we were married."

Cale snorted. He didn't care what she thought.

Bessie laughed when she read the letter. "She still expects you to return to the fold, does she? Well, she will be waiting a long time, I do believe."

My dear sister Clive, How did you do it, being a new mother? How did you manage on only a few interrupted hours of sleep each night? How did you deal with a cranky baby that can only cry and wail? How long before you no longer have to soak and wash and hang out dirty nappies, or clean her and yourself after she's spit up what she's just eaten? I wish you were here to advise me. Some days, I'm so desperate I even wish Mother were here. Bessie is a help although she knows less about mothering than I do. And yet, Marjorie can be a little angel at times, when she sleeps peacefully, when she smiles, when she gurgles and goo-gooes (is that a word?). Those times are pure bliss. Love to all, especially my niece Peggy, Mary. P.S. Women now have the vote and I intend to use it to vote in favour of prohibition in next month's referendum.

* * *

Spring turned into summer turned into autumn. The vegetables and flowers that Cale had planted flourished, my precious hollyhocks bloomed grandly, and Mrs. Evans across the street became a new mother so I had someone to commiserate with. Bessie and I were well settled into life in Moose Jaw with all its amenities – running water and electricity, shops only a few blocks away and neighbours to visit.

Cale was a different matter. He continued to dream about buying a farm, *his* farm. Almost every weekend, he returned home with one of the Moose Jaw papers and spent the evening reading the "Farms for Sale" advertisements. There was nothing he could afford. "I'm not going to borrow from the bank if I can help it," he'd say.

Eventually, he changed tactics. "Perhaps I can rent a farm. At least I can get my foot in the door, perhaps save enough to buy a small farm somewhere."

I hoped he wouldn't find one, and said as much. It was the cause of several disagreements.

"You have a good position with the dairy," I'd say. "Why would you give that up for farming? You know how uncertain it is. Will always complains about the ups and downs of grain prices. And how will our children receive a proper education if there is no good school nearby? Farming seems a foolhardy proposition."

"Mary, you knew I wanted to be a farmer when you married me. I came to Canada to be my own boss."

"Except you won't be. There's the bank, the seed companies, the grain elevator companies, the machinery dealers, you'll be dancing to their tune, not the other way around."

"I don't intend to spend the rest of my life looking at the arse-end of a cart horse. I intend . . ."

"No, you'll be looking at the arse-end of a plough horse, that's what you'll be doing. Same end, just a different horse."

"Yes, but it will be the arse-end of *my* horse pulling *my* plough over *my* field. That's the difference."

"No, it will be someone else's field . . ." He never stayed to hear me finish. He would grab his coat and hat and stomp out of the house. I'd sit down with a cup of tea, sometimes shaking so hard with anger I'd slop the tea onto the saucer.

My dear Mary, I no longer have to worry about Harold being posted overseas. He was honourably discharged this month due to sickness. That's the good thing. However, he still suffers from some lung disease although they say it is not consumption. Thank heavens for small mercies. He received the Silver War Badge that he wears to indicate he has served, otherwise some nosy parker might stick a white feather in his lapel, thinking he is a coward. Do they do that in Canada? Maude is now working in Truro at the Royal Navy Hospital. She says there are more wounded every day. She is sick to think of all the young men being thrown away like trash. We all hope this war will end soon. Love, Dorothy.

* * *

Early March of 1917, Cale came home, happy as a lark. "There's a farm for rent east of here, near Keystown, just north of Pense. It must be on the CNR line because I don't remember seeing it when I worked for the CPR. There's good land there, black soil, flat as a pancake. The crops seem to thrive, as best I could tell speeding by on the train."

I caught my breath. A pang pierced my heart. I capped my pen and looked up from the letter I was writing to Dorothy. "How big is Keystown? And what is there at the farm?"

Cale hung up his coat. "It's not big, a grain elevator or two, a store and post office. Sort of like Belbeck. And don't worry about the house. Mr. Johnston says it is a big house and in good condition; his wife made sure to clean it well before they moved to Pense."

I scowled. "You've already talked to the owner?"

"Yes, of course. Mr. Johnston is desperate for a renter. His oldest son, Michael, is fighting in France, his younger son passed away last autumn after surgery of some sort, and his daughter is married and living somewhere in Manitoba. He's too frail to continue farming, heart problem or something, so he and his wife have moved into Pense. I will have use of all the buildings, equipment and livestock until his son returns from Europe. *If* he returns. *If* he returns in any condition to take up the farm."

I yelled after him as he went upstairs to have a nap, "You're one big foolish oaf." He didn't answer.

I gave the fire in the stove a good shake and banged the tea kettle onto it. I was most of the way through a second cup of tea, and somewhat calmer, when Bessie came down from upstairs holding Marjorie who had just woken up from her nap. Bessie sat at the table, bouncing Marjorie on her knee, and poured herself a cup of tea.

"Would you like a sip of milky tea?" Bessie asked her. Marjorie looked at me then shook her head and buried her head in Bessie's shoulder.

"I heard you arguing with Cale. What about?"

I told her. Bessie wasn't any more pleased than I was.

A few days later, Caleb bounced into the house and announced the deal was done and we were moving. At the end of the month! Only two weeks to pack!

"And what about me? What am I supposed to do?" Bessie said. "I have only two choices – go with you or stay in Moose Jaw and find a place to live. I don't know which is worse."

Cale chuckled as he turned to go outside. "You mean, if you come with us, Willie won't be able to come courting you, and if you stay, he will."

"That's not what I mean!" Bessie yelled at his departing back. She turned to me. "Well, maybe it is." She was blushing.

"It's up to you what you do, but you are welcome with us. I'll see that Cale agrees to that."

In the end, Bessie decided to come to Keystown. "Besides, this will be a test to see how serious Willie is," she said, grinning.

Packing up the house was a challenge because of Marjorie. She had just learned that walking was preferable to crawling. When she wasn't falling down and bawling her head off because she bumped into something, she was crawling into boxes and bawling her head off because she was trapped. Thank heavens, Bessie was there to help. One of my last acts was to fill an envelop with hollyhock seeds and tuck it into my handbag.

The removal truck arrived early the morning of March 31, a cold, blustery day that occasionally spit snow upon us. Bessie and I stood inside while the men loaded all our trunks, boxes and furniture and secured everything. Cale rode with the removal men to the CNR station, and Bessie and I, carrying Marjorie, got into Mr. Cox's Model T – he had kindly agreed to take us to the station.

My heart sank as we pulled away from our little house. Would we ever settle in one place that we could call "home?" At least Bessie and my precious envelop of hollyhock seeds were coming with us, so in a way, I was bringing "home" with me.

Chapter Fifteen
Keystown

We stood on the station platform, Cale talking with the drayman, Bessie smoking, and I cradling Marjorie who was screaming for no apparent reason. Icy wind knifed through my coat and icy snow crystals stung my face. Icy despair filled my heart as I looked at the miserable assemblage of buildings that was Keystown. Once, I had promised myself I would never follow a man to someplace I didn't want to go, yet time and again I found myself in some sorry excuse of a town. It didn't seem fair.

Someone called, "Mr. Higham?"

I turned to see a man, several years older than us, walk slowly and haltingly towards us, leaning heavily on a cane. Cale turned, then went to him and extended his hand. "Mr. Johnston, good to meet you."

I didn't hear the rest of their conversation. Bessie pulled me and the still screaming Marjorie towards the station's waiting room. "Let's get inside out of this bitter weather."

The station master took one look at us and hollered into the back, "Missus, there's folks out here could use some help."

A couple of minutes later, a spritely woman, wiping her hands on a towel, came into the waiting room. She saw screaming Marjorie and took her into her arms. "Come here, little one. Let's see what's the problem with you." She motioned with her head for us to follow her into the back. "I've a young one this age myself. Love him to bits, I do, but there are days . . ." She laughed. "Some days I want to send him back where he came from. Except I can't. Not that I'd really want to."

She put Marjorie on the table and unwrapped her, finally revealing the problem, one of the safety pins in Marjorie's nappy had come unsnapped and was sticking in her. She handed Marjorie, who hiccupped a few last sobs then buried her face in my neck, back to me. "Hope we see more of you, and more of this little one, too," she said as she stroked Marjorie's cheek.

"Thank you, I was at my wit's end. You've been very kind."

She smiled. "No problem. What are neighbours for, if not to help each other?"

"Your husband's looking for you," the station master called in.

Cale was standing in the waiting room. "Mr. Johnston's driving us out to the farm. The dray man is hauling our things out later this afternoon."

We climbed into Mr. Johnston's car and pulled blankets tightly around us; I did not want Marjorie to catch a chill. The rutted road was frozen hard; the car ricocheted from one rut to the next; we bounced and jolted along with it. My mood was as dreary as the flat, featureless, snow-covered land around us.

Imagine my surprise when we drove into the yard. No hovel, this house; instead, a large, two-storey home with a verandah in front and a smaller verandah and a balcony at the back. A bow window in what I presumed would be the parlour. Two chimneys. I heard Cale whistle. "Look at that barn! It's a damn sight bigger than Dad's is."

Mr. Johnston all but gloated. "Came out here in '95. Heck, it wasn't even Saskatchewan then, still the Northwest Territories. Regina was just a bunch of shacks. So was Moose Jaw. Homesteaded here and built this farm up from scratch. Right proud of it, I am." He shook his head. "Don't know what will come of it, though, if Michael don't come back."

I leaned forward. "Have you heard anything from him?"

He shook his head. "We got a letter two weeks ago, so we know he was alive then. Dreadful business, war. The wife's not sleeping well, neither am I for that matter. We're too worried." He shut off the car. "Let me show you around the house. I got the furnace going this morning and the power plant's charged up."

I couldn't believe my ears. A warm house with electricity! Dare I hope for a washing machine? A flush toilet? No, that last would be too much to expect.

We walked into the house through the back porch and found ourselves standing in a spotless kitchen with an enormous range, a large enamel sink, lots of cupboards and a huge worktable in the centre. A door led through a butler's pantry into the dining room. From there we walked into the parlour with its big bay window, and across the hall was another room. "My wife used that as her sewing room," Mr. Johnston explained.

Mr. Johnston took Cale into the basement to inspect the furnace and power plant while Bessie and I walked upstairs. There they were, four bedrooms, one with a sleeping porch off it, and a bathroom complete with a claw-footed enamel bathtub, a sink and, yes, the dreaded commode that hid the pail.

Bessie and I looked at each other in amazement. "I didn't expect something this sumptuous," I whispered.

She nodded. "Me, too. And it's clean as a whistle. Mrs. Johnston must be particular."

I giggled. "Or she had a domestic."

We heard a truck rattle into the yard. I peered out a curtainless window. "It's the drayman. I thought he wasn't coming till this afternoon." I scurried towards the stairs. "We'd best get down there and tell him where to put everything. When it comes to household affairs, men don't seem to know."

"Or care," Bessie added.

Furniture and boxes were soon helter-skelter throughout the kitchen and dining room, although I instructed the drayman and his assistant to carry the bedroom furniture upstairs before they left. We spent the rest of the day unpacking

That night, as Cale and I crawled into bed, I asked him, "Do you think you'll be happy here?"

"What kind of question is that? I came to Canada to be a farmer and now I'm a farmer." He turned and looked at me. "Of course, I would be happier if I were working my own farm, not someone else's. Why do you ask?"

"Oh, no reason in particular. Just wondering."

"Well, here, wonder about this." He began to tickle me.

"Oh, Cale! Stop that!"

He didn't.

* * *

My dear Carrie and George, What wonderful news about your new son. I can understand how relieved you are that he is so healthy. Give him a kiss and hug from his Auntie Mary. Marjorie is growing fast and is very bossy, even if she is only one year old. You asked about Bessie and Willie, well, Willie must be serious, he has driven here a couple of times already and we've been here only a couple of months. Bessie gets into such a tizzy: Is my hair straight? Do we have enough cake? Where's the good tea pot? Oh dear, I've a stain on my apron. She's quite amusing. Willie is always the gentleman, complements her on the cake and tea, then sets to arguing with Cale about politics especially now that our prime minister's government has enacted conscription, and there's talk of playing with the clocks, something called daylight saving time. As if the government can control the sun! I hope the ship bearing this letter isn't torpedoed. How low will those Germans sink to win this terrible war? I shake with fury whenever I think of it. Love, Mary.

Dear Mary and Caleb, Dad and I are pleased to learn Caleb finally has his farm, even if it is only a rented one. Little Marjorie looks so sweet in the photograph you enclosed in your letter. Please give her a big kiss from her

Granny Higham. The review board has continued John's exemption but on condition he joins the Oxfordshire volunteer regiment. Now, once a week, he dresses up in a hand-me-down uniform, shoulders his hand-me-down rifle, and parades up and down the streets of Banbury or Adderbury or Bodicote. He says it is a waste of time, he already knows how to shoot having had to keep rabbits and other vermin at bay on the farm. There is a growing shortage of food as it all goes to the troops and what is left in the shops is dearer by the day. The government is talking about rationing, as if conscription isn't bad enough. Love to all, your Mam and Dad Higham.

My dear Amelia, Harvest has begun in earnest. Cale is pleased with the crops. He hired a couple of local boys to help with the stooking and tomorrow the threshing crew rolls in. Bessie and I have been busy making pies and cakes and bread to feed all those hungry men. Remember our garden at Higher Tregurra? Mine this summer was just as spectacular. Mrs. Johnston must love flowers as much as I do, the garden already had lilacs, peonies, poppies and columbines, and a huge yellow rose bush, the flowers much smaller than our English roses but very perfumed. I planted my precious hollyhock seeds although they won't bloom till next summer, and cosmos and pansies. I have lost count of the quarts of peas, pickles, corn, and tomatoes we have preserved. A neighbour lady introduced us to saskatoon berries this summer, they're small blue berries and very tasty, they make an excellent pie. The bushes grow wild in the valley north of here, so we made a day outing of it complete with a picnic like we used to have at Loe Beach. Those were such good times, do you miss them as much as I do? Love, Mary

* * *

In early November, Cale came back from town with groceries and mail. "There's a letter from your sister," he hollered as he headed back outside. "Gotta unhitch the horses."

I cleaned the last of the bread dough off my hands and opened the letter. I gave out a yelp and called to Bessie who was in the parlour minding Marjorie. "Come here! You've got to read this!" She came out and read over my shoulder.

Dearest Mary and Bessie, please sit down before you read any further. I am secretly married to Harold. Mother doesn't know but I have told Clive and Maude. Mother threw a fit when she learned Harold was a Wesleyan and forbade me to ever see him again. You know what Mother thinks of Wesleyans. We were wed at his church in Paignton on October 20 but to maintain the secrecy I am still living at home as Dorothy Appleton and Harold lives in Dartmouth. Harold, bless his dear sweet soul, said he will convert to Church of England if that is what it takes for us to be publicly married. He must love me dearly if he is willing to do that since Wesleyans think the C of E is only a genuflection short of being Papist. I will write further as to the outcome of this romance worthy of the best Charlotte Brontë or Jane Austen novel. With much love, Dorothy.

Bessie and I looked at each other, mouths open. Then we laughed. "Dorothy's definitely an Appleton, flouting Mother! Who knew she had it in her!"

***

By now, I was expecting again, but in spite of that, and in spite of the cold and snow, we accepted Will and Emeline's invitation to spend Christmas with them. We took the train to Moose Jaw where Will met us with his Model T piled high with blankets and steaming hot rocks to keep our feet warm as we motored out to Belbeck. We were barely in the door when the girls came running to greet us. How they had grown! Mabel, now a healthy three-year-old, was dragging Miss Piggly by one arm.

Florence threw her arms around me. "I'm in Grade One. Now I can tell you a story."

Gertie and Pearl each took one of Marjorie's hands and led her around the house.

Emeline helped us with our coats. "Has Will told you our news?"

Cale and I looked at each other. "Ah, no. What news is this?"

Emeline smiled as she took Will's hand. "We are married, Will asked me in July." We stared at Will. He shrugged. "The girls love her, and they need a mother, and I need a wife. Mr. and Mrs. Hudson gave us their blessing. But that isn't all."

I stared at Emeline. "Don't tell me you're . . ."

She laughed. "No, not that. You tell them, Will."

He patted Emeline's hand. "We are moving into Moose Jaw in the new year. The girls need a better school."

"What about the farm? Are you selling the farm?" Cale asked.

Will shook his head. "No, Cale, the farm's not for sale, not even to you. I can manage it just as well from Moose Jaw as from this house. Now then, what about a drink to warm you up? It's been a cold ride out here."

Later that afternoon, John and his family, and Albert and his family arrived for Christmas dinner and, once again, the huge farmhouse was full enough to explode. It was a riotous time, what with adults talking and laughing, and the children playing and yelling and screeching as only children do.

While we were doing the washing up, Emeline paused, her hands in the dish pan. "Mary, I don't know what hospital is near you but why not come stay with us when your time nears? We would love to have you. The girls would love to have you."

I blinked in surprise. "There's a hospital at Pense, I don't know how good the doctor is." I paused. "I'll talk it over with Cale and let you know. And thank you for the offer. I was wondering how we would manage."

We stayed for three days. Bessie visited with Mr. and Mrs. Smail. "They're as wonderful as ever, although Mrs. Smail is certainly more frail than before," she said when she returned. Then, much to Bessie's delight, Willie and his family arrived for a visit. I didn't think I would see the day when Bessie blushed non-stop.

* * *

Spring hiccupped its way into Saskatchewan, battling with winter for supremacy. Winter finally admitted defeat, but grudgingly. Snow and rain alternated, coming and going, leaving the yard as muddy and impassable as those Flanders fields. The roads were no better, a sloppy mixture of mud and snow. Cale lost track of the number of times he pulled automobiles out of ditches with the horses. The drivers gave him a quarter for his trouble.

In mid-April, I took up residence at Will and Emeline's home in Moose Jaw. By now, I was as big as a house, waddling to and fro, sitting with my swollen feet up on the ottoman. Cale, Bessie and Marjorie took the train in occasionally for visits, and each time Marjorie cried when they left.

They were visiting the night of April 26. Bessie and I were helping Emeline with the washing up. Caleb was sitting at the table, rolling a cigarette and talking politics and farming with Will. Mabel and Florence were playing with Marjorie. Suddenly, I was standing in a pool of water. Bessie hollered, "Cale, call the doctor. That son you want is on his way!" At the same time, Emeline called, "Will, get the car fired up."

Cale dropped the cigarette he had been rolling, scattering bits of tobacco everywhere, as he leapt to his feet and ran to the telephone. "Save the tobacco. It's all I have till the next time I go to the store."

"Is tobacco more important than your wife and child?" Bessie yelled.

"Men!" Emeline muttered as she ran upstairs to fetch my purse and night case. All the hubbub frightened Marjorie who began to cry. Gertie, bless her soul, gave her a hug. "It's okay, Marjorie. Let's go in the other room. I'll read a story to you."

Cale hung up the receiver. "The hospital's waiting," he yelled.

Bessie helped me into my coat. "Where is Will? What's taking him so long?" He rushed in almost as she spoke. "Let's go," he yelled. Emeline handed him my night case.

Cale helped me waddle out the door and sit in the car before jumping into the back seat. Will sped us to the hospital. Cale helped me up the steps as Will handed my night case to the waiting nurse. "I'll leave you to it," he said, and left. The nurse told Cale to sit in the waiting room and then helped me into the birthing room. Our first son, whom we named Robert Caleb, was born a day later, early the morning of April 27.

Two weeks later, son and I arrived back home in Keystown. Bessie fussed over both me and baby, Marjorie was not at all amused about having all the attention focused on her little brother, and Cale boasted to everyone about his new son.

My dear Carrie and George, Was your little Harold as much trouble as our little Bob? I thought Marjorie was a demanding baby, but nothing compared to Bob. He won't stop crying or fussing no matter what I do. What a struggle to get by on no sleep. Thank heavens Bessie is here to help, she keeps Marjorie entertained and out of mischief while I try to deal with Bob. Of course, Cale went out with his mates when we returned from Moose Jaw, to celebrate, he said. He says prohibition beer is so weak he has to drink twice as much to get half the effect, so he must drink a lot to get the full effect. I certainly gave him the "full effect" when he came home, three sheets to the wind. I called him irresponsible, among other things, to come home drunk with children in the house. That man makes me so mad some times. Love to all, Mary.

* * *

After finally managing to get Bob asleep one particularly trying day, I sat down to have a much-needed cup of tea. Cale was also sitting at the table, smoking a cigarette while reading the *Moose Jaw Daily News*.

"Bob's finally asleep," I said.

"Mmm." Cale was engrossed in the paper.

"I hope this isn't a sign of how he'll be when he grows up. We don't need two curmudgeons in the family."

Cale looked up. "And who would the other one be?"

I swatted at him. "You know full well who I'm talking about."

He ducked and laughed, then put down the paper. "Ah, but that's why you married me, isn't it?" He tried to kiss me but now it was my turn to duck.

"Get on with you, you big lummox," I said, but I couldn't help but smile. He finally managed to kiss me. I slapped him away, in play. "Now, get out of here, you've got chores waiting in the barn, I'm sure."

He left, humming "Pack up your Troubles."

* * *

Dear Mary, The war on the continent is finally turning, the Germans are retreating as fast as they can go. The Prime Minister says Germany will capitulate in a month but people said the war would be over by Christmas and that was four years ago. I shall be glad to see the end of it, but when I think of all the young men who have died or were wounded, whose lives will never be the same as before, I get so angry. I don't know which is worse, the wounds of the body or the wounds of the heart and mind. And now, the hospitals are filled with young people suffering from a horrible sickness they call the Spanish flu. It strikes so fast. A person can arrive in the morning, coughing, wheezing, aching in every bone. By evening they are so sick they cannot lift their heads. By next morning they are gone. It is that fast. Worse, it is spreading quickly. The wards are overrun. I pray it does not afflict you. Love, Maude.

The Spanish flu arrived in early October. Cale read about it in the *Evening Times*. "Some guy called Harry

Land has died of the flu in Regina. Hospitals in Toronto are full. It's spreading like wildfire. I think you and the children should stay home until it plays itself out. Don't want you catching it." He started rolling a cigarette.

I finished sweeping the floor and put the broom in the corner. "And what about you? You think you're immune?"

He looked up at me. "Don't worry, I'll be careful. I'll use some of Dr. Dabell's spray solution of chlorzoxazone for the nose. He guarantees full protection. At least, that's what his ad says." He lit the cigarette. "Better go do chores," and out he went.

I yelled after him, "Wear one of those masks when you go to town. They're supposed to keep you from catching the flu."

I turned to Bessie who was rocking little Bob. "What if he dies? What will we do with two little children, one a babe in arms? Will I have to be a housemaid again?" I plunked down on the davenport.

Bessie sat beside me and put her arm around me. "I don't know, Mary. We'll just have to hope we get through this all right."

We did, but it was a long, anxious three months. Keystown and most of Pense were quarantined. Dr. Boyd commandeered the Pense hotel to use as a hospital. Schools and libraries were closed, churches cancelled services, and all public gatherings were banned. Most towns, Keystown and Pense included, blockaded the highways and closed the stations so no one could enter.

Cale called the other farms on our party line, or one of our neighbours would call us. If someone was sick, Cale went to do their chores. I worried every time he went out the door. "Wear your mask!" Bessie or I would yell after him.

Amidst all this sickness and death, one good thing happened – the war ended. Cale brought the news and the newspaper home There, on the front page of the *Moose Jaw Daily News* was the official announcement that Germany was crushed and Turkey had surrendered: "The armistice has been signed. It was signed at five o'clock am Paris time and hostilities will cease at 11 o'clock this morning."

"You should have seen the people in town," Cale said. "They were dancing in the streets, jumping up and down, yelling, laughing, crying all at the same time. Some sweet young thing grabbed me and kissed me. It's a case of 'to hell with the flu, we're celebrating' in town today. It's nothing short of pandemonium."

My dear Clive, We survived the Spanish flu but so many people did not. We read it killed more people than the war did. Two hundred and fifty-three people died in Moose Jaw alone, or so the paper says, and Cale says he heard that six people in Pense died although over half of the town was ill with it. I am so relieved that you are all well, even more relieved that no one has to fight that horrid war. Let us hope it is truly the war to end all wars although somehow I doubt that will happen. Has there ever been a time and place without war? The crop wasn't as good this year although wheat prices are still up. Cale says now that we're not sending grain overseas, he is betting the prices come down. Let's hope that's not the case. I have enclosed a Canadian dollar, use it to buy yourself something nice. Have a happy Christmas. Love to all, Mary.

Christmas came and went, and we fell into 1919. January couldn't decide if it should be bitter cold that set the house creaking and groaning, or fierce blizzards that threatened to bury us, so it did both. This may have been my sixth Canadian winter, but I still was not used to it.

Dear Mary and Bessie, Harold and I are now openly married. We no longer have to carry on the charade of being merely "courting." Give Harold full marks for successfully charming Mother into agreeing to our marriage, although part of his charm offensive was to promise to join the Church of England, which he did. We were married 26 December at St. Mary's Church in Penzance, a small gathering with Mother and Clive as our witnesses. George gave me away, and Father came without That Woman, thank heavens or Mother would have thrown the both of them out. He had the good sense to sit far away from us and Mother wouldn't even look in his direction. We are living in Dartmouth near where Harold works, in a house so small you have to keep your elbows in when you turn around. Harold, bless his soul, has promised to buy a big house one day. Love to all, Mrs. Kerswell (Oh, how I love the sound of that.)

* * *

Winter passed, followed by Saskatchewan's version of spring blustering in. Bessie and I longed for an English spring – the slow greening of the landscape, daffodils and fruit trees bursting into bloom, no snow, no slush, no mud. Caleb tried to burst our bubble. "The England you're talking about doesn't exist. There might not have been snow but I remember lots of mud and muck, and cold rain that wouldn't stop."

Bad news came a few weeks later. Cale had gone into town with our ration book to get much needed sugar, if they had any. He returned a couple of hours later and dropped a five-pound bag on the table. "That's all they had," he said.

Bessie looked up from Marjorie who was miserable because she had a cold and a runny nose. "Mind the floor. I just washed it," she scolded.

Cale retorted, "I have more goddamn things on my mind than your floor."

I didn't pay much attention, other than to say, "Mind your language around the children," because I was trying to feed Bob some mushy peas and he was fighting every spoonful. I paused the battle and turned to Cale. "Now what?"

"I met Mr. Johnston in town."

"Oh." I turned back to see Bob had now grabbed a fistful of peas and smeared them all over his face. "No, Bob, no! Now look at you."

"Mr. Johnston's son is back from Europe and wants to take over the farm and we have to leave by spring."

That got my attention. "What! Where will we go?"

"Damned if I know. I'll have to see if there's another farm to rent somewhere."

By now, I had given up on feeding Bob, so I yanked him out of the highchair and took him over to the sink to clean him up. "I suppose we could always move back to Moose Jaw and you could work for the dairy again."

"No goddamn way I'm working for them again." With that he went outside, slamming the door behind him.

Bessie and I looked at each other. "What will become of us?" Just then Bob spit up what little I had managed to get into him, and now I had a real mess to clean up.

My head ached as I washed spit-up peas off Bob and me. Maybe I should have stayed in England, I thought. The Oxenhams were a good family to work for. But what if I had married that hostler? Now I'd be listening to him drone on about the price of horseshoe nails or some such. No, I decided, I'm better off in Canada even if I don't know where we will be laying our heads come spring.

Chapter Sixteen
Boharm

Will saved us.

The Griggs spent Easter with us and in the course of the day, we told them about our predicament.

"Come farm for me," Will said.

"Not a chance . . ." Cale started but Will interrupted.

"No, no, hear me out. I'm talking about a farm at Boharm, west of Moose Jaw. I lent money to the brothers who owned it. They put the land up as security and since they haven't been able to pay – crops were poor last year, as you know – they're transferring it to me. I'm looking for someone to farm it, I can't farm both it and Belbeck. What do you say?"

Cale paused. He looked at me. I scowled. "We have to move somewhere. Mr. Johnston is kicking us out."

Cale and Will shook hands. "It's a deal. And a load off my mind." He looked at me again. "And I'm sure a load off Mary's mind." He grinned. "She's been bugging me something terrible these last few weeks."

"And with good reason! I don't like being dragged all over the country like some gypsy, with nowhere permanent to lay my head."

Will interjected. "Mary, you won't have to move far if Cale takes over this farm. However," he paused, "you might not like the house. It's rather smaller than this mansion."

I shook my finger at him. "Just so long as it's clean."

Emeline smiled. "I doubt that. They're bachelor brothers, remember? Men don't have the same standards of cleanliness as we women do. But never fear. If it's in need of a good cleaning, I'll be more than willing to help."

* * *

We moved to Boharm on a bleak, dreary, gloomy April day, no hint of warmth in the sun. The damp chill seeped through my coat and into my bones. We had shipped everything, including the wagon and us, by train from Pense to Boharm, both being on the CPR line. Will met us at the Boharm station with his Model T, and after the men and the station agent had loaded everything into the dray wagon, he drove Bessie and me and the children out to the farm.

I stared at the house before us, a single-storey, unpainted, weather-beaten building with an open porch, then turned to Will. "You expect us to live in . . . *that*?"

"I know it's not much, Mary . . ."

"That's an understatement if ever I heard one."

Will slapped his hands together to warm them. "I'll wait here for Cale. Once he arrives, I'll help him unload everything from the wagon."

Bob began to whimper. Marjorie whined, "I'm cold."

Bessie shushed her, then turned to me and pointed to the door. "Shall we?"

We found ourselves in a room that served as kitchen, dining room and sitting room. Deep scratches and grooves in the floor suggested where a settee had once stood. A threadbare rug, devoid of any discernable pattern, covered the middle of the floor. On the far wall stood a cook stove in need of a good cleaning. An overflowing ash pan hung partly out of it. A wooden table with four mis-matched chairs stood nearby. I ran my finger across the tabletop, leaving a trail through the thick layer of dust and grime. To the right of the stove was the door to a pantry; on its left was a door to one of the bedrooms. The doors to two other bedrooms were on my left. Dust, cobwebs, and mouse droppings were everywhere. The windowpanes weren't any cleaner; they were covered with several layers of fly specks and Saskatchewan dust.

"Good Lord!" breathed Bessie.

I peered into the pantry; on my left was a battered counter with doorless cupboards above; straight ahead, a stained and scratched enamel sink and a hand pump. I grimaced. "Bessie, this is disgusting! No electricity. No running water. How can we live here?"

A side door led to an enclosed porch; scraps of wood suggested it had been used as a woodshed. A row of coat hooks ran across one wall; opposite was a small washstand with a chipped enamel basin and jug.

Marjorie had been running back and forth from one room into another, when she let out a shriek. "Mousey! Mousey!" A tiny four-footed creature scurried out of a bedroom, skittered across the floor and into a tiny hole in the baseboard. Bessie shrieked. I clasped Bob tighter as he wailed, "Down, down." I was not putting him down on that filthy floor. How many more four-footed residents do we have to deal with? I thought.

Bessie called out from one of the bedrooms, "They left us a bed!"

I looked in; the iron bedstead sat askew, one caster was missing as were some balusters in the footboard. "I'd say it barely survived the war," Bessie sneered. The other bedrooms were empty although tattered and filthy curtains swayed gently in a draft coming in around the window sash.

"Wait, where's the bathroom?" I went from doorway to doorway.

"Don't tell me there's no bathroom in this house!" Bessie exclaimed. "Where are we supposed to bathe?"

I shook my head. "I don't know." No bathroom, no water closet, not even a commode with a stinky pail. Who could live like this?

"I wonder if it's down there." Bessie pointed to a trap door in the middle of the floor. The hinges squeaked as she opened it gingerly and peered down a set of steep stairs into the gloom below. "It's as dark as a tomb down there, can't see a thing." She let the door fall back with a bang. Dust flew up. Bessie flailed at the dust and coughed.

We walked outside and around the house and found the pump. I worked the handle and water gushed out. The outhouse was nearby; it was desperately in need of a good cleaning. The garden was choked with last year's crop of pig weed and thistles.

We heard the rattle of harness and wagon coming into the yard, so turned to meet Cale. He had barely Whoa-ed the horses when I lit into him.

"Cale, this place is a dump! A pig sty! No, it's worse than a pig sty. No self-respecting pig would live here. The place is filthy. And the windows leak. You can see the curtains moving in those bedrooms. We can't move in with the house looking like this, not with a toddler and baby. I won't be having our children living in this squalor."

I turned to Will. "Are there storms for the windows? How good is the well? And what is in the basement? Is there a cistern to store water?" I crossed my arms and took a deep breath.

Cale looked back and forth from Will to me. Will held up his hands. "Whoa, Mary. I did warn you but I confess, it's worse than I knew. Yes, there are storm windows, they are in the basement. Along with a cistern and a cold room for vegetables and preserves. The well has never been known to run dry. As for the dirt," and he shrugged, "I'll bring Emeline here tomorrow. She can help you clean the place. Let's unload everything. Once that's done, you can come stay with us till the house is clean."

Emeline, Bessie and I spent the next two days shooing out spiders and mice and destroying their nests. We scrubbed the walls and floors and cupboards several times, burned the ratty old rug and curtains, and threw out garbage that seemed to be piled in every corner. We were pleased to discover that, under all those layers of grime, the walls were papered with a lovely pattern. The range looked like new; Bessie had polished the chrome till we could almost see our faces in it. We washed so many layers of grime off the counter that we felt like Dr. Schliemann excavating Troy.

"Cale had better appreciate all our hard work," I said when we were finally finished. The house looked and smelled clean.

"Men! What do they know about housework?" said Bessie. "They think they're the only ones who put in a hard day's work. I'd like to see Cale get this house looking this ship-shape." She lit up a cigarette, then looked at me. "Don't fret, Mary, I won't get any ashes on the floor."

Cale, for his part, reglazed all the windows and dug a new hole for the outhouse and moved it. He descended into the depths of the basement and came up smiling.

"Basement's tight as a drum though it has a dirt floor. No mice, no snakes, no mildew, no sign of water ever getting in. We'll need more glass, though. The storm windows are in worse shape than the sashes up here. There's a lot of junk down there that needs cleaning out, but I'll take care of that once seeding's done."

Thus it was, the third week of April 1919, we took up residence on the northwest quarter of Section 34, Township 16, Range 28, west of the 2nd Meridian, just southwest of the village of Boharm.

Dearest Dorothy, I am so tired of moving. My whole life has been one move after another. Just as I get settled in, I'm uprooted. I had such hopes and dreams when I came to Canada. I didn't want much, just a nice house, a nice yard and a nice garden. All I wanted was someplace to call home. I burst into tears when I saw the house, and I've cried myself to sleep every night since. I can hear Mother saying, well dear, you've made your bed, now lie in it! Yes, I promised "for better and for worse," but it had better not get any worse than this. I pray this hovel will not be our home for long, this time I will be glad to be uprooted. At least Bessie is here with us. The children are growing fast, I have been making good use of the sewing machine making bigger clothes for them. Marjorie is talking a mile a minute, some times you can even understand her. Bob is continually getting into mischief just like George used to.

There are times I want to give him back. Love to Harold and you. Mary.

* * *

At Keystown, you might as well have been standing on a board. There, I understood why people once believed the earth was flat. Boharm was different; it seemed to be in the bottom of a great shallow bowl. The village and the farmland sat in a long, gentle swale of land that sloped up to the north and the south. South of us, I don't know how many miles away, a ridge of hills ran from the northwest to the southeast. Looking at them, I almost felt like I was gazing at the Cornish moors. All that was missing was the sound of the sea crashing into the rocky headlands of Land's End. The wind was what I heard here, some days just a gentle breeze that rustled leaves almost like a lullaby. Other times, though, – the times I didn't like so much – it roared across the land, setting everyone's nerves on edge.

I never tired of looking at the hills to the south, they changed with each season. In spring, they were green with new grass which, come late summer, transformed into a velvety brown. In winter, they were brilliant white with snow. And above, the blue sky, often cloudless but occasionally grey or black with angry storm clouds that brought rain or hail or snow. And then there were the sunsets and sunrises. I don't remember ever seeing such spectacles in England. Perhaps there were too many buildings or too much smoke in the air; I don't know, but these prairie light shows took my breath away.

My dear Clive, Bessie and I had a falling out last week when she came back from town with her hair bobbed and marcelled. I told her she looked like a boy but she just blew cigarette smoke in my face and said she didn't care what I thought. She said she was tired of washing and putting up long hair, and short hair would be so much easier to care for. Just don't go wearing trousers, I told her, and she laughed and shrugged. She doesn't seem to care what people think. Never fear, I am not cutting my hair.

However, we agree the shorter skirt length is so much more practical, we joke that one day hems might even be knee-high. Cale is busy with seeding, he's hoping for a good crop especially if wheat prices remain high. Love to all, Mary.

* * *

If I was shocked at the state of the house, Cale wasn't much happier about the state of the farm machinery. He swore a blue streak as he surveyed what there was. "No wonder those goddamned brothers couldn't make it as farmers, they didn't know how to look after anything." Worse still, there was no livestock, no cattle, no hogs or chickens, but especially no horses. "How the hell am I to farm with no horses? I'll be damned if I'm going to pull the goddamned machinery myself." Off he went to Caron, the nearest town of any size, and came back with four mules.

We raised our eyebrows. "Mules? Why mules?"

"They're cheaper and stronger than draft horses," he said, "Just because they're ugly doesn't mean they're dumb. They're every bit as smart as a horse, maybe smarter. Treat them right and they'll work hard for you. At least that's what I was told." We had those mules for the next five years, until Cale had enough money to buy horses.

There's a reason people say, stubborn as a mule. Yes, they did work hard, those mules could pull any piece of machinery with no effort. And yes, they were smart. Too smart. They had minds of their own. They stopped when it was time to eat, or when it was time to head back to the barn to be unharnessed, or sometimes just because they felt like stopping. Then they made straight for the farm, regardless of what lay in their path, even a slough which happened more than once. We heard no end of cussing and swearing. They caused Cale no end of grief and us no end of laughter.

Summer brought happy news from Maude.

My dear Mary and Bessie, I have just started my training as a nursing sister at the Royal Surrey County

Hospital in Surrey. I was so inspired by the nursing sisters I worked with during the war, and I promised myself then I would do my part to alleviate as much needless suffering as possible. I felt a little guilty about leaving Mother on her own as she is getting frailer, but Clive said she will look in on her every few days. Give my love to Cale and hug my dear little niece and nephew for me. Love, Maude.

Bessie was happy for her twin, "I'm glad one of us can achieve our dream." We both wrote back letters wishing her every success.

The crop that fall was middling fair but wheat fetched a good price, so Cale wasn't worried about paying all the bills that had piled up. Just as well, because by November I was expecting again. That wasn't the only good news. At Christmas, Willie proposed to Bessie. The wedding would be July 28 at St. John's Anglican Church.

Cale clapped him on the back. "About time you worked up the nerve! What took you so long? Damn this prohibition. We should have a good snort of whiskey to celebrate."

"Just as well you don't," I said.

I hugged Bessie. "I am so happy for you, but . . ."

"But what?"

I sighed. "I'll miss you, and it's not because you've been such a great help. You're my only family here."

She threw her arms around me. "And I'll miss you. Who knows? Maybe there's a farm to rent near Assiniboia." She smiled and turned to Willie. "Right?"

He shrugged. "One never knows."

That night, when we crawled into bed, Cale muttered, "Willie sure has it easy. Wish I had a rich father to buy a farm for me. No mortgage hanging over my head."

I was silent. How could I reply with this huge hole in my heart, a hole that formed when I left England, a hole that Bessie had filled. Till now.

"You're quiet."

"Yes."

"You're going to miss Bessie, aren't you?"

"Yes."

"It's not as if she'll be living on the other side of the world. We can go visit them from time to time."

"Yes." My voice cracked.

"Oh, come here." Cale rolled me over into his arms. I cried.

* * *

By the end of May, I was waddling like a stuffed duck. I could barely bend down to plant and weed the garden. Bessie was a great help, as usual, and I was truly concerned about how I would manage without her. However, I reminded myself that Mother had cared for seven children all on her own. If she could do it, so could I.

The baby decided to enter the world of the living the afternoon of July 8, just as a thunderstorm broke in all its fury. Lightning bolts flew every few seconds it seemed; thunder shook the house; the rain hammered down like hail.

"I'll get Dr. Gray," Cale yelled over the roar. He grabbed his coat and ran out the door.

Bessie alternated between holding my hand and keeping the children occupied. Marjorie started crying, "Mommy's hurting!" Bessie was hard put to calm her fears.

An hour later, a very drenched Cale returned with an equally drenched doctor, and a few hours later, John Brock was born. The sound of his first cry brought Cale running into the bedroom. The doctor looked up. "Greet your new son, Mr. Higham."

"Another son!" Cale exclaimed. He took my hand. "Are you all right?"

"As fine as can be expected after having been in labour for these last several hours."

Bessie brought in Marjorie and Bob. "Say hello to you new brother." Marjorie wrinkled her nose. "He's ugly. He's all red and wrinkled."

We laughed. "You looked like that when you were born," I told her.

She stomped her foot. "Did not!"

We all laughed again.

Cale took the doctor back to Caron, and when he returned he told us that, for once, the mules had co-operated. "They let me harness them, they trotted into town and never once shied at the thunder. Maybe they knew they were on a mission."

"I doubt that," Bessie replied.

* * *

Bessie and Willie's wedding was a quiet morning ceremony, just us and the entire Lamb family and a few close friends. Gladys and Mary, Willie's sisters, were their witnesses. Bob squirmed in spite of Cale's warnings, John slept, and Marjorie wanted to know why she couldn't be part of the wedding. There was no time for a party afterwards because Willie and Bessie were catching the afternoon train to Assiniboia. Instead, Mr. Lamb took everyone to the Royal George Hotel for dinner. Afterwards, we sat and visited in the CPR station gardens until the time came to say good-bye. Bessie and I hugged each other like we would never see each other again. Both had tears in our eyes.

"I love you. I'll miss you," I whispered.

"I'll write," she replied.

Cale and Willie shook hands. "Come visit us, it's not that long a train ride to Assiniboia."

The whistle blew. The bell rang. The engine huffed and puffed and pulled away from the station, heading southward.

She was gone. My stalwart companion of the last six years was gone. We had become so close during that time. So close, that we finished each other's sentences. So close, that we knew what the other was going to say before she said it. I could tell by the set of her mouth, the tilt of her head, the way she smoked her cigarette if she was happy or sad, annoyed or content. We had spent many afternoons reminiscing and laughing, a pot of tea on the table. We had spent many evenings at our needlework, chatting all the while, the coal oil lantern casting flickering shadows on the walls. And now she was gone.

* * *

Two weeks later, we received a letter from Annie. A black-edged card fell out onto the table. "In Loving Memory of John Higham," it read.

Dear Mary and Caleb, This letter bears the sad news that your Father has passed on to his reward. It happened so quietly and so quickly. He had been out riding around the farm in the trap, old Goldie pulling him as usual, to see the farming. When he came back, he said, "I'm feeling a bit tired, I think I'll have a lie-down before tea." An hour later I called him for his tea but he didn't come out so I went into the room and there he was, lying still, and I knew right away that he would never wake up, but I still called, "Pa, wake up, tea's on." He didn't answer so I sat down beside him on the bed and held his hand and wept like a child. John found me there, he put his arm around me and said he'd call the vicar. Now, your father is in the churchyard, waiting for the last trumpet to sound when the Lord will call all his faithful to him. He has left you some money in his will which will be deposited in a bank should you ever return to England and have need of it. As for me, I have a huge hole in my heart that will never be filled. Still, life goes on. My love to your dear children. Mam.

Cale stood quietly for a time. "I guess his heart finally gave out." He walked out the door. I let him go. There was no point in talking to him now. Let him grieve his own way. I found my notepaper and a pen and sat down to write a letter to her but just then little John started bawling, so the letter had to wait.

Cale never did talk about it.

* * *

We went to Assiniboia for Thanksgiving. Willie's father might have bought him the farm but he didn't buy them a fancy house. In fact, he didn't buy them any house; Willie had to build it himself. It wasn't any more luxurious than ours, but he did have a wind generator standing proudly in the yard. What a thrill to push a switch and get brilliant light from an electric lamp instead of the dim glow of a coal oil lantern.

In the midst of all our talking and eating, Willie turned to Cale. "I hear there's a farm for rent at Mazenod."

"Where's Mazenod?" Cale asked.

"Not that far from here. West of Mossbank on the CNR line."

Before I could say anything, Willie turned to me. "The house is much nicer, Mary. I thought you might be interested in living closer to us, seeing as how Bessie is your only family here in Canada."

He turned back to Cale. "It's good land. There's a half-section and the buildings are in good shape. And Mazenod's a bigger place than Boharm."

Cale rubbed the back of his neck. "Sounds interesting. Send me the details. I'll think about it."

It didn't take much thinking, although Will tried to encourage Cale to stay on his farm. "You're a good, dependable tenant, Cale. I know you could manage this farm at a profit," he said.

Will argued in vain. Cale was stubborn. He was still dreaming of owning his own farm even though there was no land around Moose Jaw for sale that he could afford to buy. "Perhaps land is cheaper around Assiniboia. The only way I'll find out is if we live in the area," he said.

For once, I encouraged him to move, anything to leave this hovel, especially after receiving one of Bessie's letters.

My dear Mary and Cale, Willie and I went out to take a look at the farm, and you'll be pleased to know the house is a darn sight better than the one you're living in now even if it is not as fancy as the Keystown house. It has seven rooms, a proper bathroom although just the dreaded commode, and a real set of stairs into the basement. Best of all, it's clean. And no mice! And no leaks around the sashes. Tell Cale that Willie says the barn and granaries are in good repair and the owner is willing to negotiate the rental arrangements. I can hardly wait until you move here, I have missed you so much. Love to all, Bessie.

By the end of October, Cale had rented the Mazenod farm but the move this time was more complicated than when we left Keystown because we had acquired a dozen or so hens, two sows (one pregnant), a milk cow, and a Hereford cow and her calf, not to mention the four mules. Cale reserved a settler's car at the CNR station in Moose Jaw, and on the appointed day he packed all our worldly possessions in our wagon. A neighbour loaded the hens and sows into his wagon and hitched the cows to the back. The children and I rode in the buggy driven by the neighbour's son.

We made quite the procession into Moose Jaw and turned several heads as we wound our way through the city streets to the CNR station. I pretended I was Queen Mary and waved royally. Some waved back and I acknowledged their wave with a regal nod of my head. I had to amuse myself somehow.

Loading everything into the car was easy, if laborious, until it was the mules' turn. They baulked, they brayed, one almost escaped. A quick-thinking train employee provided the solution. He lured them in with a bucket of grain.

"Me pa had mules, no end o' trouble. Couldn't get rid of 'em soon enough," he told Cale.

Chapter Seventeen
Mazenod

On November 7, 1921, a cold and snowy day, we took up residence on the NE quarter of Section 16 Township 10 Range 2, West of the Third Meridian. Bessie was right about the house. It was modest but clean and comfortable. We weren't in each other's face like at the Boharm house; how glad I was to leave that sorry excuse for a house. The new kitchen was big and had lots of cupboards. A small washroom off the kitchen had a huge porcelain sink and drain board, and the hand-cranked milk separator was also there. The parlour had a hardwood floor, nice to look at but it required polishing every week. The bedrooms upstairs were small but they were big enough for sleeping. Outside was a large garden with lilacs and rose bushes, although I had to wait till summer to see any roses. As I wandered through the garden I wondered if there were hollyhocks or if I would have to use some of my dwindling supply of seeds.

I also couldn't help wondering if Cale would ever be able to buy a farm. I was tired of moving. That was all I had done since coming to Canada. I wanted my own place. So did Cale. But for now, we were here, in yet another person's house, in yet another person's farm.

At least I was closer to Bessie.

Every Saturday, we bumped into Mazenod along the road that might be dusty, muddy or snow-covered, depending on the season. We shopped at Mr. White's general store for groceries, dry goods and the weekly *Lake Johnson Star*, and we gossiped with everyone we met. We picked up the mail at the post office and the latest Eaton's parcel at the train station. Occasionally, we got repairs at the Massey-Harris dealership, or medicine for the livestock from the livery stable. We ordered coal. Transacted business at the Bank of Toronto. Attended the occasional dance. Sometimes attended the Anglican Church where Bob and John were baptized. Occasionally, we made the trip to Assiniboia to visit Bessie and Willie, or they came to visit us.

* * *

My dear Clive, Here it is, April of 1922 and spring is nowhere in sight. How I miss English springs that come early and stay long. All we have is mud and rain and snow and more mud and cold and even more mud. I long to see green grass and flowers but that will have to wait till May or June when we can finally plant the garden. I still dream of a garden filled with flowers like back at Higher Tregurra. Cale doesn't mind the rain, he says the moisture will help the crops germinate. He's out in the barn now, one of his precious Yorkshire sows is farrowing and we have two new calves, one a heifer, so we'll have cream to sell. Living is rather lean these days. Bob and John are out there with Cale, probably being more hindrance than help. John follows Bob like a puppy. Whatever Bob does, John has to copy even though he's barely two to Bob's four. Enjoy your spring, please send some our way. Love, Mary and Cale.

My dear Dorothy and Harold, What wonderful news your last letter brought, a baby girl. Anne, such a lovely name you've given her. We visited Bessie and Willie last weekend and went into Assiniboia on Saturday and found a gift for her which we're sending separately. It's from both Bessie and me. All the talk here is about the tornado that hit Mossbank area in early June, a vicious storm that destroyed a farm and hailed out many crops east of here. Cale says we got off lucky, only one field has some damage. Times like this I wonder why people live here. Remember the stories Grandfather Ferris used to tell about life on the sea, one minute calm and smooth sailing and the next the sea is doing everything it can to send you to the bottom? Saskatchewan is the same, a land of extremes, not the sort for soft people and easy living. Summer or winter, there's always wind that tries to blow you away or bury you under snow, and it can be scorching hot one day and freezing cold the next. The children are growing by leaps and bounds, Marjorie starts school this autumn and she already knows her letters and numbers and is pleased to recite them to all and sundry. Cale says she takes after her mother. I don't know what he means by that. Love to all, and a hug to Anne from her Canadian auntie. Love, Mary.

* * *

The tedium of daily life was interrupted in early August by a cable from England. MOTHER PASSED AWAY TUESDAY STOP FUNERAL FRIDAY STOP DOROTHY.

I stood like a statue, cable clutched in my hand, my head spinning. She was only 65. I wasn't sure what to feel or think. Mother had been an angry, domineering woman who had tried to control our lives, and I resented that. She was the main reason why I left home. But she was still my mother. Wasn't I supposed to feel sorrow?

Bessie, Willie and one-year-old baby Roy came to visit that evening. Like me, Bessie had mixed emotions. We agreed to cable money to Dorothy to purchase a floral tribute from us, and Cale said he would go into Mazenod on the morrow to cable it.

Grief and loss hit me a couple of days later. I was rocking John – he was feeling poorly – and suddenly there she was in my mind's eye, rocking baby Dorothy when she had a cold, singing exactly the same lullaby I was singing to John, "Oranges and Lemons, Say the Bells of St. Clement's." The memory was so strong, she might as well have been sitting on the chair opposite.

I broke down. I cried like a child. I cried for the loss of a mother, who, in spite of her worst self, had loved and nurtured us. She wanted us to have a better life than she had, so she fought Father's stinginess to give us as good an education as possible. She wanted the best for us even if her idea of "best" was not ours.

* * *

We rolled into 1923. I was expecting again but worried. I'd been expecting last year, too, but it had come to an abrupt and painful loss late one summer afternoon. I didn't want to lose this baby, too. When I told Cale in November that I was expecting again, he sighed. "Mary, how many more babies are you going to pop out?"

I crossed my arms and stuck out my chin. "Well, Mr. Higham, in case you forget, you play a part in making these babies. Perhaps you're the one who needs to decide how many we have."

We didn't speak for the rest of the day.

Dearest Mary, At long last, I have graduated and am a certified nursing sister. I have included a photograph taken upon our graduation. Clive says I look terribly proud and I most certainly am. This has been my dream for such a long time and now I've achieved it. Clive asked me to sit so she could paint my image, she's a good artist, you know, and she said she will paint a copy for everyone so you should receive one soon. I am still awaiting my first posting. After what I saw during the war, I am ready for anything, nothing could be worse than the injuries of those years. I must confess that nursing Mother in her last year was a challenge. Knowing death was imminent only made her more demanding but eventually she accepted it with grace knowing she was going to her reward. With much love, Maude.

* * *

That spring, Cale finally had enough of the mules. I was in the garden checking to see if anything had sprouted, when I heard a jangle of harness and the loudest, longest streak of swearing that Cale had ever uttered. I walked around the house toward the barn. Cale was unharnessing the mules, all the while cursing and swearing a blue streak, as the saying goes. His trousers were soaked and muddy to the knees.

"What happened?"

"Those blasted beasts!" That wasn't quite what he said. "They came home straight through that goddamned slough, pulled me along behind them, wouldn't listen to a single goddamned command." And he was off again, another long string of words describing the mules' ancestry and descendants and what they could do with themselves.

When he finally cooled down and changed into dry clothes, he clapped on his hat. "I've had it with mules. I'm taking them into town and buying some horses instead."

And he did. He returned with six horses – two Percherons and four Belgians. They never once dragged him through a slough.

* * *

The baby decided the middle of the worst thunderstorm was the perfect time to be born. June 1 was one of those hot, humid oppressive days when even the air weighed down on you. The storm broke late afternoon just as the baby announced it was coming, and this time, Bessie was too far away to help. I yelled at Marjorie, "Tell your father to fetch the doctor!" She ran out the door into the pouring rain and returned a few minutes later, "He's hitching the horses now."

An hour passed, the storm had abated but still no Cale or doctor. Marjorie was little help.

"Ew! I'm never having a baby!" she squealed as she screwed up her face.

Between contractions, I told her it was all part of being married.

"Then I'm never getting married," she announced and ran out of the bedroom.

"Look after your brothers!" I yelled after her, and then I was doubled over with another contraction.

An hour and a half later, I heard the door slam downstairs. The doctor ran up the stairs and into the bedroom. "My apologies for taking so long, Mrs. Higham, I had to stitch up your husband first."

"What . . .?" A contraction interrupted my question.

The doctor put his hand on my stomach. "He said the thunder spooked the horses and they ran him through a fence. I had to stitch a few slashes before we left town. Now, as for you and this baby, you are doing just fine, Mrs. Higham."

The baby, a girl, was born just before midnight. She let out one great howl that brought Cale running. "This one's wanting her mother," the doctor said as he wrapped her. I held her to me, and once again I was amazed at how tiny a newborn baby is.

Cale stroked her sparse black hair, then looked at the doctor. "I'll be in tomorrow to pay the bill." He turned to me, "And I'll telephone Bessie, too."

The next morning, the children examined their new sister.

"She's so tiny," Bob commented

"So were you when you were born," I told him. John wanted to know if he could play with her.

Marjorie just screwed up her face. "She's ugly!"

Bob shoved her. "So are you!" and the tussle was on. Cale had to separate them.

Bessie, Willie and their little Roy, a year younger than John, arrived on Sunday. Almost immediately, Bob, John and Roy scrambled outside to get into no end of mischief. Bessie cooed over the baby and Willie and Cale debated politics. Marjorie was the odd person out.

"What will you call her?" Bessie asked.

"We think Maisie, I like the name," I replied as I rocked her.

"Remember that story that Father always told us, that the Appleton name was given to a woman named Mabilia who came over with William the Conqueror? I think it is high time one of your children had the Appleton name. John would have been the perfect one, I can not imagine why you let Cale talk you into giving him the Brock name instead."

She stopped to take a breath and pour herself another cup of tea. "Now you have the perfect opportunity to honour the woman. Maisie Mabilia Appleton Higham. It has a certain ring to it, don't you think?"

I chuckled. "It's rather long for one so small."

Bessie snorted. "Balderdash! She'll grow into it. She is an Appleton, after all, as much as she is a Higham."

* * *

Some dates stick in my mind even if I would rather forget them. November 21, 1923 is one of those days.

We had just sat down for breakfast. I was feeding Maisie and trying to get John to eat his oatmeal. We heard someone drive into the yard.

Cale set down his cup. "Wonder who that is?" He got up and went to the door.

A voice said, "Cable for Mrs. Higham."

I looked up, startled. That phrase was never a harbinger of good news. My heart pounded as Cale handed me the cable. His voice was very quiet. "Bad news, I'm afraid. Your brother's been killed in an accident."

The words blurred. I read it but didn't see it. I read it again. "It doesn't say how," I choked out.

Cale took the cable from my shaking hand. "Just that the funeral is this Saturday. We should send flowers."

My head was spinning. "Bessie. Bessie should know. We must go see her. I have to tell her."

Cale put a hand on my shoulder. "She's probably received a cable, too." He turned to Marjorie. "Deal with your brothers. And finish feeding Maisie. We have to go into town. You can skip school today, we need you to stay here and look after things while we go to town."

I remember it was a cold grey day, a day much like I was feeling. Questions ran through my head. How did it happen? His poor wife, what is she going through? And their children, to lose their father when they're so young, only 11 and 6. How would they manage without a father?

At the station, we cabled money to Clive with a message to buy flowers. We had barely started to drive to Assiniboia when we saw Willie and Bessie driving up Mazenod's main street. Bessie leapt out of the car and ran towards me. She was in tears. We hugged and cried together.

Cale put his arm on my back. "Let's go," he said.

Willie said, "Mary can ride with us." Bessie and I sat in the back seat, holding each other's hand, talking about our brother, wishing we could be with the rest of our family.

A few weeks later, we received a letter from Carrie.

Dearest Mary and Cale, Thank you for the floral arrangement and the lovely letter. They have been a calming source of consolation in this unhappy hour. The children are lost without their father, as am I. It was such a terrible death. George was driving his wagon, delivering logs, when a couple of scallywags threw stones at him. The horses bolted, throwing him under the wagon where he was hideously crushed. What is most horrible is that he didn't die immediately, he lingered in great pain for a few hours before passing away. The lads were sentenced to one of the reform schools, but oh how I wish we were back in the 1700s, they would have been condemned to death and then transported to Australia, and good riddance. The church was filled with people and floral tributes from family, friends and old schoolmates. We gave yours a place of honour. So many people stood on the street to pay their respects that the police cordoned it off so the hearse could drive to the cemetery. It was such a sad day. He was so young, only 35 years on this good earth. With all my gratitude and love, Carrie

I grieved for weeks afterward, as did Bessie. He was our only brother.

* * *

We went to Willie and Bessie's for Christmas that year. Willie's brother, Harry, and his wife and children were there, too, so it was a houseful what with six adults and eight kids all crammed into their little house. It was a mild day for December so we shooed the boys outside.

"Let them run off their energy out there," Bessie said, and we went about readying the meal. Harry had a new camera, and after dinner he insisted on taking photographs of everyone both inside and outside the house. I didn't like the one he took in the house because I had my mouth open and my eyes shut.

We settled down to an evening of card games and talk. Willie, Harry and Cale were talking about politics, especially Prime Minister McKenzie King talking to his dog. "Whoever heard of a grown man doing that?" Willie asked.

Cale laughed. "I talk to my dog all the time. Usually 'Git, Pooch' or something like that."

Willie dealt another round. "Not to change the subject, but Caleb, are you still looking for a farm to buy?"

Cale stubbed out his cigarette and appraised his hand. "Yes. You selling yours?"

Willie chuckled. "Not a chance, but I hear the MacKinnons, father and son, are selling a couple of quarter-sections of good land. You know where they live? It's that blue house a couple of miles up the road. There's a house and barn and some other outbuildings. And a slough just to the south of it and another bigger one to the north."

Cale rearranged the cards in his hand. "Oh yes, we passed it on the way here. There are trees around it, too, if I remember rightly. What are they asking?"

"I don't know, you'll have to talk to them."

The next day, we stopped at the MacKinnons on the way back home. The house didn't look like much, aside from being very blue, and I said as much to Cale. He looked at me. "Never judge a book by its cover, they say."

"I hope the book's better than the cover."

Mr. MacKinnon opened the door to us and invited us inside. We walked straight into the kitchen because there was no porch where we could hang coats or leave boots. A door led from the kitchen into the parlour. A staircase ahead of us led upstairs.

Mrs. MacKinnon already had the tea kettle on the stove. Five children, none looking older than Marjorie or younger than Maisie, crowded around the table.

Mrs. MacKinnon called to one of the boys. "Rankin, take their coats." She spoke with a strange accent, certainly not English. The oldest of the boys held out his hand to take my coat.

I started to say, "No, thank you. We can't stay long . . ."

Cale interrupted. "Thanks, a cup of tea would hit the spot."

I took off my coat, as did Cale, and helped the children with theirs. Rankin took them into the parlour. I scanned the room; everything seemed clean and orderly.

She motioned to the chairs around the table. "Sit down and have some tea. It's brisk outside, not like yesterday when it was so warm."

The kettle whistled. Mrs. MacKinnon poured the boiling water into a large tea pot with a chipped spout while she called to one of the girls. "Jessie, put out the cups." The girl went to a cupboard and set out several chipped but clean cups.

Mrs. McKinnon smiled. "I'm glad you have time for a cup of tea." She turned to Jessie. "Fetch the biscuits."

Mrs. MacKinnon soon had the table covered with biscuits and butter and jam, and poured tea. The tea was black and strong, the biscuits light, the jam sweet and rich. The house didn't look like much but it was clean, and even if the tea pot and cups were chipped, I could not fault the hospitality, the children's behaviour or the food.

After a lot of chit-chat about the weather and crops and grain prices and children and colds, Cale turned to Malcolm. "Willie says you're selling your farm. I'm interested in buying. I'm tired of renting someone else's land."

Mr. McKinnon raised an eyebrow. "How do you know Willie?"

I spoke up. "Bessie, ah, Mrs. Lamb is my sister."

Malcolm scratched the back of his neck. "I'm asking $5000.00 for the two quarters."

Cale scowled. "But I wouldn't be getting two complete quarters. There are the two huge sloughs, and the CPR right-of-way cuts across both of them. Would you take $4000.00?"

Malcolm furrowed his brow for a moment. "Well, how about somewhere in the middle, say $4500.00?"

Cale shrugged. "I'll think about it. I will have to talk to the bank because I don't have enough to pay that amount outright. I'll get back to you."

I looked more closely at the house. If Cale bought this farm, this is where we would be living. It would do; it wasn't the finest house I had lived in but neither was it the worst. Then I realized, if Cale bought the farm, I could finally have my own garden. Not someone else's garden, but my own.

I turned to Mrs. McKinnon. "Do you have a garden?"

She smiled. "Oh yes, of course. We have a large garden area north of the house, just before the trees. The soil is very good and the well is close by."

I smiled. Yes, this place would do just fine.

* * *

Cale closed the sale on a cold January day. His savings covered about half the cost and the Bank of Toronto was only too eager to lend him the rest. Cale did not like banks. "All they do is suck the country dry. Most of the farmers I know are beholden to them."

The day he closed the sale, Cale strode into the house like a conquering hero, waving the mortgage and deed. I was not in a mood to celebrate. Maisie was fighting being fed some applesauce and it seemed to be going everywhere except her mouth. John accused Bob of cheating at checkers, and they started throwing checkers at each other. Marjorie was sniveling and whining because she had a cold. I was losing my temper with the lot of them.

"Are you expecting us to move in the middle of winter?" I picked up Maisie and headed to the sink to wash her face and sponge off my apron.

"Good Lord, no. I'm not that crazy. Besides, the MacKinnons aren't moving for another month or two. They've got some work to do on their new house."

Maisie was now spitting up and the boys were punching each other. "Stop that, boys, or I'll get the switch!" I felt like I'd been through this before.

I gave Maisie to Marjorie. "Look after her!" I turned to Cale. "Where are they going?"

"Just north of Welcome School. That's where our kids will go. But just think, Mary. This will be the last move. I promise."

"It had better be."

I turned to separate Bob and John. "Stop, you two, or you *will* feel the switch. Go to your room. Now!"

Cale left me to deal with the children. And the packing. Men!

Part 2
Settle

Chapter Eighteen
Congress: The Blue House

We moved on a cool but sunny April day in 1924. Cale loaded all our possessions into the wagon and drove the 20 miles to the farm; he had taken all the livestock over the day before. The children and I came by train, changing from CNR to CPR at Vanguard. I kept thinking of Cale sitting on that wagon seat for the better part of the day, shivering in spite of his sheepskin jacket and hat, in spite of the hot rocks at his feet. We were warm, although I had the challenge of the children. Marjorie was pouting because she had to leave her friends behind. Bob and John were running up and down the aisle, that is, when they weren't arguing and fighting. Maisie, just turned 10 months, was in the midst of colic.

The station agent's wife at Vanguard took pity on us while we waited for the CPR train from Moose Jaw. She fed us lunch, gave me a break from Maisie's constant howling, and somehow enticed a smile from Marjorie.

Cale met us at the Congress station and we rode the two miles south to our new farm. I hoped the house would be as clean as when we saw it at Christmas time. I had heard rumours of eastern Europeans being dirty and lazy, but Mrs. MacKinnon must have scrubbed the house within an inch of its life. The house would have been spotless if Cale and Willie had not tracked mud across the kitchen floor while unloading the furniture and crates that now stood higgledy-piggledy in the room. The house was warm; Cale had started the fire in the cook stove and in the furnace in the basement.

"We're invited to Willie and Bessie's for supper," Cale said as he pulled the settee into the parlour.

I looked around. Here we were, in another house without electricity, telephone or bathroom. I wished I was back in Moose Jaw where we had both. I was tired of outhouses and cleaning Aladdin lamp chimneys, tired of hauling in coal and hauling out ashes, tired of hand pumps and wells and worrying that the cistern might run dry.

Never you mind, I told myself. This is now *our* home, not someone's else's home that we've rented. We won't have to move again. What's unpacked will stay unpacked. It's all ours, for better or for worse, as the vicar had intoned at our wedding. I didn't think it could get much worse. Then I remembered the Boharm house. Yes, I had seen worse. Be thankful for small mercies, Mary, I told myself.

Bob and John were no help that afternoon.

"Take off your boots!" I yelled at their backs as they raced upstairs. Marjorie wasn't far behind. An argument broke out above me.

"We're sleeping here!" That was Bob.

"Well, where am I supposed to sleep then?" That was Marjorie.

I walked up the stairs, holding Maisie who was squirming and whimpering. Marjorie stood on the landing, hands on her hips, pouting. Bob and John stood in a bedroom doorway, arms crossed, defiant. I was in no mood to put up with this.

"Stop it or I'll get the switch! I don't want to hear any more fighting." I looked around. Upstairs consisted of only two bedrooms but there was a large landing. I jerked my head in the direction of the landing, away from the door where the two boys stood. "Out! Marjorie gets the bedroom. Girls need more privacy than boys. You can sleep on the landing. Dad will put up a curtain around your bed."

"Mom, we want our own room," Bob whined.

"Be thankful you're not sleeping in the kitchen like my Ferris uncles."

Bob scoffed. "Nobody sleeps in a kitchen."

"Yah, that's for cooking," John echoed.

"My uncles did. On a straw mattress with a tatty old blanket. Be thankful you have a proper bed. Now get downstairs and help your father."

As they turned to leave, they scowled at Marjorie. She, in turn, scowled back but then stabbed her finger at Maisie. "I suppose I'll have to share with her!"

"Not while she's a baby, she'll sleep with us. Now, pull in that lip of yours, take off your coat and look after Maisie while I unpack those boxes."

I sighed and went back downstairs to face the chaos below.

Cale and I were exhausted when we finally crawled into bed. He put his arm around me. "How do you like your new home, Mrs. Higham?"

"I wish it had electricity, and a washroom would be nice, but at least we won't have to move ever again. I'm grateful for that." I rolled over to look at him. "You can promise me that, can't you?"

"Yes, Mrs. Higham, I can promise you that. I don't know about the electricity but I can build a proper porch. Now, come here."

It was a while before we got to sleep.

Cale fell asleep soon thereafter, snoring loudly, at peace with the world. I lay awake a while longer, thinking of my sisters in England, remembering the good times we had together, and wishing we could be together again. I felt a little envious; they had electricity and running water, we did not. But then I started planning my garden and the curtains I would make for the windows. The parlour could use a new rug, if we could afford it.

The clock tick-tocked half-one. The fire snapped in the stove downstairs. The house creaked a little as it settled into the night air. I sighed and rolled over, away from Cale, yawned and closed my eyes.

* * *

I had to wait until early May to examine the garden area. As Mrs. McKinnon had said, it was large, just south of the trees, with the well nearby. Cale stood beside me.

"Lots of room for taters and neeps," he said, then he elbowed me. "I suppose you'll be wanting to plant your flowers here, too."

I elbowed him back. "Of course, but I think I'll put most of them around the house. The hollyhocks, for certain. They'll be too exposed to the wind here."

I could hardly wait to plant. In the meantime, I imagined roses and hollyhocks, gladiolas and irises, paeonies and chrysanthemums, all blooming in great profusion. Cale could have his taters and neeps.

Chapter Nineteen
Envy

Some called them the Roaring Twenties. The only roaring that happened around Congress and Assiniboia had to do with prohibition, the occasional raid on some illegal still or the RCMP catching rum runners bringing illegal whiskey across the border from the United States. Even that came to an end in 1925 when the Saskatchewan government finally gave up on prohibition.

Cale was overjoyed. "Finally, I can get a drink!" He and Willie and their mates spent the night in Assiniboia celebrating. The next morning, Cale had a massive hangover and I made sure to rattle the dishes particularly loudly.

Aside from that, one year bled one into the next with nothing to distinguish one from the other. The sun rose and set. We got up, did our work and went to bed. We planted crops and gardens, watched them grow and harvested them. We sweltered in summer's heat and shivered in winter's cold. We grew older.

We got to know our neighbours that summer of 1924. I was surprised how many were foreigners. Just like at Mazenod, Boharm and even Moose Jaw, English families seemed to be in the minority. Here, we were surrounded by Norwegians, Germans, Belgians and Swedes. Why would Canada, part of the British Empire, have let in so many non-English immigrants, I wondered.

When I commented on the number of foreign families, Cale snorted, "For heaven's sakes, Mary, we're foreigners, too."

"No, we're not. We're English!"

"Damn it, what has that got to do with it? We weren't born here!"

"That's not the point."

He sniffed and stabbed his finger at me. "Mary, sometimes I think you're nothing but a bloody snob. Our neighbours are all fine, hard-working people. I don't care where the hell they're from."

"Well, I do! I want my children to associate with the right people," I yelled at his retreating back. I grabbed the broom and gave the floor a hard sweep.

We didn't talk about it again.

We had Canadian neighbours, too. Mr. McLean lived north of us, Mr. and Mrs. Peller lived west of us, and Mr. and Mrs. MacKinnon also lived west of us. They were of good English stock from eastern Canada, except Mr. MacKinnon's wife who was Russian. Aside from Bessie and Willie, the only other English-born family near us were Mr. and Mrs. Easterby. I considered them my best friends, although I did get along with the others.

Marjorie and Bob, even little John, settled in much faster than I did. In no time at all, they knew all our neighbours (whom they always called Mr. and Mrs.), and made friends with their children. I often saw them traipsing across the fields and pastures to visit them. They knew the road to Aunt Bessie and Uncle Willie's place so well they could do it with their eyes closed. They knew every cow, every pig, every horse by name and by personality. I think they even named the chickens. They waved at every train that went by. And at supper time, they regaled us with tales of their day's adventures. Supper could be very noisy.

* * *

Our house was right beside the highway between Assiniboia and Moose Jaw, and I worried about the children being hit by passing trucks and motor cars which now greatly outnumbered horse-drawn wagons. Especially Bob and John. Those two! Always getting into trouble. Bob was the ringleader, I'm certain of that, and John was only too willing to go along with whatever his big brother proposed. One cold winter day, we could not find them anywhere. We searched everywhere on the farm but in vain until we discovered two sets of footprints heading down the highway. Cale followed the footprints south and caught up with the vagrants half-way to Bessie and Willie's place.

"We wanted some of Aunt Bessie's good cookies," they said, as if that justified all our panic. They got the switch for that.

Another time, when Bob was eight and John six, Bob dared John to climb up the windmill tower, which he did. Except he couldn't climb down because his legs weren't long enough to find the top step. Bob came running into the house, "Mom, John's stuck up the windmill!" I wasn't about to climb up there and neither was Marjorie. John stayed there till Cale came home from town. Once again, they both got the switch but later I overheard them boasting that they had done something that neither Marjorie nor I could do. Or would do.

Another time, Bob and John decided to hitch one of the calves to their wagon. It did not go well. We laughed till tears ran down our faces as we watched the calf zigzag across the yard, trying to get rid of the wagon flying behind. It wasn't so funny for Bob and John. John ended up with scrapes and bruises, and Bob got the switch again.

"Cale, you have to keep those boys in hand, else they'll come to no good."

Cale merely replied, "Boys will be boys. I certainly was." He did not explain that last remark to my satisfaction.

Or Cale would reply, "I don't know where Bob gets all his ideas from."

I'd shake my head. "The apple doesn't fall far from the tree, you know." Cale said he didn't know what I was talking about.

But how to keep them off the highway? Or at the very least, warn them of its dangers? "You'll think of something," Cale said one night. And I did.

"Beware the Bologna Man," I told Bob and John one day when I caught them playing near the highway.

"Why?" Bob replied. "I like bologna."

"Yah, me too," said John, then somewhat more cautiously, "Why?"

I shook my finger at him. "Because he cruises up and down the highway with his tanker truck, and whenever he sees a little boy or girl, he snatches them up." I snatched at John, who ducked. "Then he throws them in his tank and turns them into bologna."

John stared wide-eyed, "Really!"

Bob looked skeptical. "That's bologna!"

"No, it is not! So you be careful, don't go onto the highway unless Dad or I am with you. The Bologna Man won't grab you when there's an adult around."

Much to my amazement, the Bologna Man story worked. I didn't realize how well until one day, several years later, the boys came into the house all covered with dirt and grass. "Look at your good school clothes! They're all dirty! What have you been up to?"

Both looked sheepish. John scuffed his shoe against the floor. "We saw the Bologna Man coming so we hid in the ditch."

I stifled a laugh. "Okay, at least you're safe. Now get out of your clothes so I can wash them out for tomorrow."

I learned later they had seen the fuel tanker truck drive by our house.

* * *

England still called to me. My sisters' letters, however frequent, were no substitute for spending time together over a pot of tea. I missed the soft English air, the sound of the sea crashing against the shingle beach, springs that came early and stayed long, flowers that bloomed without excessive care. Cale told me that England existed only in my imagination, and if I ever went back I'd be sure to find it wasn't all a bed of roses.

I would have loved to return but our circumstances were such that a trip to England was out of the question. We had young children to look after and no money to spend on such an extravagance, Cale used every spare penny to pay the mortgage and taxes. Perhaps next year, was my constant promise to myself, but as with every farmer's hopes that "next year" would bring the bumper crop, "next year" never arrived. But I could dream, although that dream was tempered by the thought of another ocean voyage and an accompanying week of being violently ill.

My dear Mary, we are about to embark on the adventure of a lifetime. Harry is hired to teach at a private school in Alexandria! Egypt! That ancient land of pyramids and pharaohs. Just imagine. We sail in September. Jack and Peggy will come, too, of course. Jack keeps asking if he can ride a camel to school and I tell him, No. The school provides a flat and we will have servants. I shall feel like a queen! Love, Clive.

When Bob heard the news, he said, "I want a camel!"

"Me, too," echoed John.

Marjorie curled her lip. "They stink. And they bite you." With that, she lunged at John as if to bite him. He squealed and ducked behind Bob. Bob lunged at Marjorie to bite her back.

I laughed. "I don't think camels would survive our winters but perhaps Auntie Clive will send you a photograph of one."

Clive's first letter from Egypt arrived in mid-November.

My dear Mary, Cale and everyone, We might as well be in Paris as in Alexandria. Fine businesses and broad tree-lined streets, although palm trees not chestnuts or oaks. The shops are filled with the latest fashions, English is spoken everywhere although the Egyptians are agitating to expel us and rule the country themselves. Tell Bob there are no camels in our part of Alexandria but we saw many when Harry took us to the market last Wednesday. What a cacophony of smells and sights and sounds, men in long robes jabbering in Arabic, women draped in black from head to toe, donkeys braying, and yes, camels. Camels everywhere. Marjorie is right – they are smelly and mean-

tempered. I held my nose as we walked through the market. I saw one try to bite someone. We have yet to visit the pyramids, they are outside of Cairo which is well south of us but we plan a visit there over the Christmas vacation. We will send you photographs. Our love to all, Clive and Harry.

My dear Clive, I am so envious of your adventures. The children fought over who would be the first to read your letter. Bob is still waiting for you to send him a camel. He throws a tea towel over his head and pretends he's an Arab. Of course, John has to copy him. I wonder where I would be if Father had let me go to teacher's school and become certificated, maybe I would be in some exotic location like you. Instead, I'm here in this creaky house in the middle of nowhere on the prairie. I would love to visit you, stroll down those tree-lined streets with you, barter with the stall-owners, and have a cook and a housemaid and a nanny. But such is not my lot. We are all healthy and the crops are looking good. Love to all, Mary, Cale and family.

Clive sent postcards to the children every few months. Pictures of the pyramids. A street scene in Alexandria. A Bedouin, wrapped in turban and robes, mounted on a camel. The market, a maze of stalls and people. Palm trees at a desert oasis. The harbour of Alexandria, filled with ships. Messages of *Merry Christmas*, or *Happy Birthday*, or some explanation of the picture on the card. Marjorie saved hers and faithfully wrote back to Auntie Clive. Bob and John read theirs, and promptly lost them.

* * *

Come September, we enrolled Marjorie and Bob in Welcome School. Caleb grumbled about the tuition.

"All that just to attend a one-room schoolhouse?"

Marjorie was not happy that Bob would be tagging along. "He's always getting me into trouble," she pouted.

John was not happy that he couldn't go with Bob. "Why can't I go too?" he whined.

"You'll start in two years," I told him, but that did not placate him.

My dear Maude, Sometimes I think I have five children, Cale being the fifth. I was outside weeding the flower garden, and I could hear laughing from inside the house. I walked in to find Cale walking on his hands around the edge of our dining table! I yelled at him to stop, he'd break the table, but he just shook his head and did a second circuit. Of course, Bob had to try it and promptly fell off and began to bawl. That man! I tell him if he wonders why Bob and John are always getting into trouble, perhaps he should look at the example he's setting. Little Maisie is toddling all over the house and getting into mischief just like her father. It's enough to make you pull your hair out! Marjorie is in Grade 3 and doing very well. Bob's in Grade 1 but barely gets passing grades, even on his colouring. Maybe that's why he hates school. He may not be a good student but he has a knack for anything mechanical. He's often out helping Cale work on the machinery. Love, Mary, Cale and the family.

* * *

I went into labour with our fifth child the evening of January 26 of 1926, a wintery day with snow sifting across the road and fields. Marjorie ran out to fetch Cale who was in the barn pitching feed to the cattle. When she ran back into the house, she fetched my coat and little suitcase. Cale grabbed the buffalo robe when he came in; he wrapped me in it and hustled me into the cutter. The ride into the Assiniboia hospital seemed to take forever. In spite of the robe, I shivered all the way, that is when I wasn't bent over with contractions that were becoming stronger.

The nurse took one look at me and called for the doctor, then she said to Cale, "Don't you worry, Mr. Higham, we'll take good care of your wife."

"You'd better," he yelled back.

Mary Elizabeth, soon to be known as Betty, was born the following morning. Cale arrived that afternoon; his breath was a give-away that he had been celebrating with his mates. Bessie and Willie came at the same time.

"Oh, such a beautiful darling girl," Bessie cooed. She sighed, "I would love to have a daughter but I guess that is not to be."

Maisie was not happy when we brought Betty home. She liked being the baby of the family and the centre of attention. Now she was no longer either. At first, she pouted and fussed and refused to have anything to do with the baby. She changed her mind when she saw Marjorie care for the baby; whatever Marjorie did, Maisie had to do, too.

We had good crops those first few years, not bumper crops by any means but good enough to keep the bins full. Grain prices were good, too, so Cale never worried about paying bills, or at least, didn't worry any more than usual. He took great pride in paying the taxes on time and making installments on the mortgage. "Once it's paid off and I'm free of that pesky bank, I'm going to buy a car. I've had enough of going into town in the cutter or buggy."

And he did. In autumn of 1927.

He bounced into the house after taking a load of grain to town, threw his hat toward the hook, grabbed me by the waist and whirled me around the kitchen. I gasped for breath as he let out a whoop. "I've paid off the mortgage! The farm's all ours! Time to enjoy life a little."

A few days later, Cale drove a new Chevrolet into the yard. I walked into the yard, drying my hands on a dish towel, and stared open-mouthed. Bob and John hopped up and down around the car.

"Can I drive it, please? I'm nine, I'm big enough now," Bob whined.

"Me too, me too," echoed John.

Marjorie brushed her hand over the hood. "Wow!" was all she said. Maisie did the same.

Cale hopped out and yelled, "Everyone in. We're going for a ride!" He opened the passenger door and swept a great bow to me. "After you, madam." We roared out of the yard and down the highway to show off our new car to Willie and Bessie.

I almost killed Cale with that car. Not intentionally, of course. Cale came into the house, grumbling. "Damned car won't start. I need you to push the starter button while I crank."

I climbed into the driver's seat and looked at all the buttons and levers. "What do I do?" I asked.

Cale pointed to one of the buttons. "Push that one while I crank."

I pushed the button as commanded, and watched Cale's head bob up and down as he turned the crank. Suddenly the car sputtered and coughed and roared into life, then, much to my horror, started to go forward. Cale yelled, "Hit the brake! No, the clutch! Hit the clutch!"

The car was lurching forward, pushing Cale backwards. I was frantic. "Which one's the clutch?" I yelled.

"The left-most pedal," he yelled back.

I pushed it to the floor. The engine coughed and died as the car jerked to a stop. My heart was pounding. My hands were shaking. Cale ran around and opened the door.

"Good God, woman, what were you trying to do? Kill me?"

I climbed out of the car. "If I'd wanted to kill you, I'd have done a better job of it. It's all your fault. You should have told me what to do before I got in."

"Last time I ask you to help." He got into the car and slammed the door.

"Good! I don't want anything to do with that beast except ride in it." I doubt he heard me, he was already driving away.

* * *

My dear Mary and Cale, We are back in England for a year's respite, Mousehole to be exact, just a short drive from Penzance and better shops. You can write us at 2 Commercial Road. It is so good to be back home even if it is only temporary. The children will have proper English schooling while we're here, and a better sense of where they belong. It's nice to travel to foreign lands but really Mary there's no place like home, back among your own kind. I now have to be my own cook and maid but that's a small price to pay for being back. The beach is only a short walk away, the children have already found "treasures" there. Love to all, Clive.

* * *

The following year, 1928, we had one humdinger of a crop, as they say. The wheat ran 35 bushels to the acre. Even farmers who'd been here since the region opened up for homesteading said they'd never seen the like. The men pitching sheaves into the threshing machine couldn't keep up with the stream of hay ricks coming in with yet more sheaves. The grain poured out of the spout and filled granaries to overflowing. Farmers hauled so much wheat to the elevators that they soon stopped accepting deliveries. We piled wheat on the ground and hoped we could sell it before the snow came. Grain prices were good, too.

"Maybe that smooth-talking agent back in England wasn't such a shyster after all," Caleb said.

* * *

My dear Mary, We are back in Egypt, arrived a month ago, back in the same flat. Harry started teaching last week but the school is struggling to pay salaries, and there's talk of laying off some of the Egyptian cleaning staff. The children are coping well, better than I am, but then children seem to be far more adaptable than us "old" folks. Of course, I can't complain about the weather here, I had forgotten how awful English winters are and how cold English houses are. Love to all, Clive. P.S. Thank Marjorie for her beautiful letters. I love hearing from her.

Chapter Twenty
1929

Some years I would prefer to forget. Nineteen-twenty-nine was one such year.

It started off well enough. Our sixth child decided to enter the world of the living on a Sunday in March. I was putting a large roast of beef and Yorkshire pudding on the table. Bessie was dishing up the vegetables. Marjorie was getting the children settled. Cale and Willie were discussing politics as usual when the baby announced his arrival.

Little Maisie, five years old, giggled and pointed. "Mommy pee-peed."

Marjorie was tying a bib around Betty's neck. "No, she didn't. That's the new baby coming." Bob and John sat there, open-mouthed, eyes big and round.

Thank heavens Bessie and Willie were there. Bessie took charge. She sent Marjorie off to get my little bag and a blanket. Cale ran out to get the car and blew back in on a gust of icy wind. As he helped me out the door, he turned to the boys. "Now you listen to your Aunt Bessie and do as she says. If she tells me when I get back that you were bad, you'll be across my knee in no time. Do you hear?"

Bob and John nodded. "Yes, Dad."

Cale tied down the curtains on the car windows, but they barely slowed down the wind, and I shivered in spite of my coat and the heavy blanket. Little skiffs of snow snaked across the road, threatening to form drifts. Cale muttered, "I thought March was supposed to go out like a lamb."

"I hope the road is still clear when you return home," I said.

The 15-minute ride to the hospital seemed to take an eternity, especially when another contraction bent me over. We arrived there safely and the nurses bundled me into the delivery room. The birth was easy; it was my sixth after all, not counting the two miscarriages. Just before midnight on March 24, the baby was born. I heard the doctor say, "It's a boy, Mrs. Higham." The nurses washed and swaddled him, then gave me the tiny red-faced bundle to hold.

"Hello, little one. What will you grow up to be?" I whispered to him. He merely bumped his head against my neck and gave a little whimper.

Bessie and Willie came with Cale the following day. Bessie stretched out her hands. "Let me see my new nephew." She held and rocked him as if it were her own.

"Have you chosen a name for him?" Willie asked.

I shook my head. "Not yet, we have time."

Cale was happy to have another boy. "Good, another one to help with farming."

Later, Bessie told me Cale was worried about how he could afford to feed, clothe and school six children on a farmer's income. I wondered that, too. It would be tight but we had managed so far.

Baby and I came home a week later. Bob and John were delighted to have a brother.

"Now, we're even," they said; they thought it was very unfair there were only two boys to three girls.

Maisie wanted to help change nappies and wash the baby. Betty seemed to think I had brought home a doll for her to play with. Marjorie merely saw her duties grow to include minding yet another younger sibling.

We named him William George, William after my great-uncle who had designed the famous schooner Mary Rhoda, and George after my brother who had been killed in that tragic accident. I wanted to call him Bill, but Bob and John started calling him "Wee Willie" to distinguish him from their Uncle Willie. They wouldn't stop wittering on about "wee-wee Willie;" they thought it was hilarious. Out of pique, I started calling him George, and soon everyone was calling him that.

George's birth was the last good thing that happened for a long time.

* * *

Our world began to fall apart a month later. I was at the stove, stabbing at the potatoes to see if they were cooked for dinner, when I felt a tug at my skirts and heard a scratchy little voice behind me. "Mommy, my throat hurts."

I turned to see Maisie standing behind me, holding her throat. "It hurts to swallow," she whispered.

"I'll make you some honey and hot water, that should help it feel better. Go sit down and I'll bring it to you when it's ready."

I didn't think much of it; all our children had ailments at some time or other. Besides, three-year old Betty was now demanding my attention, banging her spoon on the table to let me know she wanted more milk, and George was crying that it was feeding time.

"Bob, give Betty some more milk." I handed Maisie her little cup of hot honeyed water. "Does that help it feel better?" Maisie nodded a yes as she drank. I called to Marjorie to finish getting dinner ready while I fed George.

Maisie wasn't any better the next day.

A week later, Maisie did not come down for breakfast. Marjorie said, "I think she's really sick, she's not hungry. She's very hot and she says her knees and elbows ache."

That was quite unlike her. She usually tore down the stairs with the others. I put Marjorie in charge of finishing breakfast and went up to see Maisie.

"They hurt real bad," she said when I asked. I put my hand on her forehead; she was running a fever. I looked at her elbows, they were red and swollen. Now, I was worried.

I told Cale to go into town to fetch the doctor.

"It's only a sore throat, she'll get over it," he said.

"It's not her throat that's sore, it's her joints. Get the doctor and don't argue about it."

He gave a mock salute. "Yes, ma'am! Any more orders?"

"Don't be wise, just go."

The doctor arrived that afternoon. I took him upstairs to where Maisie was resting. He sat on the bed beside her. "Now, little Maisie, what seems to be the trouble with you?"

"My knees hurt, my elbows hurt," she whimpered.

"Well, let's take a look at you. Open wide." The doctor peered into her throat, then checked her ears. "Now, I'm going to take your temperature so hold this in your mouth but don't clamp down too hard."

"Mm-mm," Maisie replied.

"Now, let's look at those knees of yours." He motioned to me to pull back the blanket. He carefully touched the knees. Maisie moaned. "That hurt, did it?" he asked.

Maisie nodded, "Mm-mm," the thermometer still in her mouth.

The doctor took the thermometer, looked at the reading, then shook it down and put it back in its case. "Yes, you're running a bit of a fever. Now, I want to listen to your heart. This might feel a bit cold especially since you've got a temperature." He put his stethoscope to Maisie's chest, listened for a moment. "Good. That's all. You rest now and mind your mother."

"Will I die?" Maisie asked.

The doctor smiled and patted her hand. "Heavens no. You'll soon be right as rain, but you will have to rest until you're feeling better."

We walked downstairs, my mind racing. What could be the problem? The doctor frowned as he faced us. "I think she has rheumatic fever. Did she have a sore throat earlier?"

"Yes, she's been complaining about it for the better part of a week. But rheumatic fever? Are you sure?"

He nodded. "I am fairly certain. Her sore throat was probably a strep throat, and rheumatic fever can flare up afterwards as a result of the infection."

He began walking to the door. Cale handed him his hat. "Is there anything you can do for it?"

"No, I'm afraid not. I wish I had better news. It will just have to run its course and that could take several weeks, even months."

"Months!" I exclaimed. "But she's to start school this autumn!"

The doctor shook his head. "School may be out of the question for this year. It depends on how fast she recovers. She'll have to stay in bed. You could put cool cloths on her joints to reduce the swelling." He paused. "Even when she's better, there could be complications."

"Such as?" Cale asked.

The doctor picked up his bag and stood at the door. "Rheumatic fever has been known to damage the heart. If that happens, she could experience shortness of breath or heart palpitations. Only time will tell."

I took a keep breath. "You listened to her heart. Did you hear anything amiss?"

"No, not yet. Those complications often develop afterward."

We were silent for a moment. "If that happens, how long will it go on?"

"For the rest of her life, I'm afraid. I wish I had better news for you, but you should know the worst."

We thanked the doctor. Cale said he'd pay the bill next time he was in town.

We looked at each other. I was almost in tears. "I don't believe it. How do we tell Maisie she has to stay in bed all that while? She's as rambunctious as the rest of the kids. What if she's not well enough to go to school this fall? She was so looking forward to it."

Cale put his hand on my shoulder. "Let's hope for the best." He grabbed his hat and put on his wellingtons. "Gotta go check the hogs, one's about to farrow."

We broke the news to the children at supper. After a moment's stunned silence, Marjorie spoke.

"Just because she can't go to school doesn't mean she's too sick to learn. We've got *The Canadian Reader*. We can teach her to read."

"Yes, we can teach her," Bob and John echoed.

Marjorie scoffed. "You? Hah! You can't even read properly yourself."

"Can, too!" Bob retorted. "Yeah, me too!" John echoed.

Marjorie yelped. "Bob kicked me!"

"Did not!" Bob retorted.

Cale stabbed his finger at Bob. "Stop it! Stop it, all of you. There'll be no fighting at the table."

Bob made a face at Marjorie, but the sparring ended.

Come September, Maisie cried when Marjorie, Bob and John left for the first day of school, wearing their school clothes and carrying their books. Tears streaked her face. "I want to go to school, too. It's not fair!"

I comforted her as best I could. "Don't worry, we'll have your school right here. Marjorie will start teaching you to read when she comes home tonight. Why don't you practice your letters for now?"

I made up the davenport, then gave her a pencil and a sheet of my precious letter paper. She soon filled the sheet with her letters, then threw them on the floor.

"I'm bored!"

I put my long-ago training as a practicing teacher to use by teaching her to knit and embroider. After a few attempts, she threw down the needles and wool. "I'll never learn to knit."

When I tried to correct her stitching, she yelled, "You're mean! I hate you!"

Where had I heard that before?

Somehow, I managed to keep her occupied but it wasn't easy coping with a cranky Maisie, a nine-month-old George and an almost three-year-old Betty, all at the same time. Trying to keep her quiet in bed once warm spring weather arrived was impossible. She was six going on seven, an age when children are full of energy, when they want to run and play. Maisie whined continually, enough to try the patience of Job. The only time she didn't whine was when Marjorie taught her to read. By Christmas, Maisie had memorized all the stories and poems in *The Canadian Reader*.

My dear Clive, This has been a trying summer with Maisie recovering from rheumatic fever. I worry what her future will be with a dicky heart but now just try to keep her quiet! Cale, bless his prankster heart, keeps her well entertained. Last week, he took her outside one night, it was clear and the stars were bright, and he told her the names of the stars and constellations. She asked him how they got their names and he told such tales! I don't believe the half of them but if it keeps her happy, well he can tell her all the tall tales he wants. Then yesterday, after a shower, she asked him why there was a circle of mushrooms in the grass. That's a fairy ring, he told her, the fairies danced there last night. It brought to mind the stories our Granny Ferris told us when we were kids, remember them? A thought just popped into my head. Do you see the same stars in Egypt? Love, Mary, Cale and family.

Maisie didn't recover until almost November. Come the following September, a year after she should have started school, she was well enough to attend, much to her delight and my relief.

* * *

We should have taken it as a sign that 1929 would not be a good year for crops when a severe dust storm hit in late May. It was Monday, wash day. I had just hung the last load out on the clothesline when John came running into the house. "Big dust storm's coming, Mom!"

I grabbed the basket. "Marjorie, help me get the clothes off the line. Maisie, stay with George, I don't want him getting outside." One-year-old George was always in need of minding.

The wind hit us hard, battering us sideways as we ran to the clothes line. A wall of black rushed towards us from the west. Russian Thistles bounced across the yard. "Where's your dad?" I yelled at John.

He pointed west. "Harrowing over across the tracks. I think I see him coming in."

The wind twisted the clothes around the line, making it difficult for us to gather them. We blinked against the sharp dust that stung our faces, our mouths, our noses. Occasionally, a clothespin flew away. Marjorie held a couple of shirts. "Mom, they're still wet."

"We have to take everything in, otherwise they'll be covered with mud. We'll finish drying them in the house."

I heard horses and the clatter of the harrows as Cale drove the team into the yard. John and Bob rushed over to help him unharness the horses and put them in the barn. I sighed with relief; at least he wouldn't be caught out in the storm.

I bent to pick up the heavy basket of still-damp clothes. "Marjorie, grab the other handle, help me carry this into the house."

She turned her face away from the wind. "I can't breathe, Mom."

I grabbed a pillowslip out of the basket. "Here, put this over your face. It'll protect you from the dust."

I saw Cale and the boys rushing to the house, Cale leaning against the wind, holding his hat on his head with his right hand, his left hand holding his kerchief over his mouth and nose. We rushed toward the house, stumbling and almost dumping the clothes. We ran inside and shut the door.

The dust cloud hit and blotted out the world. The house shuddered against the wind. Marjorie got the coal oil lamp down from its shelf and set it on the table. I lifted the glass chimney, and Maisie wrinkled her nose against the pungent smell of kerosene. I struck a match and lit the wick. The lamp shed a ruddy glow around the kitchen but even in its pale light we could see dust seeping in around the windows and hanging in the air. We'd be dusting once it ended, I realized.

We did a lot of dusting those next several years.

Summer was no better. The rain was sparse. The crops struggled. The garden suffered. The flowers wilted in spite of the pans of dishwater I put on them. My beloved hollyhocks were barely as tall as I. Water in the sloughs shrank first to mud, then to cracked earth, the first time that had happened since we moved here.

Cale wasn't too worried at first. "We've had the occasional dry year before. The rains will come next year, you wait and see."

Come mid-July, George was colicky. One day, when the house was hot as an oven, I took him outside and walked among the poplars on the north side of the yard. The cool shade was a welcome relief from the relentless heat. The rustling leaves seemed to whisper, "Sh-sh, sh-sh." The calm and coolness of the double row of trees brought to mind the columns that flanked the central nave of St. Feock's church. I had walked between them so many times. That little stone church was cold even on the hottest Cornish summer.

The coolness must have calmed George; he was no longer wailing his head off. He burbled a few little sobs and relaxed into sleep. I walked back and forth, dreading heading out into the sun.

I watched the girls in the garden, weeding the potatoes. I doubted Betty was of much help, but Marjorie was extremely patient with her. As for Maisie, just try to keep her out of the garden. She was always in it, especially when Cale was working there. She followed him around like a puppy dog; he could do no wrong in her eyes.

I heard the boys laughing. They were at the well, pumping a pail of water. They carried the pail between them to the garden, taking care not to spill a single precious drop. Under Marjorie's direction, they poured a bit of water on each potato plant. We had to husband the well water; the last thing we needed was the well to run dry, even if it was alkaline.

I worried about my flowers but it was important to water the vegetable garden; we needed the vegetables to see us through the winter. I hoped the perennials would survive, surely there would be rain next year and they would flourish then.

I could no longer delay going back into the house. It was time to start preparing supper. The sun beat down mercilessly upon me as I left the cool shade. I feared the house would be hot as an oven.

It was.

* * *

The drought took its toll. That autumn, the sheaves where thin and the stooks were few and far between. The threshing crew was here for only a few days as opposed to 10 days or more as in the past. We barely got 10 bushels to the acre, worse than any harvest since we'd moved to Congress.

Our potato crop was poor in spite of our best efforts; the other garden produce was similarly sparse. Marjorie and I canned what we little we had but the larder was far from full when we finished.

Cale came back in a foul mood the day he took a load of grain up to Congress. He stomped into the house, slamming the door behind him and swearing a blue streak. I clapped my hands over Betty's ears so she wouldn't hear. Amongst all the unmentionable words, I finally gathered that wheat was selling for a fraction of what it had been last year.

"Too goddamned much grain in the world. Nobody's buying. Do you know they're paying?" He sat at the table, dug out his cigarette papers and tobacco tin, and started rolling a cigarette. "Twenty-five cents a bushel! Twenty-five bloody cents! Can you believe it? Last year, I was getting over a dollar a bushel and now it's down to twenty-five cents."

"Can we make it through the winter?" I asked.

Cale finished rolling his cigarette and lit it. He peered into the tea pot, then poured himself a cup of by now tepid tea. "We should be able to. It will be tight till next year, though. I'll make sure we have money for taxes. I'm not going to lose this farm."

I sat down, too, and poured myself a cup of tea. We'd been through slack times before. At least we had a garden and livestock, and we could always hope crops and prices would be better next year. I heard baby George start to fuss and, as I got up to tend to him, Betty who'd been running around the kitchen, tripped and fell against the table leg and began to howl. I called to Marjorie to deal with George, then picked up Betty and hugged her. "Would you like to hear the story about the one-legged chicken?"

She hiccupped a couple of sobs. "Chickens have two legs," she protested.

I smiled. "Not this one, and she had such adventures. Her name was Matilda and she lived on a farm much like ours. One day she was out in the yard, chasing grasshoppers to catch for her baby chicks . . ."

Cale finished his tea, then went outside. It would take more than a story to bring a smile to his face.

That wasn't the end of the bad news. At the end of October, we heard that the New York stock market had crashed. We weren't worried, what happened in New York wouldn't affect us, so everyone said. How naïve we were. Soon, businesses closed down, factories shut down, men were out of work, and people panicked.

Hard times were upon us.

Chapter Twenty-One
The Dirty Thirties

Nineteen-thirty arrived. "Next Year" did not.

May was cold, damp and stormy. The wheat germinated but then just sat there, not growing. Warm weather finally arrived at the end of May along with a terrifying and destructive storm. It ripped branches off our trees and scattered a neighbour's haystacks across his field. Another farmer lost shingles off his barn roof. In mid-June, a hailstorm tore through just south of us. We got a bit of hail, nothing the crops and gardens couldn't recover from, but south of Assiniboia some farmers lost almost half of their crops.

The weather didn't improve as summer progressed. Just like the previous year, the soil baked and cracked. Crops struggled to grow, then withered and burned in the sun and the heat. Crops were worse west of here where the land was lighter. Our garden struggled in spite of the pails of water that John and Bob hauled from our well, the well I feared would run dry. Willie said he hadn't seen it this dry since just after the war. "At least then they paid us a decent price for what little wheat we harvested."

Come harvest time, farmers joked you could walk for a mile to get to the next stook, but it was no joke. Cale finished threshing in less than a week. He stalked into the house, slamming the door behind him, and swearing a blue streak.

"All that goddamned work and for what? The granary's not even full." He yanked the chair away from the table, sat down, and rubbed his stubbled face.

"And to make matters worse," he rubbed his neck, "to make matters worse, you know what they're paying for wheat? Twenty cents! Twenty goddamned cents!" He slammed his fist on the table so hard the tea pot jumped. "How the hell can I pay the taxes on twenty-cent wheat?" He began to roll a cigarette.

My stomach clenched. If he couldn't pay property taxes, we would lose the farm. I shuddered at the thought of moving again.

"What are we going to do? How will we manage?" My voice choked. I turned away from him and put the kettle on the stove.

Cale ground the butt of his now-finished cigarette into the overflowing ashtray. "Damned if I know, but I'm bloody well not going to lose this farm." He rubbed his forehead, then fiddled with the saltshaker. "Whatever money I get, is first going to pay the taxes. We'll just have to make do on what's left over."

The kettle was boiling. I poured water into the tea pot and set cups on the table. I sat down and took his hand. "I hope this drought doesn't last forever."

He squeezed my hand. "I hope so, too. Is the tea ready?"

I nodded and poured.

Willie and Bessie came for supper the following Sunday. Marjorie and Maisie washed the dishes while we sat around the table, talking.

"There's talk of the government setting up some sort of relief program," Willie said.

Cale blew cigarette smoke into the air. "The government's going to pay my taxes? That'll be the day! I can't see Regina just handing out money."

Willie laughed. "Right! Can you hear them saying, 'Here, have some money. What? Pay it back? No, heavens, no. It's a gift. Wait, here's more.'?"

They both laughed. Cale opened two more beers for them.

Joke all we might, the situation was no laughing matter. We could only hope next year was better.

* * *_

It wasn't. "Next Year" didn't arrive in 1931, either.

Again, there was no rain to speak of. Whatever crop that managed to grow was eaten by hoppers or cutworms or sawfly, or it was choked by soil blown into drifts like snow. Cale complained that what little grew was hardly worth harvesting since wheat prices were still rock bottom. Somehow, he managed to find money to pay the taxes.

My dear Dorothy, I don't know how much more misery we can take. We are desperate for rain, this entire south country is nothing more than a desert. Some farmers to the west of us have walked away from their farms, their situation is that bad. I am tired of having to dust every day, and we put the glasses and plates upside down in the cupboard to keep the dust out of them. The crops are nothing to speak of, even the oats are doing poorly, and the pasture has more dust and Russian Thistles than grass. The garden is doing all right but only because the boys haul pails of water to it every day. We live in fear of the well running dry. Cale worries more each day about money and the livestock. Some days, it's better not to talk to him, he is so cranky. Last month, he accepted work on a relief project fixing up the highway that runs by our place. No money, just chits for groceries, food and coal. I feel so sorry for all the men who are laid off and riding the rails in search of work. Every few days, a couple of them stop at our place and ask for a sandwich or a bit of work, sometimes a place to sleep overnight, and we give them what we can. Their stories are heartbreaking. By the time they leave, I am in tears. All I can do is wish them well and a safe journey. Love, Mary.

My dearest Mary, I was crying by the time I finished reading your letter. You are going through such difficult times. Life isn't exactly rosy here but at least we are not in the midst of drought. I'm grateful that Harold is still working, as are most men in southern England. Unemployment is really bad up north, so many mills and mines closed down, so many destitute families, and the government dole is no substitute for work. I wouldn't be surprised if riots break out, people can take only so much hardship. Harold thinks the government is ruining the country and I'm inclined to believe him. So much for politics. Love, Dorothy.

My dear Mary, We are finally, at long last, back in England for good, same address as before in Mousehole. Things in Egypt weren't any better than anywhere else in the world. The school is closed, it had been struggling ever since the Egyptians took over running their country. England is in turmoil, too, not like the good old days when it ruled the waves, as the old song says. Harry is looking for a teaching position, he talks about retiring but I don't know on what. We have very little money set aside and no pension, and England is far more expensive than Egypt was. What terribly distressing news from you, I hope the rains you so desperately need come soon. Love to all, Clive.

Marjorie was disappointed when she read Clive's letter. "Everyone at school was so jealous that my aunt was living in Egypt."

Bob sulked. "Now I'll *never* have a camel."

I was glad that Clive and her family were happily back in England, but also a little sad. Her letters had given me an exotic escape from my daily, exhausting, hum-drum existence. I used to imagine myself standing awe-struck before the grand pyramids, or puzzling out the Sphinx's mysterious smile, or walking arm-in-arm with her down tree-lined streets to stores offering the latest Paris fashions or listening to Harry bartering with a vendor in one of the markets. I would miss that.

* * *

The Thirties dragged on. One year after another with no snow and no rain. With too much sun. Too much heat. Too much wind and dust. Too many grasshoppers and cutworms and gophers. Too many nights when a red sun set in a haze of dust. Too many winters when the only drifts in the trees were of dirt. Too many summers with the fences filled with tumbleweeds. Little in the way of crop. Even less in the way of income. Somehow, Cale always managed to find enough money to pay the taxes. For everything else, we scrimped and scrounged.

I did my best to cope. I turned the collars on Cale's shirts; those that were too worn, I cut down to make shirts and blouses for the children. I took apart the relief clothes, those that still had wear in them – some were fit only for the rag bag – and remade them. I was not about to let the children go to school with torn knees in their trousers or ragged shirts. We may not have had much money but we still had our pride.

At least I knew how to remake clothes. Some women did not. Bessie often called on me to teach the members of the Leeville Homemakers Club how to make patterns, or how to modify a pattern to fit a growing child or turn the fabric of a worn-out man's suit to make new clothes. I was shocked to discover a couple of women didn't even know how to knit so I taught them how to knit mittens from the yarn unraveled from men's socks. After all these years, I was finally able to use the training I had received at the Practicing School, although I never thought for a moment that I would be teaching grown women.

My dear Mary, Thank you for the dollar you sent. I know you can little afford it, times being what they are. It's thin living here for everyone, even those who have work. Fortunately, Harold is still employed but for how long, we don't know. We have a small garden where I grow a few vegetables, but I wish we could have chickens and pigs as you do. Meat is extremely dear as are vegetables, what there is in the shops, and there's precious little to choose from. We carry on. Love, Dorothy.

The vegetable garden struggled in spite of the pails of water that Bob and John carried from the well. My hollyhocks soldiered on, although they weren't as tall as usual, nor did they bloom as profusely. The flower garden was the one bright spot in this otherwise dismal world of dust and grey, thanks to the dishwater and Saturday night bath water that I poured on them. For me, it was a promise of better times to come even when we had all but given up hope. The flowers brightened other people's lives, too. Many a time, someone driving by would come into the yard and ask for a "tour," and I always gave them a small bouquet of whatever was blooming to take with them.

When we weren't hauling water to the garden, we were fighting the multitude of creeping and crawling and flying things bent on eating what grew. The girls and I spent many an afternoon picking worms and grasshoppers off the plants. We managed to save enough beans and peas from their hungry mouths to put up several jars for the winter, and we filled the root cellar with potatoes and turnips. The chickens were fat after a summer of gorging themselves on grasshoppers. We might be poor but we wouldn't starve.

As the drought continued, Cale was even more worried about the livestock. What little feed there was, was poor quality. The horses got thin, they couldn't work as hard, they got sick and sometimes they died because we couldn't afford either the vet or the medicine. He refused to take up the government's offer to send them to northern Saskatchewan, and that left him no alternative except to apply for relief oats. His mood did not improve when he learned he had to pay the freight.

The continual wind and dust were the worst. The wind battered and shook the house and rattled against the windows. It stripped the remaining few bits of blue paint off the house. It bounced Russian Thistles across the yard and into fences and trees where they hung and caught dust in great drifts. It tore away the soil and the crop with it. The dust blew in around doors and windows and covered everything. We breathed it. We ate it. It was in our hair, in our beds, everywhere.

I lost track of how many times I stood in the house, wishing that, for just one day, the wind wouldn't howl and the dust wouldn't blow. That the clouds that gathered would bring rain, a good soaking rain to benefit the field and pasture and garden. That Cale would not have to worry about money and crops and taxes. That I wouldn't have to make a meal out of nothing, and clothes for the children out of someone else's tossed-out clothes or slips for the girls and shirts for the boys out of flour sacks. That I wouldn't have to dust and sweep and then, an hour later, do it all over again. That I wouldn't have to worry if there was still water in the well and how we would water the livestock and cook and wash if it went dry. Again.

The thirties changed Cale. He was so happy-go-lucky when we first married, a jokester, a trickster, always laughing and finding humour in everything, or joking with the neighbours, or teasing the girls when they were little. Now, he was moody, grumpy and angry. Angry at the agent who, he said, conned him into coming to Canada. Angry at himself for falling for his sales pitch. Angry at the government for abandoning farmers. For once, he and Willie agreed on politics, that all governments, be they Liberal or Conservative, had forgotten farmers. Angry at the wind and the dust and the bugs and the Russian Thistle that grew when nothing else would. I wish George could have seen how Cale used to be. All he saw now was a grumpy old man.

I lost count of the number of times I saw Cale shake his fists at the dust clouds or the swarms of grasshoppers. Or the times I had to clap my hands over the children's ears so they wouldn't hear him swearing at everything. The times we had argued, usually over nothing. The times he came back from town with only the meagerest of grain cheques in his hand. Being on relief didn't help his mood. Cale, like other farmers, took great pride in providing for his family; taking relief implied he was incapable of doing so.

The only good thing in our life was our six rambunctious children who talked and laughed and got into all sorts of trouble. Marjorie was the most serious, possibly because she was the oldest, but she could talk a mile a minute, outdone only by Betty. Once they got to talking, it was next to impossible to get a word in edgewise although Maisie did her best.

Bob was a curmudgeon before his time but sharp as a tack and with a wicked sense of humour that I did not always appreciate. He could fix anything. John adored Bob and tried to emulate him in every way, but he had a kind and gentle side, especially when it came to looking after his "little sister," meaning Maisie.

Maisie, in spite of her dicky heart, refused to take life easy. She was always in the midst of whatever shenanigans the others were getting into. I worried constantly about her health but, scold her as I might, she refused to slow down. Betty refused to be left behind, no matter what the others were up to.

And George, little George, I could only shake my head. He, more than the others, even Bob, was always playing tricks or getting into mischief. But he, like Bob, was very good at taking things apart and putting them back together in working order.

The dinner table was always bedlam. Marjorie and Betty tried to out-talk each other with Maisie trying to break in. Bob and John told jokes or described their latest antics; George teased his sisters.

And the goings-on! My mother would never have allowed such things. Cherry-spitting contests, for example. Bob usually started it. Marjorie would spit one back and soon cherry pits were flying back and forth until I yelled, "Stop it. This is not a shooting galley."

Or George would kick Betty under the table, and Betty would yell and kick back. Cale would holler, "Quiet, the bunch of you, or your mother will get the switch."

That worked when they were young.

And people wondered why I had grey hair!

* * *

In 1934, Bob quit school. He was 16 and hated both school and the teacher. He started working for a farmer near Carlyle in southeastern Saskatchewan where the drought wasn't quite as bad. He sent home some of his wages each month. A year later, John quite school and went to work for a farmer near Yellowgrass, southeast of Regina. He, too, sent home some of his wages. Marjorie started working about the same time, candling eggs at the Assiniboia Creamery. Like Bob and John, she gave Cale part of her wages.

The drought took a break in 1935. Rain fell. Crops grew, although not the bumper crops of previous years. The sloughs produced lots of good hay for winter feed. We breathed more easily that fall. We argued less. Cale paid the taxes. I ordered a few things from Mr. Eaton's catalogue.

Everyone said the drought was over. It wasn't.

Chapter Twenty-Two
Bad News

In December of 1930, I had received a letter from Maude filled with her usual breezy gossip about Clive and Dorothy and their children. She was back in England after living the past few years in Switzerland where she had nursed an invalid woman.

Dearest Mary, Dorothy and family were over on Sunday. It was nice but I tired quickly. I went to a whist drive the other night and won second prize, a nice box of chocolates. I felt quite pleased with myself as it was the first whist drive I have been to. I drink a pint of stout every day so I ought to be getting fat, don't you think. Love, Maude.

We were visiting Bessie and Willie one Sunday, when Bessie said, "I'm worried about Maude. I'm sure there is something wrong. It's just this feeling I have, I can't explain it. Dorothy's worried, too. Did she write you about Maude?"

I nodded. "Yes, she says Maude has lost weight and she's listless."

Our worries only increased with Maude's next letter in early January.

Dearest Mary, Well, are you done in after all your Xmas revels, expect you were glad when it was all over. It is cold here this week, plenty of ice, so the kids are getting plenty of sliding, they love it, they stay out until it is pitch dark. Expect Bessie told you I have not been well, am going to a T.B. hospital in Torquay, so was hoping to be over there this week as Dorothy has started school and I don't like to think she has to look in on me. She has been jolly good to me. I'll let one of you know when I go over. I meant to send all the kids a card but was too seedy to bother, I hope they don't mind. Dorothy sends her love, and I will write one of you when I get to Torquay. Don't worry, I am fairly fit and better than a week ago. Lots of love, Maude.

Bessie had received the same letter with the same news. We feared it was only a matter of time.

The fateful news came in late June. I heard a car pull into the yard. A few minutes later, the car drove away and Cale came in the house. He handed me a cable. "I'm afraid it's bad news."

I took the paper, unfolded it and read. "MAUDE PASSED AWAY FRIDAY STOP FUNERAL MONDAY STOP DOROTHY"

The world stopped turning. I was numb. I heard nothing. I sat down hard. I looked up at Cale. "She's, she's . . ." I couldn't say anything else.

"Bessie," I said suddenly. "Bessie. She must be devastated." I stood up. "Cale, we must go see Bessie. Now."

Cale turned to Bob and John. "Finish hoeing the garden. And Marjorie, look after the girls and George. We'll be back later." We got in the car and drove to Willie and Bessie's.

Bessie was in a state. Her eyes were red. We hugged and wept together. She took a handkerchief and wiped her eyes. "I knew something was amiss. I just knew it in my bones. You know what they say about twins – what one feels, the other one does, too? I knew long before I received the cable."

I held Bessie's hand. "I wish we were back home so we could say our farewells properly. Sending flowers just doesn't seem like we are doing our part."

But that was all we could do. The next day, we cabled money to Dorothy for flowers.

Marjorie, Maisie and Betty were as saddened at Maude's death as Bessie and I were. "I liked getting her letters. She wrote about such interesting places and people," Marjorie said. "They always made me hope to see Europe one day, maybe even see it with her."

In early September, Marjorie received a letter from Dorothy.

Dear Marjorie, I have today sent off to you the gold drop and chain of Aunty Maude's, which I am sure she would be pleased if you had it. It belonged in the long ago to your grandmother. At that time, the gold drop formed a part of a pair of earrings which were designed in the shape of a fuchsia. Granny Appleton had a brilliant idea. She had the earrings separated and so made into four parts and a link added for a chain to go through. The two big drops were given to Aunty Amelia and me, while the two small drops were given to Bessie and Maude. I am sure you will prize this and regard it as an heirloom which you will one day be able to hand on to your own daughter. I have sent Maisie a parcel of things of Anne's, I hope they will fit her. I have packed a trunk with all the best things of Aunty Maude's which Mrs. Crebs will be able to take back with her. Aunty Maude used to love your letters. Much love, Aunty Dorothy.

The promised locket arrived a month later. We were in town – it was Saturday, and we'd gone in to buy groceries. We stopped at the post office and when Cale came out he carried a package as well as letters. Marjorie squealed with delight. "The necklace! Please, can I open the parcel now?"

"No, you have to wait till we get home," I said firmly.

For her, it was the longest car ride ever.

As soon as we walked in the door, Marjorie ripped the paper off in shreds, then gasped. "Oh, my! It's beautiful."

There, in Marjorie's hand, was the prized amethyst drop on a gold chain. She looked up at me, her face full of delight and amazement. "Can I put it on now, please?"

"Okay, but just for a moment." She handed me the necklace and I carefully fastened it behind her neck. She ran over to the mirror above the washbasin and examined it carefully. "I will treasure it always."

I didn't have the heart to tell her how envious I was, that Mother had given a drop to all my sisters but not to me.

Not to me, her eldest daughter who had cared for all my sisters and brother when they were little. Perhaps that was how she punished me for "abandoning" her, as she called it.

Mrs. Crebs arrived home with the trunk in October. It was like an early Christmas when Bessie invited us over for supper and the "great unveiling," as she called it. All of the girls were so excited; they had been guessing what the trunk would contain and what they would get out of it. They were especially envious when Bessie pulled out a beautiful leather coat that fit her perfectly. Marjorie stroked it as if she were touching the Crown Jewels.

She turned to me and pronounced, "One day, I will have a coat just as beautiful!"

"Me, too," chimed in both Maisie and Betty.

Bessie passed on at least half of the dresses to me. "I have a closet-full already, and these are hardly the sort of thing to wear while working in the garden."

She held one of Anne's dresses up against Maisie. "This colour looks absolutely gorgeous on you, young lady. I think you should have this dress. I know Aunty Dorothy would want you to have it."

I felt like the poor cousin accepting all those clothes but Bessie, bless her heart, made it sound as if we were doing her a favour by taking them. We came home that night with an armload of dresses. I kept my sewing machine very busy over the next month modifying them to fit the girls. That year, they were well-dressed for school.

This may sound uncharitable but I was always a little jealous of Bessie and not just because Mother had given her one of the amethyst pendants. They always seemed to have a bit more cash on hand than we did. Willie had never had a mortgage because his father had bought the land for him. However, to give them credit, they did not brag about their good fortune. Bessie often said they'd be in the same situation as us if they had six kids to feed and clothe and send to school.

Chapter Twenty-Three
1937

We thought we had seen wind and dust but 1937 was the windiest and the dustiest. The rain that summer didn't amount to a teaspoonful. The wind howled all day long. It scooped up our fields and seed and flung them into Manitoba. By August, the crop was so thin you could drive a lorry across the field and the only green thing you would crush was Russian Thistle.

July was hotter than anything I could remember. The sun hammered down, relentless, merciless, making the world one giant oven. Heat waves shimmered on the horizon. Mirages spread water where we knew there was none. Horses and cattle stood in the shade – what little there was – heads down, tails swishing away flies. The leaves on the trees drooped, too hot to move. Even birds were quiet. Sloughs dried up, leaving behind a thick skin of white alkali broken by dead, alkali-encrusted reeds. We wrinkled our noses against the acrid stench.

We sweltered and sweated. The house grew hotter each day. I hated lighting the stove, it only made the house hotter, but I had to cook. Cale set up the tent in the trees, and George slept out there most nights rather than suffer through hot, breezeless nights in the house. We prayed the well would not go dry.

John came home in June. "The drought's not quite as bad at Yellowgrass as here, but the crop's still poor. Mr. Aitkens had to let me go, said there was barely enough money to buy groceries for his family, never mind pay and feed me."

In July, Cale decided we should go to Carlyle Lake and visit Bob. "No point in staying home. The drought and hoppers have taken care of the crop. Bob says the drought isn't as bad there, they've even had some rain," he said.

Cale tied the tent onto the running board of the Chev and put the coal oil stove in the box on the back. I packed food: boiled eggs, pasties, cheese, some relief apples in relatively good condition, fried chicken, bologna, bread and tea, and the tea kettle.

John told me to pack a frying pan, too. "I might catch a fish," he mused.

Maisie and Betty packed bedding and a change of clothes for everyone. Betty whined, "How can we go swimming if we have no bathing costume?"

I told her she could take off her shoes and socks and wade in the lake. Marjorie had to stay home because she was working.

The five-hour trip seemed longer because the heat shortened everyone's temper. Betty and George sniped at each other, then George complained, "Why do I have to sit in the middle where I can't feel the breeze, Maisie and Betty are hogging it all."

Cale threatened to stop and explain to them in no uncertain terms why they should stop complaining. A tyre puncture just outside Pangman slowed the journey even more.

Eventually, we saw Moose Mountain rising to the north of the road. I stared at it, hardly believing how green it was. A few minutes later, we arrived at the Carlyle Lake campground. The children exploded out of the car. Cale, John and I climbed out, stretched and took a deep breath of air that had not been cooked to death.

The air was soft, cool, moist. Green grass carpeted the ground. Leaves rustled in the breeze. Water lap-lapped against the beach. Wild flowers peeked out from under bushes. We were in heaven, or at least the Garden of Eden. I didn't want to leave.

The next day, we picked up Bob and drove to Kenosee Lake. Maisie and Betty took off their shoes and socks and waded in the water. Bob, John and George rolled up their pant legs and ran through the water, pushing each other.

I yelled, "Be careful! Don't get your clothes wet!" They didn't hear me or, if they did, they chose to ignore me. I decided to let them have their fun.

I sat on a bench in the shade, grateful to be somewhere cool. As I listened to the lap-lap of the water I was suddenly back in England. I saw the green and fertile fields of Feock and Higher Tregurra in my mind's eye, as strong as if I were standing there. A pang went through my heart. How could I have left all that for this, a place that had only heat and drought and hardship and despair and hopelessness. I wanted to go back home, back to England, to roses and daisies and poppies in abundance, to gentle rain, to cattle stomach-high in forage, to rivers and streams that flowed ceaselessly, to everything that this place was not. But I could not, and anger and resentment rose within me.

But anger at whom? Resentment at what? I had chosen to come here. Should I be angry at myself? Resent my past decisions? What good would that do? It would not make the rains come or the dust stop blowing.

Screams interrupted my reverie.

"Snake! Snake!"

Betty and Maisie were running madly out of the water, shrieking, splashing water all over their dresses. Bob waded over to where they had been, reached down into the water and pulled up some weeds. He ran after the two girls, threatening them with the 'snake,' and finally threw it at them. Maisie turned around, stuck her tongue out at him. "Bully! Meanie!"

Bob and John doubled over laughing.

It had been too long since they'd had opportunity to laugh and play like that. Was that the fault of the drought? I thought of the many times we had gone to Lake of the Rivers to swim and canoe. Willie called it a mud hole, and there certainly was no sandy beach like here at Carlyle and Kenosee Lakes. The girls always grimaced and whined at the feel of mud squishing up between their toes, and the boys called them scaredy-cats. That didn't stop them from splashing all and sundry, running around as only children can do.

We'd often camped at St. Victor, too. An hour south of Assiniboia brought us to a line of hills with rocky outcrops. Not the hard rocks of the coasts of Cornwall that broke the bones of men and ships when dashed against them, but soft gritty rock on which ancient people had carved numerous symbols. We camped across the road in a valley, then walked across the road to the rock carvings. The older children climbed straight up the rock face. We yelled at them, "You'll fall and kill yourself!" but they ignored us. We adults laboured up the grassy slope, the little children scampering before us, to the top where we stood and admired the view.

The fields of southern Saskatchewan lay before us, the little village of St. Victor and Montague Lake only a mile away and Assiniboia barely visible on the distant horizon. No views like that in Cornwall unless you were on the moors. The children each had their favourite carving and they raced across the rocks to examine each one, a bear's foot with long claws, a man's face, a human hand, deer hoof prints, what looked like a bowtie. Bessie and I wondered if these were sacred like the springs and wells and hawthorn trees of Grandmother Ferris's stories. Unfortunately, there was no Grandmother Ferris equivalent here to tell us their meaning.

I sighed thinking of those pleasant times when we did not have a care in the world. When life sat lightly on our shoulders. When everything seemed to be going so well. When the future seemed rosy.

We stayed two more days at Carlyle Lake. It was over too soon. We left reluctantly because we knew what we would face when we got home – heat and dust and wind.

*　*　*

Just when we thought the year couldn't get any worse, Maisie came running into the house. "Mom, there's worms everywhere! They're eating everything!"

I ran out to see. It was like a horror movie. The ground was alive, moving, crawling, undulating. Army worms were everywhere. They crawled up the sides of buildings. They squished underfoot.

Betty was screaming. "One crawled up my leg!"

I heard Cale in the barn swearing a blue streak, punctuated by the frequent thump of the shovel hitting the barn floor. The horses and cattle were skittering and stomping around the barn yard. The chickens and turkeys were running back and forth, eating what to them was manna from heaven. It was anything but, for us.

"Get the bucket, fill it with kerosene. We have to kill them before they eat our garden." I ordered.

Maisie made a face. "They're icky!"

"Do it! Now!" I commanded. The girls soon returned with two buckets filled with kerosene.

We picked worms and drowned them in buckets of kerosene. Cale and George stomped and shoveled them out of the barn and the feed and water troughs. It was futile. They kept on coming like there was no end. They ate everything, the garden, our meagre crops, leaves on the trees and bushes, my flowers, even the Russian Thistle. They covered the road and squished under tires, leaving a greasy slick that caused more than a few cars and trucks to skid into the ditch. Finally, all we could do was cover the well and let them march on.

The worms left on the third day. I was exhausted. We all were exhausted. I collapsed on a kitchen chair and cried like I hadn't done since I was a child. I cried out of worry and despair and hopelessness: for my children, their future, our very survival.

Marjorie stood beside me, her hand on my shoulder. "Don't worry, Mom, we'll make it somehow."

I wanted so badly to believe her but how could I when our farm, our lives were in ruins. If we lost the farm, where would we go? Why did it take tragedy to make me realize how attached I was to this place? Never mind that it was a dreary little house on a dreary little farm stuck out on the dreary prairie. This was where we had lived for 13 years, where our children had grown up and made friends, where Bessie lived just down the road, where we knew all the merchants and they knew us. Cale had pinned all his hopes and dreams on this little farm. Would he be able to, would he want to, start all over again somewhere else? I now understood why Cale worried so much and fought so hard to keep the farm. It wasn't just a dreary little farm, it was home. Our home.

Supper that night was a gloomy affair. We sat in silence except for the occasional request to pass the food. We listened to the wind howl and the dust hammer against the windows. The wind still howled when I went to bed. I tossed and turned until Cale crawled in much later. He turned his back to me. I rolled over and put my arm around him. He grunted and held my hand. We fell asleep that way.

The worms left us with nothing that year, no crop, no garden, no money, no hope. We were left facing another winter of relief and hand-outs: rotten apples from Ontario, salt cod from Newfoundland, and worn-out, ill-fitting, hand-me-down clothes from who knew where. Another winter of poor feed from the government, of watching the horses and cattle grow thin and weak. Another winter of worrying about finding the money to pay taxes and the coal bill and school tuition. Another winter of making do when there was nothing to make do with.

We were exhausted, exhausted from worrying, from arguing, from trying to keep the children properly fed and clothed when we had little money to do so. After so many years of drought, it seemed pointless to hope that next year would be a good year, that next year the rain would come and the grasshoppers would stay away, that we would have a good crop and money and no worries.

Those days finally came, but by then we were worn out. We were old before our time.

Chapter Twenty-Four
Intermission

I remember the first good rain we had in 1938. It began as a clear sunny day in early May but we could smell rain in the air. They say you can't smell rain, but they're wrong. You can. The air is different, it has a fresh, tingling, dewy, intangible quality that is hard to describe but once you smell it, there's no forgetting it.

"Rain's coming," Cale said.

The clouds started to roll in from the southeast about 8:00 pm, low grey sheets that gradually covered the sky. We awoke in the middle of the night to the sound of a few drops pattering on the roof. By morning, the rain was hammering on the roof and sheeting down the windows.

For two days, it rained. We lived with the sound of rain dripping off the eaves and running into the rain barrel, and water dripping off wet slickers hanging in the porch. With the smell of wet coats and the feel of damp sheets and blankets that took ages to warm up when we crawled into bed. With mud, and wellies that tracked mud into the kitchen in spite of my calls of "Take off your boots, you're tracking mud all over my clean floor!" We didn't mind any of it.

"It's a million-dollar rain!" Cale declared.

It wasn't a million-dollar crop, however. The clouds seemed to be apologizing for having ignored us for so long. They dropped too much rain, and the crops were badly rusted. At least we had a crop. And money. For the first time in nine years, we did not have to worry about money.

The garden loved all the rain that fell that summer. My flower garden thrived, and once again my precious hollyhocks grew taller than me and bloomed profusely. We had an abundance of vegetables, and whenever we tried to give some of the bounty to a neighbour the response was always, "No thanks, we have too much already."

The girls and I spent August and September canning vegetables until every shelf in the basement was crammed full of sealers. There'd be no hunger this winter.

We had snow that winter, enough snow to make drifts in the trees. The kids dug tunnels and caves and played Fox and Goose. Cale or Bob or John had to shovel it away from the porch door, from the path to the outhouse, from the path to the barn, from around the barn door. We rejoiced there'd be moisture in the ground for next year's crop. For the first time in years, we knew hope. For the first time in years, the threat of losing the farm no longer hung over our heads.

* * *

In early May of 1939, Cale received a cable. MOTHER PASSED AWAY MAY 13 STOP FUNERAL WEDNESDAY STOP LEN. Cale held it for the longest time before sitting down at the table and rolling a cigarette. He swept the fallen bits of tobacco back into the can, snapped the lid on, struck a match and lit the cigarette. He let out a long slow stream of smoke. Finally, he spoke.

"She was quite the mother." He turned to me. "Did I tell you she worked as a cook for a wealthy family in London? She wasn't even 20 when she ran away to London to escape her drunken dad, yes, the same one I'm named after." He took another long drag of the cigarette.

I poured us each a cup of tea and sat down at the table. I'd never heard him talk about his parents like this.

He chortled. "Can you imagine? A country girl who'd never been outside of Lower Heyford, goes to London and talks her way into a position with a wealthy family. She was some woman." He drank some tea. "She had a backbone of steel, no one dared cross her." He chuckled again.

"All of us kids learned that the hard way. Especially my cousin, Al Varney. He was working for Dad and managed to get into a spot of money trouble, so late one night he stole £140 in Dad's cash box and a couple of Mom's rings. The coppers found the rings and the cash box, minus some money, in a manure heap in the cow shed. He was found guilty and sentenced to three months hard labour but not before Mom got hold of him and tore a strip off him."

Cale scratched the stubble on his chin. "She usually spoke the standard English she'd learned in her few years of schooling, but when she was angry she fell back into her old Oxfordshire tongue. I can hear her now, scolding Al. 'I've a mind to give you a clout up yer yed!'" He paused and drank the last of his tea.

"I wouldn't be surprised if she did, clout him on the head, that is. I bet Al found the hard labour easier to bear than Mom's rage."

Cale finished his cigarette, stubbed it out in the ash tray, and stood up. "Got to finish harrowing the field, see you at supper." He kissed me, then paused at the door. "Guess I should wire some money to Len for flowers."

* * *

At the same time, everyone was aflutter with the news that King George VI and Queen Elizabeth were coming to Canada in May, and they would be in Regina on May 25. Cale and I had talked a little about driving into Regina to see them, but it came to a head the day John returned from high school and announced he would be going on the special CPR train taking all school children into Regina.

Betty stalked to a chair, plopped down on it and crossed her arms. "It's not fair! Why does John get to go to Regina and we don't?" She stuck out her lower lip as only Betty could.

Maisie stuck her tongue out at John. "Yes, just because he's in Grade 12 and only the Grade 12s get to go." She pouted, too.

George jumped up and down. "Please, Mom, can we go into Regina, too? Why should John be the only one to go? Please?"

I shook my finger at them. "Go change your clothes, all of you. Maisie, when you're changed, go tell your dad and Bob that tea's ready. As for going to Regina, I will discuss it with your dad. So, no more whining. Now go change your clothes, there are chores to do."

I yelled after them as they disappeared up the stairs, "Girls, the eggs need picking up and the chickens need to be fed. George and John, the pigs and cows need feeding."

At supper, the children continued to pester us about going to see the King and Queen. Marjorie was quite put out that she would not be able to go. "The bank certainly wouldn't give me a day off!"

Eventually Cale lost his patience. "Quiet, the lot of you. I don't want to hear any more of this. Your mother and I will talk about it."

Cale went out after supper to finish up some harrowing. When he came back in an hour later, he washed up, then turned on the radio while I started to embroider a pillowslip. He fiddled with the dials. "Hmm, the signal's weak. I'll have to get new batteries next time I go to town."

Through the squawks and static, we heard the King and Queen were already sailing to Canada on the Canadian Pacific *Empress of Australia*, and were due to land in Quebec on May 17. I chuckled as I threaded a needle. "They'll have a different reception than we received when we landed in Canada."

Cale snorted. "Yes. I doubt they'll have to take off their shirts and get their chests thumped."

He finally gave up on the radio and turned it off. He smoked his way through a cigarette while we sat in silence save for the clock ticking. We could faintly hear the boys outside, talking and laughing. Bob was probably getting them into some mischief. A couple of robins were singing and sparrows were chirping. Betty and Maisie were sitting at the kitchen table, doing their homework under Marjorie's supervision.

Cale chuckled and I looked up. "What's so funny?"

He lit another cigarette. "I was just thinking about you and Bessie, how horrified you were when the old Prince of Wales was cavorting with that harridan, as you called her."

I put down my embroidery. "At least he had the good sense to abdicate rather than let her rule him. I tell you, Cale, she'd be the one wearing the crown, never mind whose head the Archbishop had put it on." I picked a skein of green embroidery thread out of my work basket. "But that was hardly fair to his brother, what with his stammer, although you'd never know to listen to him now. He wasn't trained to be king. And they have two little girls. Just think, one of these years, we'll have a queen. Don't know if that will be in my lifetime, though."

Cale stubbed out his cigarette. "I think we should go. Seeding's all but done and I think the old Chev's up to a run into Regina."

A week later, we packed the tent and food into the car, and on May 25 drove into Regina, after having left John at the station to catch the train. We camped there over night and awoke to a chilly, overcast day that, try as it may, could not stamp out the crowd's enthusiasm. Maisie and Betty shivered in the cold. I hugged them close to me. "Here, stand beside me. Just be thankful it's not raining like it was yesterday in Winnipeg."

People had come from all over the province, even from the United States, and the streets were thronged, just as in 1912 when everyone came to see the Duke and Duchess of Connaught. We found a place on 11th Avenue among the crowds. Everyone was in a festive mood, laughing and buying candies and flags from the vendors walking up and down the street. I heard one calling, "Flags! Greet the King and Queen in royal style. Just a nickel apiece!" Cale bought five.

Just before noon, we heard the far-off sound of a train whistle. Excitement ran through the crowd like a wave. People leaned out to peer down the street, little children ran out and scampered back at their mothers' commands. We had to wait more than an hour before we heard cheering and applause. First came the Royal Canadian Mounted Police in red serge, mounted on their horses, and then came the King and Queen in a magnificent open car, smiling and waving in spite of the chill. King George was resplendent in military uniform and Queen Elizabeth was in a beautiful white dress and hat. We waved our flags. Men waved their hats. We all cheered, "Long live the King! Long live the Queen!" The roar of the crowd was deafening. I had tears in my eyes.

And then they were gone.

Betty looked up at me. "Is that it? Can we see them again?"

I shook my head. "No dear, that's it. But what a story you will have to tell your children. Not everyone has a chance to see royalty, even if only for a moment."

We drove back to Congress that afternoon, and met John on the evening train. He was unimpressed with the day's events, "They're people, same as us, what's all the fuss about?"

We settled back into daily life on the farm.

My dear Mary, We are all so envious that you saw the King and Queen. What a splendid day that must have been. Now you have seen royalty twice. Perhaps I should have come to Canada, too, they will never come to Cornwall. But royal visits are the least of our worries now. Harry says Chamberlain's agreement with Hitler isn't worth the paper it's written on. He has great arguments with the neighbour who thinks Hitler is Germany's saviour, so we suspect he is a closet Nazi like the Duke of Windsor. But England seems to go blithely on as if all is well in the world which I doubt very much. I hope Hitler is satisfied with Czechoslovakia, although Harry thinks otherwise. He worries that we'll soon be at war again. What is this world coming to? Didn't enough young men die in the last war? Love, Clive.

Apparently not. In September, the storm clouds broke in Europe. We were at war.

Again.

Chapter Twenty-Five
World War II

On September 1, Hitler invaded Poland. Two days later, England and France declared war on Germany. Canada joined the war on September 10. My heart sank, the room faded out around me as we listened to Prime Minister Mackenzie King broadcast Canada's declaration of war.

This morning, the King, speaking to his peoples at home and across the seas, appealed to all, to make their own the cause of freedom, which Britain again has taken up. Canada has already answered that call. The people of Canada will, I know, face the days of stress and strain which lie ahead with calm and resolute courage. There is no home in Canada, no family, and no individual whose fortunes and freedom are not bound up in the present struggle. I appeal to my fellow Canadians to unite in a national effort to save from destruction all that makes life itself worth living, and to preserve for future generations those liberties and institutions which other have bequeathed to us.

I could barely breathe. Not again, I thought. I knew what would happen. The last war, the so-called War to End All Wars, hadn't ended war. No war ever would.

Cale listened, head shaking. "Here we go again," he said. He snorted in disgust. "I suppose they'll be saying this war will be over by Christmas, too. Not bloody likely, except for all those young men who end up getting themselves blown to bits."

I didn't know what to say. I did not like the idea of our young men marching off, all full of pride and dreams of glory, to return broken in body and spirit, if they returned at all. I had seen it all before. I did not want to see it again.

The next day, I told Bob and John, "Don't you dare sign up! Don't you dare cause me to worry and grieve." But I saw the look in their eyes, the look that comes when adventure in whatever guise beckons. Something in me knew they would not listen.

A couple of weeks later, just as I was cooking breakfast, Cale came storming into the house. "Where the hell are those goddamned boys? There are chores to do!"

George came downstairs just then, yawning and rubbing his eyes. Cale turned to him. "Get those lazy brothers of yours down here. Tell them to hurry up, I need them out in the barn."

George shrugged. "They're not upstairs. Aren't they out with you?"

Cale snorted. "They're not. Now, get your shoes on and get out to the barn. The cows need milking."

Betty had been setting the table; she suddenly stopped with forks and knives in hand. "Wait. The other day, I heard them talking about joining up, the army or whoever would take them. Maybe they're in Assiniboia at the recruiting office."

That was the last thing I wanted to hear. When Betty told Cale what she had overheard, he got in an even more foul mood.

"Damn boys, just when I need them, they take off to get themselves killed in some goddamned war."

Cale's inquiries at the recruiting office left us none the wiser. They had not gone there. I stewed and fretted all day. I stewed and fretted even more when Mr. McLean said he had seen two men that morning walking north along the tracks toward Congress. "I thought they were just a couple of hobos looking for a handout," he said.

Weeks passed with no word from them. We worried ourselves sick. Were they murdered? Killed in an accident? Already overseas fighting somewhere?

* * *

Bob and John weren't the only ones to disappear. Cale came in from the field a few days later and, as he washed his hands before having tea, he announced, "The Zimmermans have done a runner."

I was taking bread out of the oven. "What do you mean?"

Cale snorted. "I mean, done a runner. Scarpered. Vamoosed. I heard it from Hans Olson. He heard they packed everything into their old truck a couple of nights ago and took off. No one knows where."

I thumped the bread out of the pans just as the kettle began to steam. I poured water into the tea pot and set it on the table. "Really? Well, they were struggling same as everyone else around here. I didn't think they were that bad off, though. I wonder if it's because they're German. Everyone's suspicious of Germans now. Tea will be ready in a few minutes. Sit down, I'll cut some bread."

Cale sat at the table and started rolling a cigarette. "Don't think so. The story is they were in arrears on their taxes and their mortgage." He paused. "You know what that means. They've forfeited their land and it's available to someone who wants more."

He grinned and waggled his eyebrows at me. "Like me. I'll have a bigger farm and you'll have a bigger house."

I stopped in mid-slice, turned and waved the knife at Cale. "And where are you going to get the money for that, Caleb Higham? We're skint, you know that. We've barely enough money to buy groceries and gas for the tractor, never mind your beloved Chev. And what about taxes? You're worried enough as it is about paying taxes for the land we already own, never mind more taxes for more land."

Cale lifted the top of the tea pot and peered in, then swished the pot around and poured tea into his cup. "Good God woman, it's not up for sale yet. I don't even know who's holding the mortgage. Hans thinks it will probably go for back taxes plus whatever is owing on the mortgage. Think of it, Mary. It's a half-section of land, twice what we have now. Even in the good years, this half-section is barely enough to support us. That place has some things going for it. The house is newer and bigger, I thought you'd like a nicer house, and the water's good, no more having to haul water from McLeans."

I carried the plate of bread and the pot of butter over to the table and sat down opposite Cale. I'd been inside the Zimmerman's house and liked it. It didn't have electricity or a bathroom or running water but it had a large kitchen with a pantry, a big dining room, two bedrooms on the main floor, and lots of room in the upstairs.

"Well . . ."

"Good, because I'm going into town tomorrow to make inquiries."

"Already! I have half a mind to throw this cup at you."

Cale grinned. "What? Waste some perfectly good tea?"

True to his word, Cale went into Assiniboia the next day. He waved a wad of papers at me as he came in the door. "The place is ours, well, sort of ours. We're only renting it, but one of these days when we have money, I'm going to buy it."

Two weeks later we moved into the Zimmerman's house. Mr. Olsen and Mr. McLean helped Cale pack everything into the wagon and the Chev, and then carry everything into our new house. I directed traffic.

"The girls sleep in that bedroom. Put our bed in the front bedroom. Put the kitchen table there, no not against that wall, against the other wall. Take the boys' beds upstairs. Now, where are the dishes and the sheets?" It was bedlam until everything was sorted.

The next morning, Marjorie came out complaining of bites. "They're all over my arms and legs."

"Mine, too," Maisie and Betty echoed. George had been bitten, too.

I took one look at the bites and almost dropped the frying pan. "Bed bugs! This house is infested with bed bugs! Well, no wonder the Zimmermans left in a hurry!"

I ordered everyone to haul the mattresses outside into the sun and pick every bug off them. I washed the sheets in boiling water, and sent Cale into town to get sulphur to disinfect the house. It took a couple of weeks, but eventually we rid the house of those disgusting bugs and we could sleep through the night without being bitten.

Bob and John were still missing.

* * *

Just before Christmas, we received a letter from John.

"Dear Mom and Dad, Don't worry, we're fine although we've had some adventures and have met up with some less than honest characters. We rode the rails to Vancouver looking for work but everyone is here doing the same thing and there are few jobs to be found. The Salvation Army was our salvation, so to speak, they kept us out of jail when Vancouver's "finest" arrested us for vagrancy. I'm now working for a farmer north of Kamloops and Bob is working at another farm up the valley. We're meeting in Calgary in the spring. I promise I'll do better at writing and letting you know how we're doing. All my best, John

Don't worry! How could we not? Cale threatened to tan their hides when they got back. I reminded him they were grown men now, rather too large for Cale to turn over his knee. But at least they were safe.

In May of 1940, George came running into garden where I was planting cosmos seeds. Between gasping breaths, he stammered, "Guess who's walking up the lane?"

"Who?" I couldn't imagine Bessie or Willie walking the three miles.

George gloated. "John!" He saw the look on my face. "Uh-oh, I'd better warn him he's in trouble." He turned and ran down the lane.

I waited in the garden, seed packets in hand, and watched John approach. He looked thinner. Just as I opened my mouth to scold him, he smiled.

"Hi Mom. I'm home."

Cale did not kill the fatted calf to welcome the prodigal son home, but I did make Cornish pasties for supper. He told us of his "adventures," as he called them, all the while wolfing down two pasties. He was mid-way through the third when he paused, looked first at me then at Cale, and set down his fork. He took a deep breath.

"Before I go any further, I should tell you I've signed up with the Air Force."

Stunned silence, then Cale roared, "You've done what?"

John got the same stubborn look I'd seen on Cale countless times. "Look, you know I've always wanted to fly, ever since I saw that plane fly along the CRP line back in 1927. Now's my opportunity to learn how to fly and maybe, while I'm at it, shove a bomb down Hitler's throat. What's wrong with that?"

"You'll get yourself killed, that's what's wrong with it," I yelled back.

Betty bounced up and down on her chair. "Can you take us for a ride in your plane? I always wanted to ride in an airplane."

I stabbed my finger at her. "There'll be no riding in an airplane for any of you."

Bob returned a few weeks later, full of wise cracks and stories about his "adventures." I was happy to have him home safe and sound. My mood changed when he said, "I've signed up for the army."

"You'll get yourself shot," I snarled.

John punched Bob on the arm. "The army? You're going to walk into Germany, are you? Well, you'll have to wait till I bomb Germany into submission."

Bob punched John back. "You're not going to get me in one of those flying crates. I intend to keep my feet on good old terra firma. Won't have as far to hit the ground." The two of them laughed.

I did not.

* * *

By now, Hitler had run roughshod over France and Belgium and was camped on the English Channel. Everyone feared he would invade England. Instead, every night Hitler sent his planes over to bomb Britain into submission. Thus began the Battle of Britain and the Blitz. The Royal Air Force fought back, the bloody and vicious air fight that sent many men on both sides to their deaths. We listened to BBC radio transmissions and watched the Pathé newsreels at the movies showing the dogfights. It was unnerving hearing the rattle of gunfire, the scream of planes spiraling downward, the explosions and plumes of smoke as they hit the ground. The BBC announcer made it sound as if he was at a rugby match.

"Our boys have downed another one!"

"And there goes another Nazi Messerschmidt!"

We knew different. We knew it was a matter of life and death.

My dear Mary and Cale, London is taking the brunt of the bombing but the Germans spare no one. Plymouth is bombed and reduced to rubble. We fear we may be next although what they have to gain by bombing Penzance is beyond me. There's talk of forming a Home Guard and Harry's says he'll sign up for it as he's too old to fight. There's talk of rationing so our little vegetable garden will come in handy. We'll be planting more next year, if the Germans don't bomb our little plot first. Love, Clive and Harry.

Cale scoffed. "Home Guard? How does anyone think a bunch of old men can stop an invasion?"

Dear Mary and Cale, The Nazis are bombing everywhere. We hear air raid sirens every night. We wince every time we hear a plane, every time we hear an explosion. We now have black-out curtains on all our windows and so far, Adderbury has been spared but so much of the Midlands is rubble now. The Germans may think they can bomb us into submission but Herr Hitler obviously doesn't know who he's dealing with. We carry on as we always have. Much love, Flo and Len.

Each night, Cale and I listened to Lorne Greene, the "Voice of Doom" as everyone called him, read news of death and destruction. It didn't matter that we hadn't lived in England for almost 30 years, it was still our home. We had family living there. Places we knew and loved were being destroyed or under threat of destruction. The possibility of John and Bob going overseas to fight hung over us like a black cloud. What if they never came back?

Chapter Twenty-Six
Two Years of Worry - Two Years of Terror

John's call came in September of 1940.

George had driven me into town because Cale, Bob and John were busy with harvest. As soon as I saw the typewritten envelope, I knew what it was. I was silent on the way home; I was torn between giving it to John and tossing it in the cook stove.

George glanced at me as he drove. "What's wrong, Mom? It's not like you to be quiet."

I shook my head. "Nothing. Just keep your eyes on the road."

Once home, I walked out to the field where they were working and handed John the letter. "John, your call has come." I could not say anything more. I dared not say anything more lest I burst into tears.

John took the envelope and opened it. He read it then looked up. "I'm to report to the recruiting office in Calgary as soon as possible." He held up a slip of paper. "They've sent a voucher for the train fare."

I was silent. John put his arm around me. "Won't worry, Mom. I'll be fine."

I didn't believe him.

We had a very quiet supper that night. The next morning, we took John to the Congress station. We didn't say much on the drive there. We said even less while waiting on the platform. Some of our neighbours' boys, all about John's age, were also there with their parents, waiting for the train. Like us, no one talked much.

The train arrived, chugging and whistling, bell clanging. It's a death knell, I thought. Cale shook John's hand, "Good luck, son."

I hugged him and whispered, "Write, or you'll worry me into an early grave."

He smiled. "Will do." He picked up his valise, turned and climbed into the passenger car. I saw him find a window seat. He waved as the train chugged its way out of the station.

We drove home in silence.

A few days later, we heard on the radio that the troops were being evacuated from Dunkirk. Hitler now owned all of Europe. And my son, perhaps two of them, wanted to go there.

Only four children were at home now: Maisie and Betty were going to Assiniboia High School; George was still at Welcome School, and Bob was helping Cale with the farming. Marjorie was no longer living at home; the Bank of Toronto had transferred her to Meyronne, 40 miles to the west.

George was proving to be as much of a handful as his older brothers, always up to high jinks. "He must get that from you," I accused Cale one night.

He guffawed. "As I recall, you are fond of practical jokes, too."

I didn't let that lie.

Dearest Mary and Cale, What is this world coming to? Last night, the Germans bombed Coventry, wave after wave of bombers intent on destroying that beautiful city. Even though the city is 35 miles north of us, we could hear the continual thump thump of bombs exploding and see the glow of the flames in the night sky. The cathedral is a ruined shell, all that remains is the choir and the wall. Hundreds, maybe even thousands, of innocent lives taken, factories destroyed, ancient buildings burned, and for what? I've half a mind to cross the Channel myself and give that Hitler a good piece of my mind. Len says the RAF will do that for me. Love to everyone there, Flo and Len.

Dear Mom and Dad, I'm in Toronto, 20 in our group including one from Georgia. He asks what winter will be like and we Canadians string him such a line. Bob would be proud. We march a lot but then we're not all farm boys used to walking distances. When we're marching, every time our drill sergeant sees a pretty girl on the sidewalk, he screams "Eyes Right!" and we all get a good look at her as she blushes and waves. Lots of classes in this, that, and the other thing, including how to take the antiquated Ross rifle apart, didn't they learn in the last war it was a sorry excuse for a rifle? Good thing you made us boys learn to darn, I'm the only one how knows how to mend socks. Love to all, John.

Winter was setting in. I kept myself busy with housework, dusting and cooking and washing to keep my mind off what John was training for. Cale said he had never seen the house so clean.

Dear Mom and Dad, The Air Force can't decide where it wants us. We were in Nova Scotia for a couple of weeks supposedly to guard ships but they never told us from what. Now we're back in Toronto for more training although I thought we already knew everything. The medical exam is next week and when I pass it, I will be off to learn how to fly. Toronto winters are horrible, slushy snow or rain and always gloomy. Give me a good crisp Saskatchewan winter day. Mr. Man from Georgia says he's never been so cold and I tell him this is nothing. Love, John. P.S. give my sisters a hug. Any word about Bob's call?

I sat with my head in my hands after reading that letter, the tea growing cold in the cup. Why on earth does he want to fly? It's bad enough being shot at on the ground, but up in the air? There's no way anyone could survive a crash.

I poured another cup of tea and telephoned Bessie. She understood my worries all too well. Roy had also enlisted, and was training as a mechanic to repair airplanes.

"At least no one's going to be shooting at him as long as he's in Canada, but if he's posted overseas, well . . ." She didn't say anything more.

We took great comfort in each other's company during those days of worry.

Bob received his call a week before his birthday. All he said was, "Guess I'm off to learn how to shoot people."

Cale replied, "Just make sure they don't shoot back at you."

Bob laughed. "That's the whole idea, Dad."

That night, as we turned into bed, Cale said, "Can you see our stubborn-as-a-mule Bob taking orders? He'll be court-martialed before the week is out."

"I hope that's what happens. I don't want him going overseas to be cannon fodder like the last war."

Cale put his arm around me. "It's out of our hands, Mary."

I sighed. The next morning entailed another sad and quiet trip to Congress. Another group of young lads waiting to board the train. And now, another son gone.

I cleaned the house again.

Dear Mom and Dad, I passed my medical and now I'm in pilot school. A doctor said I could be a "average" pilot. Average! I'll show him! I am finally fulfilling my boyhood dream. What a thrill soaring over the countryside, but I have to remember it's a long way down if something goes wrong. Thanks for letting me know about Bob, I'm sure he will learn to be yelled at and told he's an idiot. I certainly did. Love, John.

I worried more. I didn't need John to remind me that it was a "long way down," I was already well aware of that and what his fate would be when that happened. I put that letter in a bureau drawer along with his others.

Dear Mom and Dad, Damn doctor was convinced he'd heard a heart murmur during my physical. I was about to tell him where he could stick that icy cold stethoscope but then remembered he had the power of life and death over me, so I told him he must have been hearing things, after all, how much hard work have I done on the farm without keeling over, and I doubted marching in the army was harder on the old ticker that hefting sheaves onto the hay rick. Anyway, I talked my way out of a dismissal and now we march a lot, we salute a lot, we crawl through and over and under a lot, we shoot at targets a lot, and we take a lot of shit from our sergeant. Regards to everyone, Bob.

Cale laughed when he read the letter. "Bob could always string a convincing line especially when he wanted to do something. I think he's actually enjoying it."

"Well, I'm certainly not!" I walked over to the stove and gave the grates a good shaking. "The ash bin needs taking out, if you're through giggling."

Hi Mom and Dad, We're still marching up and down the streets of Kingston, I don't know what idiot thinks we'll meet Herr Hitler and his gang of thugs here, but orders are orders. Now we're ordered to learn about rifles. We've taken them apart and put them together so many times I could do it in my sleep. Not that the damn sergeant gives us any time to sleep. Gotta go, we're being called to parade or something equally useful. Bob.

John returned in late August of 1941 on a 30-day leave. What a day that was! We met him at the Congress station. Several young men in various uniforms spilled out of the passenger car. And then, there he was. I couldn't help myself. I ran to him and hugged him. "Welcome home, son."

I didn't know what to make of him. Something about his bearing was different, as if he had grown up somehow, not in size but in attitude, as if he was ready to take on Hitler personally.

The girls, however, all swooned, and took turns trying on his uniform jacket and cap. George just seemed bemused by all the fuss; after all, John was only his older brother, nothing special. My joy was tempered by the knowledge that, 30 days hence, John would be posted overseas. I dreaded that day. I hoped it would never come.

It did. That September went by too fast. So many people to visit, so many stories to tell, so many jokes, so much laughter, so many beers and whiskeys and cigarettes, and so many late nights, but behind it all a looming darkness, that this was all temporary, that it would come to an end, that soon there would be no stories, no jokes, no visiting, no laughter, only emptiness and loneliness and worry.

Cale and I drove John to Moose Jaw on the dreaded day. It was a long silent ride, none of us could think of anything to say. We waited at the station till the train arrived and watched him climb into his car along with scores of other young men. I choked back tears as we waved him good-bye.

"Take care, son," I whispered to the departing train.

Would we see him again? I prayed he would not be like so many of those brave young pilots who had defended England during the Battle of Britain and the Blitz.

For the next week, I picked apples and put up jars of apple jelly, spiced apples, apple sauce and apple butter. "Mom, I'm getting tired of this, we have enough to feed all of Saskatchewan," Betty whined.

"Never mind. There's still potatoes and carrots to dig, and cabbages to pick…"

* * *

It's a mother's burden to worry about her children. When they were little, I worried over every cut and scrape, every cough and sniffle. I worried when they walked across the field to Welcome School on cold winter days, when they biked into Assiniboia to attend high school, and when they walked down the highway to visit Uncle Willie and Aunt Bessie.

Hi Mom and Dad, Still in Kingston, nothing yet about being posted overseas, but now doing something more productive than marching up and down the streets ogling all the pretty girls. I get to play with explosives! I'm driving trucks loaded with ordnance, guess the bigwigs think a farm boy knows how to drive a big truck especially one that might go kaboom. Germany, beware! Worst that can happen is I hit a bump or go off the road and blow myself to kingdom come. Bob.

October 15, ▮▮▮▮▮▮, Dear Mom and Dad, I survived crossing the North Atlantic, terribly rough, seasick all the way. Glad to be on solid ground. Slept so soundly I slept through the Huns bombing the heck out of this city. Have been assigned to bomber squadron, leaving tomorrow for ▮▮▮▮▮▮▮▮▮. Love, John.

John piloting a Wellington bomber over Germany and Bob driving a truck full of explosives was far more dangerous than biking into Assiniboia.

The nightly news didn't help my mood. I didn't want to hear Lorne Greene drone out the names of the missing and dead each evening in case John's name was among them but I had to listen to make sure John's name *wasn't* on the list. I didn't want to read the stories of bombings and battles in the newspapers but it was hard to ignore the headlines in large bold print. I didn't want to see the Pathé newsreels at the Olympia Theatre showing swarms of bombers or fighter planes spiralling down in flames but I searched those pictures wondering if one might be John's plane. I didn't want to get the mail in case there was no letter from John but I desperately wanted the mail in case there was one so I knew he was alive, at least on the day he wrote it. I didn't want people to ask if we'd heard from John because then I would have to put on a brave face and say he was doing well, even if I didn't know how he was doing.

Dear Mary and Cale, John was posted near Adderbury for a fortnight. What a handsome lad he is, I see why you're so proud of him. He told us so many stories about Saskatchewan and Canada, I now understand why you live there. We took him around to meet Caleb's relatives, I'm amazed he remembered everyone's names. Even though he's heard them all through our letters, it's not the same as meeting them. Len is right proud of him, he told John he would stand him for his first beer, that was the least he could do seeing as how John was putting his life on the line for us, but any pints after that were on his own tab. We were sad to see him leave but he promised he'd return.

He's a capable young lad and I'm sure he will make it through the war just fine. Love to all, Flo and Len.

Cale laughed after reading the letter. "I bet Len wasn't the only one standing John for a beer."

I wrote back to Flo and Len thanking them for taking such good care of John.

February 28, "somewhere in southern England," Dear Mom and Dad, I'm assigned to ▮▮▮▮▮▮▮▮. *Our new commander is "Moose" Fulton, already DFC and AFC, a no-nonsense guy but fair. The men who have served under him think the world of him. Lots of nurses to chat up every night, none as pretty as my sisters, or as smart. John*

Yes, I could see him "chatting up" the ladies. He cut a fine figure in that uniform.

Maisie wondered if one of those nurses was his girlfriend. "He just might come home with an English bride. You'd like that, wouldn't you, Mom? Another English woman to have tea with."

I muttered that I just wanted him home.

March 5, Hi Mom and Dad, Home successfully from my first raid on ▮▮▮▮▮▮▮▮▮▮▮▮. *We gave the Huns a bellyful and our squadron is unscathed. How's George doing with his arithmetic? John*

June 6, Hi Mom and Dad, Had a bit of excitement last trip out. Wimpy, my plane, suffered first damage over ▮▮▮▮▮. *It was an anxious time but we're all fine. Leave coming up in a few days. Plan to go visit Aunt Dorothy in* ▮▮▮▮▮▮▮. *Love, John.*

My stomach clenched when I read that. Cale said, "At least he made it home."

"Yes, *this* time, but what about next time?" I retorted.

"There's nothing we can do about next time," Cale replied.

I strode out to the garden, grabbed the hoe and chopped at the weeds like they were Hitler himself. On and on, down the row and up the next until I was out of breath. I finally stopped and stood there, hoe in hand, looking down the road, remembering the days before war when all I worried about was John or Bob making it home safely after a "night on the town." Oh, for those carefree days!

Dearest Mary and Cale, John was here for a week, what a fine young man he is, polite and full of piss and vinegar, definitely has Appleton blood in him. He and Anne hit it right off, like two peas in a pod, they are. Anne showed John the sights of Cornwall, what hasn't been bombed, that is. I asked him about the bombing raids but he just shrugged and said he wasn't interested in talking about them. What burdens must those young men must carry inside them knowing their plane will be raining death and destruction. Oh yes, I know it's all in a good cause to tell Herr Hitler to go to you-know-where with his Third Reich nonsense, but just like here a lot of innocent people fall by the wayside because some megalomaniac has decided to rule the world. Well, John and all those brave young lads are showing him that we will not be beaten and good on them! Dear, I'm getting all worked up. Harold is just back for tea so I will sign off for now. Love to all, Dorothy.

John wrote about the visit of King George VI and how he had commended the squadron for doing such admirable work. Maisie looked up after reading the letter. "I wonder if John told His Majesty about seeing him in Regina."

Cale muttered from behind *The Assiniboia Times*. "Bet the king says the same thing to every squadron he visits."

Hi Mom and Dad, I did such a fine job of not blowing myself up that I'm now a sergeant. Lack of incompetence is sometimes rewarded. Looks like you can stop worrying about me heading overseas. I'm in charge of training new recruits and do they ever need training! Most don't even know where their arse is. After months of being yelled at, it's my turn to yell at them. I tell them get used to it, they'll face much worse than my insults once they go overseas. Got a letter from John the other day, not much news other than he's alive. Bob.

I breathed more easily about Bob knowing he was staying in Canada and no longer driving a potential bomb.

Dear Mom and Dad, Had quite the ride last night. One engine failed just as we approached ▮▮▮▮▮▮▮▮ *but continued on and delivered our presents to Herr Hitler's gang. Made it home safely but couldn't have done it without this great crew. We were never so glad to see home and get some much-needed R&R. Still waiting for next op. Love John.*

I handed the letter to Cale after reading it. "I wonder how many other "nasty rides" he's had and not told us about?"

Cale smiled. "When you write back, tell him you only want to hear about the weather or the flowers or the pretty nurses in the canteen. He's fighting a war, he's bound to have a few nasty rides."

Then he put his arm around me. "For what it's worth, I worry, too."

My dear Mary, Do you know you have a hero in the household. John came here for a week of R&R but it was cut short when he received a telegram saying he was awarded the Distinguished Flying Cross and had to leave "forthwith" to receive it. What was that all about, I quizzed him. He shrugged and wouldn't say much but eventually Anne wormed it out of him. One of the Wellington's engines failed and the plane went into a dive but he pulled it out and they went on to drop all their bombs. They still had to get back to England or risk spending the rest of the war in a POW camp, and the plane was losing altitude fast so they started tossing out everything except the essentials and made it back, barely skimming across the tree tops as they came into land. Weren't you frightened, I asked. He shrugged and finally said, they were too busy trying to survive to be frightened. Besides he had confidence in his crew, the best he called them. I tell you, my heart was pounding just listening to him describe that night. I don't know how those lads do that night after night after night. I'd take my chances being a conscientious objector. Give my love to Cale and the others. Dorothy*

What mixed feelings after reading Dorothy's letter. On the one hand, I was so proud to know my son, *our* son, was a hero. But at the same time, my heart was in my throat. I tried to imagine the terror they must have felt, the fear of ditching in the Channel.

"Yes, but imagine their relief when they landed safely," Cale said. Then he chuckled. "I bet they went out and got rip-roaring drunk to celebrate."

"It's not funny!"

"Mary, take it easy. I think he's done his 30 ops, so he should be home soon. They always give them R&R when their shift is done, at least that's what I hear."

I hoped that Cale was right.

My hope was dashed when we received a letter a week later.

August 15, Hi Mom and Dad, We've been enjoying time off "somewhere in northern England," as they say, being entertained by all the locals who can't do enough for us, it seems. Have no idea what the brass have in mind for us. Probably going back on ops but awaiting assignment. Will write again soon. Love, John.

I didn't know what to think or feel. He had survived the first 30 missions, what were his chances of surviving another 30? I'd endured eleven months of worrying. Could I endure another eleven months.

I cleaned the house, again.

The morning of September 3, I heard a car drive into the yard and then the station master's voice. Oh no, the cable that I long feared had arrived. I froze in mid-sweep. My heart was in my throat. We had just heard about the raid on Saarbruecken the previous night. Had he been part of that raid? Had he been killed? Was he among the "Missing in Action?" Oh no. Please, good Lord, no!

Cale looked glum as he came into the kitchen, the dreaded yellow paper in his hand. He stopped, pursed his lips, then broke into gales of laughter, grabbed me and whirled me around.

"He's in Canada, him and his crew. They're safe. He's safe."

"What? Wait! Put me down! Let me see!" My hands shook as I grabbed the cable and read ARRIVED OTTAWA 2430 HOURS STOP GOING ACROSS CANADA ON TOUR STOP LOVE STOP.

I clasped the cable to my chest. Tears ran down my face. "He's home. He's safe!"

Cale smiled. "Yes, he's safe." He hugged me tightly, one of his hands stroked my hair. "Yes, Mary, he's safe."

Chapter Twenty-Seven
The Tour

To everyone in Canada, John was the conquering hero, Pilot Officer John B. Higham, DFC. To me, to us and to his friends, he was simply Johnny. And he was coming home.

But first there was the tour across Canada to promote the war effort. John and his crew were flown to Toronto where they were mobbed by the workers at the DeHavilland plant. Then they were flown to Montreal and a motorcade through the city.

Someone in the RCAF telephoned us to say Pilot Officer John B. Higham and crew were arriving in Regina on September 7 and invited us to attend. Cale assured him we would be there.

"Flt.-Sgt. Karl Sveinson's mother will also attend," the man told us.

We drove into Regina on Sunday, all seven of us crammed into the cantankerous 1927 Chev. Bob was home on leave, and Marjorie and Maisie were able to come. The Bank of Toronto managers were only too pleased to give them the day off when they learned they were sisters of the now famous Pilot Officer John B. Higham.

"I told Mr. Bingham if he didn't let me come, I would quit," Marjorie said, then she giggled. "I knew he wouldn't dare fire me, I'm the best teller he has."

Maisie nodded. "Mr. Eisnor couldn't stop pumping my hand when I told him my brother was home. You know what he said? Your brother's done yeoman service for Canada and we are eternally grateful to all of them. And then he broadcast it to everyone who came into the bank. It was almost enough to make me blush."

Bob laughed. "It would take more than that to make *you* blush, Maisie."

We arrived at the airport by 11:00 am Monday morning. Everyone who was anyone was there: army, navy and air force officials all dressed in smart uniforms that clanked with their medals, Lieutenant-Governor McNab, Regina MLA Hon. Hubert Staine, Regina's Mayor Williams, and I forget who else. They fell over themselves greeting us. However, the person I wanted to meet the most was Mrs. Sveinson, the mother of John's wireless operator, Karl.

"Please, call me Mary," I told her.

She clasped my hand. "And you may call me Margret. Karl spoke highly of your son, how calm he was even under the worst bombardment."

I patted her hand. "John said the reason he could concentrate on flying was because he had the best crew in the entire squadron."

She nodded. We two mothers bonded as only mothers can whose sons have risked their lives in war.

We heard the drone of the plane before we saw it.

"There it is!" someone yelled.

We all turned our heads to watch the plane circle and land. It seemed to take forever before it turned and coasted up to the terminal. The airport attendants pushed stairs up to the plane and we waited anxiously for them to open the door.

Maisie aimed our little box camera at the plane. "Wouldn't you know it? I want to take snaps as John comes out and this camera won't work!"

One of the newspaper camera men heard her. "Don't worry, Miss Higham, I'll take some photographs and send them to you."

The door opened and out he came, followed by his crew. My son! He looked older, not just because a year had passed since I'd last seen him but because of the weight of the responsibility that had rested on his shoulders.

I could not wait any longer. He had barely set foot on the ground when I ran forward, threw my arms around him and kissed him. "Welcome home, son," I said.

He held me at arm's length. "Mom! What are you doing here? I didn't expect to see you until tomorrow at Congress."

"Silly boy! Do you really think we'd stay home and wait another day, after having waited a whole year to see you again?"

By now, we had all crowded around him, hugging him, kissing him, shaking his hand. Bob gave him a brotherly punch in the arm.

"Decorated, eh? We'll make sure that doesn't go to your head."

John put his arm around George. "My, you've grown."

He swept his arm toward his crew. "Let me introduce you to my crew," he said, and with that we met Flt.-Sgt. Karl Sweinson, Flt.-Sgt. Siggy Lee, Flt.-Sgt. Don Morrison, and Flt.-Sgt. Artur Loach.

The official reception began. John and his crew stood at attention and saluted the RCAF officials. The Lieutenant-Governor, Hon. Hubert Staine, and Mayor Williams all made speeches, extolling "our boys" and how well they were fighting for freedom. There was a luncheon, John and crew were interviewed at the Hotel Saskatchewan, and finally a motorcade to Wascana Park with more speeches. This was the first time I heard John speak publicly, and he spoke well, sharing the attention and fame with his crew. I was so proud of him.

We drove home that night.

The same thing happened when John and crew arrived at Congress the next day. More speeches and another cavalcade up Assiniboia's Main Street to the Court House where we heard yet more speeches. But it was different here because this was John's home, people had known him from when he was a lad. To most of them, he was not so much a hero as just plain old "Johnny" who'd happened to do something good.

Then they were gone, to Edmonton, Calgary, Lethbridge, Vancouver, Victoria and other places. They made a special trip to Kamloops to visit Mrs. Fulton, the mother of their beloved squadron commander "Moose" Fulton. He had been reported as missing in July but, as John told me later, everyone knew he had died that night. John had met the mothers of many fliers who had died in the war but he said this was the most emotional meeting. He wrote to me a few days later.

Dear Mom and Dad, I was one of the last people to see him before he took off, and Mrs. Fulton wanted to know every detail of the raid. She still clings to the hope he will be found, and who was I to tell her otherwise. We just talked of how much we loved and respected him, and that gave her great comfort. Love, John

John and crew returned to Moose Jaw on September 18 for one last event at Prairie Airways. Cale and I were invited to sit on the platform with John, his crew and all the dignitaries. As usual, John introduced his crew and told the workers how they were making a significant contribution to the war effort.

"It's because of people like you, working as hard as you do, that we are able to prevail," he said. He paused while the assembly responded with clapping and cheers.

"And I'm going back. I've lost friends over there. I've got a score to settle with the Germans."

The workers cheered again but all I could think was, no, I don't want you to go back. I want you to say home where it's safe.

Moose Jaw was the last stop on their tour. John said good-bye to his crew and he came home to the farm. He had barely mentioned he had a 30-day leave when I told him exactly what I had wanted to say in Moose Jaw.

He shook his head. "I have no choice, Mom. I have to go where they post me. If it's overseas, then overseas I go, regardless of what you say."

John's leave was coming to an end when he received the letter about his next posting. He crumpled the letter, threw it onto the table and swore as I thought only Cale could swear. Good thing there were no little children nearby.

"I've been posted to some goddamned torpedo bombing squadron on Vancouver Island."

I breathed a sigh of relief. "Calm down, son. You survived your first set of missions. Do you really think you'd survive another 30 missions? The work out west is probably just as important, there's the Japanese to worry about now."

He grumbled something to the effect of "probably not" and stomped out of the house. He didn't return until evening but he was much calmer. "You're probably right, Mom," he said.

He left for Vancouver Island in late October.

Chapter Twenty-Eight
Vancouver and Victoria

Dear Mom and Dad, Come visit me on Vancouver Island. You'll love it! It's just like England here. Green and rain and flowers everywhere. The cherry trees are in full bloom, wish you could be here to see them. I'm out on patrol most days, not nearly as exciting as flying over Germany, you'll be glad to know. Have yet to see a single Japanese ship or sub. I heard from Bob, he's still screaming at recruits; I pity them. Guess you're getting ready for seeding. Love John.

I held his latest letter from Patricia Bay as I considered the invitation. Maisie took the letter from my hand; she was home from Wolseley for Easter.

"Why don't you go, Mom? How many times have you said, you wished you had seen the mountains when you were working at Strathmore? Now's your chance."

I took the letter, folded it and put it into the envelope. "I don't want to go on my own."

"I'll come with you. I would love to see more of Canada. The farthest I've been from home is Carlyle Lake. Come on, Mom, live a little."

"I'll think about it."

Maisie wouldn't let it drop. She told everyone about John's invitation at supper time. Cale looked across the table at me.

"Why don't you go? Seeding's over. Betty's big enough to look after things while you're gone."

Betty immediately objected. "Why do I have to be the one to stay home?"

Cale pointed his fork at her. "Because you're still in school and exam time is coming, that's why." Betty pouted.

On June 10, Cale drove Maisie and me into Moose Jaw to catch the CPR Dominion Train. After we picked up our tickets and left our baggage to be checked, we did some shopping then had an early supper at the Royal George. We walked across the street to the station and stood on the platform as the train huffed and puffed its way in. Maisie gave Cale a hug before we boarded.

"Thanks, Dad, for persuading Mom to go."

Cale chuckled. "I had nothing to do with it. I learned a long time ago that your mother has her own mind about things."

I gave Cale a quick peck on the cheek. "I'll write when we get there."

The train pulled out at 7:40 pm and we headed west across the prairie. I watched the land go by, and nudged Maisie as we stopped briefly at Boharm.

"John was born two miles south of here." I shook my head at the memory of that squalid house we lived in for two years.

We were eating breakfast when we pulled into Calgary for a brief stop before heading west. As the server cleared off our table, Maisie said, "Let's go to the observation car so we can see the mountains."

All the seats were full, but a couple of young men in uniform leapt to their feet when they saw us. "Take our seats, please," one said, although he was looking at Maisie when he spoke.

She smiled. "Thank you, although I could thank you better if I knew your name."

Both stood at attention and snapped a salute. "Master Corporal Michael J. Evans, at your service, ma'am," said the one.

"Master Corporal Edward H. Goodwin," said the other. They stood at ease, and one winked at Maisie and grinned. "But you may call me Mike. And he's Ed. What do your friends call you?"

Before Maisie could reply, I said, "Thank you, Master Corporal Evans. This is most kind of you," and took what had been his seat. That did not stop them from continuing to chat up Maisie who, in her turn, did nothing to stop them. In fact, she flirted with them quite openly.

"Have you been to the mountains before?" Ed asked Maisie.

Before she could reply, I asked, "Where are you being posted?"

"We're going to Kamloops. We have 30 days' leave before we're sent to England," Ed replied.

Mike interjected. "Although why, I don't know. It's not as if we'll see any fighting on the continent."

He turned to Maisie. "And where are you bound?"

Once again, I interrupted. "We are going to visit my son on Vancouver Island. He's with the RCAF. Perhaps you've heard of him? Pilot Officer John Higham."

The two men stared open-mouthed. "Yes, ma'am. We read all about him and his crew. You're his mother?"

They turned to Maisie. "And you're his sister? Very pleased, honoured to meet the both of you."

After that, all we had to do was raise a little finger and they brought us tea or biscuits or anything we wanted from the car's little buffet, although the tea was a poor weak substitute for real English tea.

My dear Cale, Remember how you used to boast about seeing the Rockies from Calgary when working for the CPR? Well, now I can do you one better. I have gone through them! I have a crick in my neck from gazing up at the snow-covered peaks, I never imagined anything could be that high. Maisie is trying to take snaps with our box camera but how do you capture something so immense and so majestic in one snap? I told her to never mind, we could probably buy some postcards once we get to Vancouver. Going through the Spiral Tunnels left me gasping. Did they even exist when you worked for the CPR? Imagine, the locomotive came out below us before the observation car at the end had even entered the tunnel. Now we are west of Roger's Pass but only after going through another long and smoky tunnel. I have to stop writing now, the porter has come through making up the berths so I will mail this tomorrow when we arrive in Vancouver. I have so much to tell you when we get home. I hope Betty is feeding you well, if she isn't Bessie will be sure to. Love, Mary.

We arrived in Vancouver 8:30 the next morning. After retrieving our luggage, we caught a taxi to the Sylvia Hotel, a beautiful ivy-covered hotel overlooking English Bay. I opened the window in our room and looked out over the Bay.

It may have been decades since I left Feock, but the sights and sounds took me back there as if I had never left. Small sail boats skipped back and forth across the bay; larger cargo ships were moored farther out, waiting for their turn to load or unload their cargo. Their sonorous horns and bells echoed against the hills and forest. Families were everywhere on the beach, their little children squealing and laughing as they ran back and forth into the water. Young couples, the boy often in uniform, walked hand-in-hand along the shore; I wondered if they were saying a last good-bye before the lad went overseas. Ocean waves thrummed against the beach, the soft humid air rich with the aroma of sea filled my lungs. My heart ached with homesickness.

I called to Maisie. "Come here. Breathe that! *That* is the smell of home."

She stuck her head out the window and sniffed. "It certainly doesn't smell like the home *I* know." She looked at me, her eyebrows raised. "Is that how England smells?"

I considered for a moment. "It's how I remember." I paused. "Of course, Helston didn't smell like that at all. It smelled more like our barnyard. No, this is the smell of Feock and Land's End and the Lizard, places of my childhood." I sighed, then shut the window. "Let's go walking."

We spent the next two days seeing the sights of Vancouver. We walked through Stanley Park, which was almost next door to the Sylvia, where we admired the totem poles and gazed in astonishment and envy at the enormous trees, the lush dense underbrush, and flowers, flowers everywhere.

I sighed. "I wish we could grow flowers like that back home."

"I wish we didn't have to haul so much water to your flowers." I gave her a stern look but Maisie only giggled. "Just teasing, Mom. I enjoy your flowers, too."

We walked all the way to Prospect Point and saw the Lions Gate Bridge, opened only a couple of years previously, and the two mountain peaks that gave the bridge its name – two peaks that looked for all the world like two magnificent lions at rest. Several passenger and cargo ships sailed under the bridge as we watched. One stood out from the rest; it was painted grey and bristled with guns, a stark reminder we were at war.

That wasn't the only sign of war. Many of the men were in uniform, most were in navy dress but air force and army uniforms were also present. Everywhere, we saw posters reminding us to buy Victory Bonds, or buy fish so meat could be sent to the armed forces. Even at the Sylvia, we were instructed to ensure the black-out curtains were tightly drawn no later than sundown.

I was leery about taking the ferry across to Vancouver Island. It may have been 30 years since I crossed the Atlantic, but I still remembered that horrible journey as if it were yesterday.

Maisie consoled me. "Mom, they have pills you can take."

The staff at the Sylvia directed us to a pharmacy where we bought some. I don't know if it was the pills or the calm sea, but I was fine.

The war confronted me shortly after arriving on Vancouver Island. We had boarded the Victoria-bound bus at the Swartz Bay ferry terminus, and had barely left when a lady pointed westward and said to her little son, "That's where the plane crashed last week."

My head swiveled where she pointed, and I asked her, "Why did it crash? Did the pilot survive?"

She nodded. "Oh yes, the pilot walked away from the plane, said he'd been in a lot worse."

A well-dressed man interjected. "I think the landing gear didn't engage and the plane landed on its belly. That was all."

"My son's in the RCAF, he was posted to Patricia Bay last autumn. I'm hoping to visit him while we're here."

The man pointed back with his head. "Then, that's where he's posted."

The bus dropped us off at the James Bay Inn. Again, we were confronted with the war. The porter carried our bags to our room on the second floor, and as he put them down, he asked, "Do you have gas masks?"

I was taken aback. "No," I stammered.

"Never mind, we have extras at the desk for guests. I will bring you two and show you how to put them on in case of an attack."

Maisie clasped her hand to her chest and sat down hard on a chair. "Do you really expect an attack?"

The porter shrugged. "You never know. Japanese submarines have been sighted off the coast, and there are rumours of them sending bombs across the ocean on balloons. We can't be too careful." He scowled. "And as you know, there are, no, there *were* lots of Japanese living here, but the government has started removing them and confiscating their property so they can't aid the Japanese navy. Like I said, we can't be too careful." With that, he left.

Dearest Clive, I am beginning to understand what you are going through. Everyone here is on edge, believing it is only a matter of time before the Japanese invade. People carry gas masks with them, we see bundles of clothing piled on street corners waiting to be sent overseas, rationing seems worse here than back home, and every street lamp and billboard is covered with posters urging us to buy Victory Bonds, to use lard instead of butter, to enlist, and not to gossip. "Loose Lips Sink Ships" said one poster. At least half the men on the streets, and several women, too, have enlisted in one of the armed forces. Maisie takes great delight in flirting with the men. I tell her that is no way for a young lady to behave but she just laughs and says there's no harm in it. Love to Harry, Mary

In spite of the threat of invasion, we enjoyed ourselves with some sightseeing.

Dearest Bessie, Maisie and I have become quite the tourists. We took afternoon tea at the Empress Hotel, as splendid a hotel as anything that Penzance can boast. It alone is enough to justify the claim that Victoria is more English than England. The hotel sits on the harbour, across from the province's stodgy old Legislative Buildings. Remember how Mother always fussed over tea? Well, the Empress met her standards and then some. Good strong English tea served in a china tea pot with matching china cups and numerous little sandwiches and cakes. I might as well have been Queen Elizabeth herself, the surroundings and the service were that good. Maisie spent her time flirting with our waiter and persuaded him to bring us a few more little sandwiches. Tomorrow we are going to Butchart Gardens where I will probably walk my feet off. Is Cale eating well? Give my love to Willie. Mary.

My dear Cale, I'm writing this while soaking my feet, they're sore from walking so much today. We spent the day at Butchart Gardens north of Victoria, an oasis of flowers and shrubs in an old abandoned quarry. The daffodils and tulips are long finished and it's much too early for the roses but paeonies were in full bloom as were irises and foxgloves and so many others. Maisie gushed over everything and mused about digging up one or two of the paeonies to take home with us. There are so many no one would notice, she said. She had to stop and rest several times to catch her breath, her heart isn't getting any better. All the beautiful gardens were an unpleasant reminder of how we have to struggle in Saskatchewan to grow anything of beauty. Here, flowers just spring from the ground and grow like weeds. We can never match that in dry old Saskatchewan, try as we may. Have George and Betty been studying hard for their exams? I hope you are eating well. See you in a few days. Love, Mary.

We never did meet up with John. He was always out on a mission when I called the base at Patricia Bay and they refused to tell me when he would return, although the officer I spoke to said he would relay my message to him.

All too soon, we were on the ferry back to Vancouver, and on the train back to Saskatchewan. Cale met us at the Moose Jaw station. "Welcome home," he said as he took my suitcase.

"Dad, Victoria is beautiful, Mom says almost as beautiful as England. And the flowers! We saw Anne Hathaway's cottage, well not the real one, a replica . . ." Maisie talked the whole way home.

We rattled up the lane into the yard. Cale shut off the car, and I climbed out and looked around. I heard the breeze rustling through the trees, smelled dry dusty air, saw a dust cloud hanging behind a truck going down the highway, heard the cows lowing and the chickens clucking. Cale and Maisie carried our suitcases into the house, and the screen door slammed behind them.

I walked into my flower garden. The ground was dry, the paeonies needed to be dead-headed, bachelor buttons needed to be thinned, my hollyhocks were growing tall and straight, and Johnny-jump-ups were blooming everywhere, as were dandelions. The dahlias and gladiolas were well along, and the columbines were beginning to bloom. It wasn't as luxurious as the gardens in Vancouver and Victoria, but it was my garden.

I turned and looked at the house. Compared to the luxury we had experienced in Vancouver and Victoria, it was a sorry excuse for a house. It needed to be painted. It had no electricity, no running water, no bathroom. It was freezing cold in winter and boiling hot in summer. The upstairs where the boys slept was unfinished.

And yet, as beautiful as those cities were, as spoiled as we had been, here we were safe. We didn't have to worry about being bombed. The only planes flying over head were from the Commonwealth training base at Mossbank. We didn't have to spend sleepless nights huddled in bomb shelters worrying if our house would still be intact come morning. We didn't dread a knock on the door from a warden saying he'd have to fine us because our black-out curtains were leaking light. We didn't even need black-out curtains. We didn't have to fear an invading force sitting only a few miles away, waiting to conquer us. I decided safety felt more important than beautiful gardens. I wished my sisters and Cale's family, everyone in England, everyone fighting in this war, could be as safe as we were.

The screen door slammed. Footsteps echoed on the porch. Maisie stood on the top step. "Mom, you coming in? Dad's got the tea made."

"Coming," I replied.

Two years later, the war ended. Europe was in ruins. Returning soldiers suffered from wounds in both body and mind; their families suffered with them. We learned of the concentration camps where millions of Jews had been slaughtered like vermin. The wounds of war went deep. We wondered if they would ever heal.

Chapter Twenty-Nine
The Family Scatters - The Family Expands

"Hi Mom, I'm coming home for a week to go duck-hunting."

An innocent-enough statement from John, but it got me thinking. Even though he now lived in Winnipeg, he still thought of this farm, six miles north of Assiniboia, four miles south of Congress, as his home.

Without realizing it, I, too, had slipped into thinking of this place as home. However, I wasn't sure if it was home for me the same way it was home for the children. I had lived in so many other places that I could never quite believe that another move wasn't just around the corner.

Our six rambunctious children had grown up here. The youngest two had been born here. They laughed and fought and dreamed, made friends and got into all kinds of mischief here. At times, they drove us mad.

And then they left, one by one. Instead of eight sitting around the table, now only Cale and I sat there. Our house that once exploded with energy was now quiet. The house felt less like a home and more like a mausoleum. Some times it was so quiet, we could hear ourselves think. It just didn't seem normal, somehow.

I missed them. The girls had finally become helpful around the house and yard. I could depend on them to see what needed doing and to do those chores without grousing like they did when they were younger. Same for the boys. Cale trusted them to drive the horses and the tractor on their own. He let them drive the old Chev, and even the new Dodge that he bought in 1942, although he always inspected it carefully when they returned from town. But I didn't miss them just because they were helpful. I enjoyed their company.

Why do they have to go so far away, I wondered. Why couldn't they find their future closer to home? Perhaps this was why my mother was so distressed when first Amelia and then I left. But I was only sad to see our children leave, not angry like Mother was. I didn't disown them like Mother disowned me. I could never do that.

I should have seen it coming, that they would leave. Ours weren't the only children leaving to find their future elsewhere. This place could hold only so many farmers or shopkeepers.

Marjorie was the first to leave. The Bank of Toronto transferred her to Meyronne, 40 miles to the west, in January of 1940. In September of that year, John was called up for training, and the following April, Bob received his call. That left only Maisie, Betty and George at home.

Maisie started working for the Bank of Toronto in Assiniboia in 1941, right out of high school. She worked there just over a year until the bank transferred her to Wolseley, well east of Regina, shortly after John's tour finished. Now only Betty and George were home.

Just because they were away didn't mean we lost touch. I wrote to them at least once a week. They weren't as conscientious with their correspondence.

The Bank of Toronto transferred Marjorie to Edmonton in the autumn of 1943. I wondered if we would ever see her again. Cale reminded me that she wasn't going to the other side of the world.

Dear Mom and Dad, I met a soldier at a dance last night. His name's Henry – what an ugly name and I told him so. He's shorter than me but he sure can cut a figure on the dance floor. Oh, by the way, he's an American, but a nice one. He's herded a bunch of horses here that the American government wanted to turn into dog meat except he decided the horses were too nice for that so he and some other Yanks brought them to Canada. For the life of me, I don't know what they plan to do with the horses now that they're here. Especially if they're like Major. How many

263

times did you sell him, Mom? And how many times did the new "owner" return him and want his money back? That horse was incorrigible! No one believes me when I tell that story. Love, Marjorie.

Dear Marjorie, If you don't like Henry's name then perhaps you should find someone else to go dancing with. A nice Canadian boy, for example. Love, Mom and Dad.

George left that fall, too, but not because he wanted to. We sent him to Notre Dame school in Wilcox because I thought he was being corrupted by his best friends who were lads from what I considered to be less than respectable families. Also, he was not doing well in school; perhaps the discipline there would change that.

George hated Notre Dame.

Hi Mom, Dad, I thought our house was cold in the winter, but I've never been so cold in my life. We might as well be living in a granary because the wind blows in through every nook and cranny. And the food! Everything is boiled: potatoes, meat, cabbage, you name it, it's boiled. The same thing every day. The teachers aren't any better than at Welcome School, except for the math teacher. Finally, someone who explains the mysteries of math in a way I can understand. I got 83% on the last test. Tell Dad all that tuition isn't going to waste. Love, George.

He wanted to come home to be with his friends, and if they hadn't been such a bad influence, I would have let him.

Cale disagreed with me about George's friends. "Maybe George is the bad influence. You're always saying he gets up to no good."

"And where would he learn that, I wonder," I retorted.

Cale shrugged.

Harvest was good that year, and we settled into winter. The news from Europe was encouraging, the Allies had landed and were slowly battling their way towards Germany. Marjorie, Maisie and George came home for Christmas. I looked through the garden section of Eaton's catalogue and planned what garden seeds I would order for the coming spring. We watched spring creep out from under the snowdrifts and become green grass and dandelions.

George didn't come home that summer.

Dear Mom and Dad, The CPR is hiring staff for the Banff Springs Hotel so some of us are going to see the mountains. I'm on the dish-washing brigade, don't know what I'll be paid, probably a pittance. I'm supposed to study Latin as well as work. I know what you're thinking, that son of yours is going to spend all his time carousing with his friends and chasing girls. George.

He never did pass Latin.

Hi Mom and Dad, Just when I was wondering what I would do when the war ended, Trans-Canada Airlines came knocking. They are desperate for pilots and what better place to find them than the RCAF? It didn't take me long to say yes to their offer, so in a week I'm off to Toronto to learn how to fly civilian airplanes. Maybe one day, I'll fly you across the country. Love, John.

"You'll never get me in one of those contraptions," I told Cale.

"Oh, I don't know. It might be interesting to see the countryside from the air," was Cale's reply.

We never did agree.

That same year, Maisie was transferred from Wolseley to Rosetown. I worried about her, and not just because her heart wasn't getting any better. She always had been an incorrigible flirt. First, there was the lad who worked at the Assiniboia Co-op. Then there was the young Frenchman; I was so relieved when Maisie was transferred before he had a chance to propose. Every place she was transferred after that – Rosetown, Kyle, Meyronne and finally Lafleche – she had a boyfriend. I shook my head over her.

One night at supper, I told Cale about my worries. "What will come of those girls! They are running around like wanton ninnies."

He pulled a handkerchief out of his overall pocket and blew his nose

"Good heavens, Mother, you worry too much. I bet you sound just like your own mother. Besides, I think the apples haven't fallen far from the tree."

"Whatever do you mean?"

He shoved the handkerchief back in his pocket and then pointed his finger at me

"Think about it. Amelia ran off to Australia against your mother's wishes. You came to Canada, also against your mother's wishes. You got Bessie here under false pretenses. George married a woman your mother considered unsuitable. Dorothy married her husband secretly." He shrugged. "And you find it surprising the girls are living it up a bit?"

I had finished stirring my tea and was swinging my teaspoon back and forth as Cale spoke and, just as he finished, it slipped out of my grasp, flew clear across the table and hit him on the forehead. He yelped and rocked back in his chair. "What the bloody hell!"

I gasped. "Are you hurt?"

"No. I'm just thankful you weren't driving the car." He got up.

"Chores to do," he said. He grabbed his hat and left the house, muttering all the way.

Hi guys, Guess what? I'm married. That's me and your new daughter-in-law, Kay, in the photo. I met her at a dance on the base last year. We had a good time so I asked her out on some dates and here we are. She's a lot of fun, you'll like her. There's talk of discharging us soldiers now that the war is over, although John says there's no way I'll be "honourably" discharged. Ha, Ha! Don't know if my experience in "Yelling abuse at recruits" or "driving explosives without getting myself blown up" will get me a job anywhere, but I'll have to start looking soon, especially now that I have a wife. Best, Bob.

I perused the wedding photograph. "What do you think 'a lot of fun' means?" I asked Cale.

He looked up from the recent issue of *Country Guide* and shrugged. "Could mean anything. Maybe she's up the duff?"

"Heavens, I hope not." I looked more closely at the photograph. Bob looked fine in his army uniform but his bride -- what a dumpy looking woman!

"She doesn't appear to have much class."

"Mary, no woman has any class, according to you." He went back to his reading.

I was aghast when I learned she was only 18. Bob was eight years her senior! I breathed more easily when nine months came and went with no grandchild, but then I began to worry if I would ever have a grandchild.

Betty joined the Canadian Women's Royal Navy Service as soon as she graduated from high school in 1944. She ripped open the letter from the WRENS recruiting office and squealed with delight. "Guess what? I'm going to St. Hyacinth for my training! All the way across Canada to Quebec! Wait till I tell my friends."

Hi Mom and Dad, I've finished my training, and here's the official portrait to prove it. Don't you have a beautiful daughter? I'm being sent to New York to learn to be a radio operator. And guess what? I'll be learning some Japanese language. The Americans want us to listen in to the Japanese transmissions and translate them. Don't think my high school Latin will help with that. Love, Betty.

My dear Betty, Thank you for the photo, I've put it on the sideboard. Please take care in New York, it's a big city with men who are only too eager to take advantage of you. I don't want you learning any American ways. We've had some good rains, my flowers are growing well. Bessie was here the other day, she took home a huge bouquet. Love Mom.

With Betty in New York, I worried even more. She was as much of a flirt as Maisie was.

Dear Mom, Don't worry so much. I've met only nice people. American soldiers are a mixed lot, just like Canadian soldiers, some are nice and some are not. But I have met a doctor, and he's quite dashing even if he isn't in uniform, as you can see from the enclosed snap. Japanese is a hard language but I'm getting the hang of it or at least as much as I need to know to intercept their transmissions.

I'm coming home soon for some leave and then I'm being sent to Washington, the state, not the city. Love, Betty.

Hi Mom, Your curmudgeonly son is now gainfully employed. I'm working as a machinist at the Canada Starch Company in Port Credit. I get to look after the machinery that produces all the corn starch you use so much of, so think of me next time you open that box. My boss reminds me of my old sergeant, always yelling at us, but the guys I work with are good sorts. We celebrate Friday night at the nearby bar. Kay is working at a restaurant part-time. The pay's the pits but she gets good tips. Hey, that rhymes. Still no grandchild on the way, in spite of your urging. Bob.

Our children were gone, but there was much in the house to remind me of them. There was the radio that John and Bob had persuaded Cale to buy, that Cale listened to every evening. The notch that George had sawn in one of the wooden chairs, quite accidentally, he said, as he apologized profusely. The cup and saucer the girls had given me for Mother's Day in 1935, bought with pennies earned by handing in jars of gopher tails. The doll, Pansy, that Maisie had won when she was six years old. John's RCAF uniform carefully stored in my old trunk. I treasured them all.

Days, weeks, months passed. Cale continued raising purebred Yorkshire pigs and showing them at fairs. He proudly displayed the ribbons they earned, especially the ones he won at the Moose Jaw fair. I attended the Leeville Homemakers Club meetings along with Bessie but never wanted to be on the executive. With the children gone, I took over feeding the chickens and turkeys, and picking up the eggs.

I was most at peace tending my flowers. Once, when George was home for a visit, he photographed me standing in front of my beloved hollyhocks. I framed that photo and put it on the sideboard along with all the children's photos.

Winter came. We visited Bessie and Willie or played cards with the Easterbys. Sometimes we went into town to see the latest movie at the Olympic Theatre. Foals and calves and shoats and baby chicks announced spring's arrival.

Betty came home after she was discharged from WRENS in early 1946.

"Now what do you plan to do?" I asked her.

"I'm not sure, Mom, but maybe hospital work of some sort." That autumn, she started training at Regina General Hospital as a laboratory technician.

"Nursing is out," she said, "I can't stand the sight of blood and gore."

We must have done a good job, Cale and I, raising our children. Except for Bob, they had all finished Grade 12 and were now well employed at proper jobs earning good money. I was so proud of them, well, maybe with the exception of George but he was still young, only 17, he had time to figure out what he wanted to do with his life.

The only sad note was they were scattered across the country. Now what was there to hold me to this place, other than Bessie and Cale?

I soon found out. Before long, I started hearing about boyfriends and girlfriends.

Hi Mom and Dad, I'm now based in Winnipeg, flying from here to Vancouver via Calgary. I'm too busy flying to see the scenery, especially through the mountains where the winds can be tricky. I'm working with a great crew again, wonder how I can be so lucky. One stewardess in particular has caught my eye, a brunette with shapely legs. Dad will appreciate that last tidbit. Her name's Shirley. How're the crops? Love, John.

Shirley? What a name! At supper, I said to Cale, "I hope this woman has more than shapely legs to commend herself."

Cale paused, a piece of roast beef impaled on his fork. "Give John more credit than that, Mother."

Dear John, What do you mean by "tricky winds?" Thank heavens no one is shooting at you. As for this Shirley, I don't care about her legs. What sort of woman would want to be a stewardess? Why not a proper profession like nurse or teacher? The crops are looking good, Cale hopes for a good harvest this year if we don't get hailed out first. Love Mom.

In his next letter, John wrote that her father was a respected doctor in Ottawa. I sighed with relief.

"At least she comes from a good family," I said to Cale at the supper table that night.

He just shook his head and waved his knife at me. "Pass the butter, Mother."

Bessie arrived on our doorstep in early July, all in a tizzy. "That boy of yours!"

I put the kettle on for tea. "Which one?"

"George! He was supposed to come work for us this summer. Instead, he's working for Maisie's boyfriend at Meyronne. He left us in the lurch with no one to help. You do know Maisie has a boyfriend, don't you? Here, let me get the cups."

I paused, tea caddy in hand. "She's mentioned a young man who comes into the bank quite a bit to check his account, I think she said his name is Garnet. At least that's what she told me the last time she phoned. She didn't refer to him as a boyfriend, though."

I grilled Maisie the next time she phoned.

"You'd approve of him, Mom. He's quite proper. I met his mother, his father died a few years ago and now Garnet runs the farm. We get along really well, we've gone to a few movies, but I don't know how serious he is." She chuckled. "The bank is transferring me to Lafleche, so he'll have to drive 13 miles if he wants to court me. That will tell how serious he is."

A couple of months later, Garnet drove the 40 miles to our farm to ask permission to marry Maisie. He was very nervous, constantly shifting in his chair, shuffling his feet and clearing his throat. He even spilled a bit of tea. His shoulders eased when Cale said, "Of course you may marry Maisie, but I warn you, she can be a handful."

Garnet nodded. "I've found that out already."

I told Cale that night, "He's a fine young man. Did you see how he took off his hat when he came in the house?

And how he called us Mr. and Mrs? And how neatly he was dressed? I think Maisie's made a good choice."

Cale grunted. "Good, otherwise I'd have to listen to endless complaining."

I didn't dignify that with a response.

Maisie and Garnet were married June 29, 1946, at St. Boniface Anglican Church in Assiniboia, and we hosted the reception at the farm. I cried a little as I waved them goodbye when they left for their honeymoon.

Hi Mom and Dad, You'd better sit down to read my news. I've proposed to Shirley and she's accepted. You'll be pleased to know I did the proper thing and asked her father for her hand in marriage. The wedding's planned for next February at the Barnhart's church in Ottawa. Do you think you'll be able to attend? We'd love to have you, and Dr. and Mrs. Barnhart want to meet you. If not, we'll come west sometime after the wedding so you can meet Shirley. Love John.

John and Shirley were married February 4, 1947, at St. James United Church in Ottawa. We couldn't attend; we just didn't have the money.

That winter of 1946–47 was especially bitter. A three-day blizzard in February shut down everything, including the trains. It was a week before the CPR had cleared the line and trains could run again. John had to wait until March before he and Shirley, now Mrs. J. Higham, could visit us.

Shirley turned out to be a pleasant woman, well-spoken and well-dressed. She set the table and mashed the potatoes while John carved the roast beef and I dished up the Yorkshire pudding. After supper and the washing up – Shirley dried dishes, – we retired to the living room where John gave us their wedding photographs.

I pointed to one of the bridesmaids and said, "Why didn't you marry this one? She's prettier."

Shirley gasped, then ran out of the living room. John snapped, "That was a cruel thing to say, Mom."

I saw Cale shake his head. "Woman, for someone who claims to be of such good class, sometimes you have no class at all."

I had no idea what he meant by that, and told him so.

That same month, Maisie called. "Mom, you're going to be a grandmother! Sometime this autumn, October the doctor thinks."

A month later, John phoned with the same news, "Baby will be born in November, if we're counting right."

Dearest Dorothy, We're grandparents to not one but two grandchildren. Margaret was born to Maisie on October 3, just seven days before my own birthday. I told Maisie she was the best birthday gift ever. Maisie and Garnet came to visit two weeks ago with baby Margaret. It was the greatest thrill to hold new life in my arms. Last Saturday, John called to say they have a baby girl, too, born November 7. They're naming her Susan, but they live so far away I doubt I'll ever hold her as a baby, much as I would love to. These grandchildren make me look at this country differently. Here is the only place they will know as home, and they are beginning to fasten me to it because I want to see them grow up. Oh listen to me getting all maudlin. Winter has set in and we have lots of snow, but I hope not as much as last winter. Garnet and Maisie are planning to come for Christmas, George, too, he's working for Garnet now. Love Mary.

By now, Marjorie was working in Toronto.

Dear Mom and Dad, What an enormous, noisy, smelling city. I thought Edmonton was bad. At least Toronto doesn't have winters that go on forever. Oh, by the way, remember that American I met in Edmonton? Well, he's here, and he's pursuing me madly. I still hate the name Henry, so I've started calling him Mitch – his last name is Mitchell. He's in the US Air Force now, not quite sure what he's doing in Toronto, it's all hush-hush. Love Marjorie.

Cale just shrugged when I showed him Marjorie's letter. "She's too sensible to do anything foolish. Besides, she talks a blue streak, I doubt any man could get a word in edgewise even if he did want to propose. So stop worrying."

This Mitch must have been able to interrupt Marjorie's prattling at some point, because a year later, we received news.

Dear Mom and Dad, you'll never guess! Mitch has proposed! Your spinster daughter will be a spinster no longer. He said he'd make a respectable lady out of me, and I told him, good luck, my mother couldn't, what makes you think you can! We're getting married in Toronto in October, the 18th to be exact, at St. James Cathedral. I only wish you and Dad could be there, then the wedding would be perfect. And I've asked Betty to be my bridesmaid. Love Marjorie.

I wrote her a couple of weeks before the wedding.

Dear Marjorie, This will be the last time I address a letter to you as 'Miss.' Dad suggested that John pays the bill for your supper and then Dad will repay John. Here is wishing you the best in your new adventure and that you will be so very happy. We had hoped the both of you would have paid us a visit but we are still looking forward to meeting Mitch. Love, Mom and Dad.

Hi folks, Well, you'll finally get to meet Kay because we're moving back to Assiniboia. Pay was good at the Starch Works but couldn't stand the boss, or maybe he couldn't stand me. We had words and I told him where he could shove his job and I was off to be my own boss. Any farms for sale around your place? Or maybe to rent? We'll be there in a couple of weeks. I'll call you when we get to Moose Jaw, it'll have to be collect, hope you don't mind. Can we bunk at the house until we find our own place? Bob.

My initial impression of Kay was reinforced when I finally met her, especially when I saw she smoked and drank. Such unladylike behaviour! But to give her credit, she helped me with housework, and even fed the chickens and turkeys without being asked. Within the month, she was cleaning houses for people in Assiniboia, and I was told she was very good at it.

Bob was another matter. It's not that he was lazy, he certainly worked hard helping Cale with the farming, but he didn't seem particularly motivated to find a farm. He and Cale had a "dust-up," as Cale put it. I don't know what words they had exchanged, but soon thereafter Bob started enquiring and within a few months he found a farm to rent a few miles south of us.

Perhaps mothers feel differently about things than fathers do. Cale seemed indifferent to where Bob lived. I, on the other hand, was glad to have one of our children living so close.

As for Betty, she seemed fated to be always the bridesmaid, never the bride. First, she was Maisie's bridesmaid and then, when she was working at Sunnybrook Hospital in Toronto, she was Marjorie's bridesmaid. I despaired of her ever finding a husband, but eventually, in December of 1953, she married Fred. T. Brooks, Jr., whom she had met when she sailed back from Europe in 1952. Another wedding we couldn't attend for the same reasons – too far away, and costing too much money that we didn't have.

With the birth of grandchildren, my ties to this country became stronger. They connected me to this place but, in spite of it all, I still felt a yearning to go back to England. That finally happened in 1952, but it took the scare of my life to get me there.

Chapter Thirty
Cancer

I'd been having a little discomfort in my left breast for some time. At first, it was just a mild ache but I dismissed it as the result of having lifted something heavier than I should have, perhaps that 100-pound bag of flour that Cale had brought home. After a while, I realized it hadn't gone away; in fact, it seemed to be more pronounced, especially when I washed myself. Perhaps I should ask the doctor about it, I thought, but then something would come up and I didn't.

Cale and I were in bed – we weren't the least bit interested in sleeping – when I cried out, "Ow, careful, it's sore." He pressed gently on my left breast. "Here?"

"Yes." I pulled the sheet and blanket up over me.

"How long has it been sore?"

"A few months."

There was a moment's silence. Cale lay back down, then turned toward me. He stroked my arm. "You should get that looked at. I have to go into town tomorrow, I could drop you off at the doctor's office while I get the repairs."

It was mid-May, 1950; Cale had just finished seeding.

The doctor asked me a host of questions. How much did it hurt? Had I felt any lumps? Was there a discharge? Was there a history of cancer in my family?

My heart skipped a beat when the asked me that. Cancer? I might have cancer? I hesitated before saying, "My paternal grandfather had cancer."

"Hmmm," he replied.

Finally, he asked me to undress so he could examine me. He poked and prodded (and apologized when I winced), hummed and hawed, and occasionally shook his head. When he finished, he said, "I'd like to see both you and Cale in my office when you've finished dressing."

I felt like I was back in the head mistress's office at the Practicing School, waiting to be disciplined for some infraction. I sat in the doctor's office until finally the nurse ushered Cale in.

The doctor took a deep breath. "Mrs. Higham, it's too early to tell for certain but I think you may have breast cancer. Now, there's no need to worry right now. If it is, and I do stress *if*, it can be treated with radiation therapy. But we will cross that bridge when we come to it. *If* we come to it. However, we need to be certain and for that you will have to go into Regina, the Grey Nuns hospital, for X-rays. That's the only way we can tell for certain. Once we have the results, we can then make plans for further treatment, if necessary."

I was stunned into silence. Cale spoke. "If it is cancer, then what?"

"Surgery, maybe. Radiation treatment, certainly. I don't know."

I tried to choke back the lump in my throat. "When do we go into Regina?" My voice sounded small, tight, not mine at all.

The doctor smiled. "I will phone Regina today, although it might be a week or two before they can take you. I will impress upon them the urgency of the situation."

Cale and I walked out and got into the car. "We need some groceries," I said. It was all I could think of to say.

We bought groceries, got the mail, and headed home. I was worried. Could it really be cancer? Cale didn't say much either. I decided not to tell the children until we knew for sure but somehow, deep within me, some part of me knew it was cancer. I did not need any X-rays or other tests to tell me that.

Two weeks later, we drove into Regina. We'd gone into Regina many times before, to go to the Exhibition or for Cale to show his pigs, but never under these circumstances. I checked into the Grey Nuns Hospital and a nurse directed me to the X-ray clinic. It was all terrifying. I hadn't slept well since seeing the doctor.

The doctor examined me again. He hummed and hawed, just as our doctor had. He called in a nurse who took me to the X-ray room. "It will take some time because we require several pictures," the nurse explained.

When the ordeal was over, Cale and I did some shopping then drove back to Moose Jaw to spend the night with the Griggs before returning to Assiniboia. They were quite concerned for me. Emeline couldn't do enough. "Have some tea, Mary," and "Is that chair comfortable enough?" and "Would you like to have a nap? Your bed's already made up."

I assured her, "I am just fine. I am not about to tip over just yet."

Cale interjected, "She's too stubborn!" Everyone laughed.

"And yes, I would love a cup of tea."

"I should write the children, let them know what's happening," I said as we drove home the next day.

Cale shook his head. "No, wait till we know for sure, then tell them. No point in having them worry especially if it doesn't turn out to be whatever the doctor thought it might be."

The dreaded phone call came a week later. Cale and I sat in the doctor's office, my heart pounding, my stomach churning. I twisted my hands in my lap. The doctor did not look reassuring as he looked up from the file on his desk. "I'm sorry, Mrs. Higham."

The world closed in on me. I felt numb, cold. I could see the doctor's mouth moving but no sound was coming out. Suddenly, I was aware of silence. The doctor was looking at me, his head slightly cocked, one eyebrow lifted.

I blinked and shook my head. "Excuse me, Doctor, I, uh, I, would you mind repeating that?" I was clutching Cale's hand.

The doctor nodded. "I understand. It's a lot to take in." He closed the file.

"The X-rays show a large mass in your breast, and it seems to have spread to some of the adjacent lymph glands. You will have to undergo surgery to remove the breast, or at the very least remove the lump – the surgeon will decide which is better at the time – and then radiation therapy to kill the cancer cells."

I swallowed. "Are, are you certain?"

He nodded. "I'm afraid so, Mrs. Higham. The Grey Nuns can do the surgery next month, they have an opening for you on . . ." – he opened the file and consulted a paper – "on July 10. Once that has healed, probably within the month, then radiation treatments will begin. That means by mid-August at the latest you will have your first radiation treatment."

He looked at both of us with a wan smile. "Radiation has proved to be very effective at killing cancer cells, although it does have some side effects. However, they will explain all that to you in Regina." He stood up and guided us out of his office.

I was all confused. My head was in a muddle. Even though part of me had suspected the result, I had hoped against hope that I was wrong. Now I faced surgery. And radiation. It was too much to take in all at once. I stumbled as I walked down the steps; thank heavens Cale was there to catch me.

As we drove home, I stared down at my hands, now clenched on my lap. I turned to Cale. "I'll have to write the children now, won't I?" I really didn't know what to do.

Cale gripped the steering wheel so hard his knuckles were white. He nodded. "I think you have to."

Those were the hardest letters I ever wrote. Each time I wrote the word "cancer" in a letter, dread and fear tightened my throat and made my hand shake. I worried how Cale would manage if . . . I refused to finish that thought. I would make it. I had to. I had grandchildren to visit. I had to see Betty and George married. I just couldn't . . .

The children wrote and phoned incessantly. Kay, bless her heart, often came to help clean or would bring some cooking, "Just thought I'd drop in for a visit, Mom, and I brought you some cookies, I made too many for Bob and me, and I know Cale likes them."

Maisie and Garnet and little Margaret came as often as they could. George came up from Estevan whenever he had a chance, that is if he wasn't going to Winnipeg to visit John.

Bessie visited me more often than usual. One day she said, "The Leeville Homemaker's club is donating money to the cancer fund. It was an easy decision and everyone contributed more than they might have otherwise, because of you."

I didn't know if I was pleased or ashamed. I refilled her tea cup. "Because of me?"

Bessie shrugged. "And if it was, what of it? The important thing is we collected a substantial amount."

* * *

We drove into Regina on July 9 for surgery. When I woke up, the doctor told me they also had to remove some lymph nodes. I was sore. I hurt. The stitches and bandaging pulled and itched. During this time, Cale stayed with the Griggs in Moose Jaw so he could drive in to visit every day.

My room mate was an Anglican nun, Sister Bernarda, also enduring radiation treatment. Her faith and optimism in the face of cancer helped me through the ordeal and all the worry it brought.

"God has brought us together for a reason," she said. "We are each other's strength as we go through this together."

Radiation treatment began in mid-August. The doctor had explained the procedure but hearing about it was nothing like going through it. I barely slept the night before it began. I walked into the hospital with a stone in my stomach, my heart racing.

"You can change in here, Mrs. Higham." The nurse drew aside a curtain and ushered me into a small cubicle.

"Please put on this gown. You may leave your clothes here but take your handbag with you. Pull the curtain open when you are done. I will be back when everything is ready."

She left me there. I took off my clothes and hung them carefully on the hook then put on the hospital gown. It was dreadful. Something that is made to fit everybody fits nobody. I pulled the curtain open and sat on the bench and waited. I heard footsteps, muted voices, doors opening and closing, machinery humming. Finally, footsteps came my way. The nurse appeared. "We're ready for you, Mrs. Higham."

I stood up, took a deep breath, picked up my handbag and followed her down the corridor to a door. The sign on the door read, "Caution, Radiation. Authorized Personnel Only." She opened the door and motioned me inside.

I was in an anteroom. Two more nurses and a technician stood before a control panel of knobs and dials and gauges. Behind the panel was a window. I looked through it to where I would be shortly – a table with a huge contraption overhead, looking for all the world like a big bomb. I would be there soon. I tried to swallow but my mouth was dry.

The nurses and the technician turned to me. "Come in, Mrs. Higham. There's no need to worry. Let me explain what we are about to do."

I heard his words but it was all mumbo-jumbo. All I understood was that soon I would be lying on that table and the huge bomb would bombard me with rays that would kill the cancer in my body. One of the nurses led me through the door into the room. She lowered the table with a foot pedal and arranged a sheet. "Please lie down on the bed on your back."

I did and felt the table rise up. "Now, Mrs. Higham, we have to position you just so in order for the rays to hit exactly where the cancer is. We will use these pads to hold you in place." She smiled a rueful little smile. "It may not be the most comfortable position but we will do the best we can."

The other nurse was now there. She looked at my chest and my neck. "Ah, I see the marks." She reached overhead and turned on the machine. I saw a red light come on, I saw a red cross dance across my chest as she shifted the bed back and forth. "Please roll a bit to your right so I can put this pillow under your shoulder. Yes, that's good. Good, let me put a pad there. I'm going to move your shoulder down a little. Please hold it there."

I must have grimaced because the nurse smiled and patted my arm. "I know, Mrs. Higham, it's not very comfortable but we will make this as quick as possible." I felt the table move back and forth, then side to side a little.

"There," the nurse said. She bent over so I could see her face. "Now, I have to put this lead apron on you to protect the rest of your body from the X-rays. It is very heavy, I'm afraid."

It was. The nurses made a final check. "We will leave the room now. You will hear whirring and buzzing as the machine warms up. You may feel a burning sensation as the rays penetrate. That's perfectly normal, so please try not to move. But you can breathe normally."

I didn't see how I could move, I was so penned in with pads and pillows. I closed my eyes.

I heard the door close. I was alone. I heard the machine whir and buzz and whine. It got louder. I felt a sharp burning on my chest. Then it stopped. I heard the door open.

"You did very well, Mrs. Higham. Now, we have to reposition you for the next dose."

They repeated the entire procedure several times, working their way up from my chest to my neck. They left once they had finished propping and bracing, leaving me alone again with that machine. With the whirring and buzzing and whining and the burning sting.

Finally, the ordeal was over. The nurse lowered the table and helped me up. I stood, unsteady on my feet. "Take my arm, Mrs. Higham. I'll walk you to the change room."

I found my footing and my voice. "No thank you. I am quite capable of walking on my own."

I changed into my clothes and walked into the waiting room. Cale stood up as soon as he saw me, came over and looked at my neck. "It looks like you've been in the sun too long, Mary."

I struggled into my coat. "The doctor said it would look like severe sunburn. Did you get the pain medicine?"

Cale nodded. "Yes, and a string of instructions from the pharmacist. I'll help you back to the car."

"I'm perfectly fine," I snapped, but after a few steps I was quietly accepted Cale's arm. I was very glad of a bed and rest when we arrived at the Griggs. The doctor warned me I would feel tired, and I did. It had taken more out of me than I cared to admit. I had to go through this again in two days, every two days for the next 10 days. I dreaded it but what else could I do? I wasn't going to let this cancer get the better of me if there was something I, or the doctors, could do.

By the time we got back to Assiniboia, 10 days later, my neck was covered with ugly burns. Kay had supper waiting for us, and a day later Maisie came to stay for a few days. Everyone phoned. George came home for a visit. John did, too; he flew in from Winnipeg for a few days.

That was only the first session. I had to endure five more. They didn't get any easier. The burns didn't get any less severe.

It was the hardest summer I had endured for many years. On the days when I could not bear the worry any more, I found solace in my flower garden. It wasn't just the weeding and the dead-heading that distracted me, it was seeing life and beauty around me, persisting despite all the trials that beset them. I inhaled the heady smell of lilacs, then in their turn peonies and finally roses, knowing full well the flowers and the smell would eventually fade, but they would return next year. The hollyhocks stood tall despite prairie winds that tried to break them down. Asters, dahlias, cosmos and gladiolas grew and bloomed in spite of bugs. Even those pesky dandelions insisted on growing and flowering despite my best efforts to kill them.

Letters from Sister Bernarda gave me courage. I was in awe of her acceptance of everything, even when she wrote that her cancer might have returned. She had faith enough for the two of us.

Dearest Mary, God has given me a challenge but He has also given me the strength to endure. I am quite convinced that in His goodness God has blessed us both in the mutual prayers we offer for each other. In the hours of trials and suffering it has pleased Him that we should be a comfort to each other. Best regards, Sister Bernarda.

And Kay, bless her soul, seemed to know when I was at my lowest. I lost track of the number of times she arrived with a casserole or some cinnamon buns or some muffins. She'd greet me with a smile. "Sit down, Mother, I can make the tea." She'd stir up the fire in the stove and set the kettle to boil. Somehow, our little chats left us smiling and even laughing. We never mentioned our worries, and I know Kay had her own worries. She and Bob still had no children after six years of marriage. She probably wondered if she would ever have children.

Maisie did what she could but it was more difficult for her, living some 40 miles away. She wasn't well, she never had been after that bout of rheumatic fever so many years ago. Her heart was giving her more and more trouble, she could hardly walk up a flight of stairs without having to rest. She was also worried about her new son, Richard. His had been a difficult birth.

And Bessie, dear Bessie. I don't know what I would have done without her. She was always there, sometimes with a funny story that left me laughing, sometimes with a shoulder to cry on when I just couldn't bear it all any more, and always with a place of refuge.

I don't know how Cale put up with me that year. I confess I was hard to live with. Cale and I had some terrible arguments, more so than usual. They often ended with him stalking out of the house, slamming the door behind him, and then I would proceed to slam cupboard doors or sweep the floor within an inch of its life. Occasionally, I would burst into tears. Cale would stand there, then come and hold me. I'd blubber out, "I'm sorry."

He'd stroke my hair and say, "It's okay." Then we'd sit and have a cup of tea.

In early December, we returned to the Grey Nuns for a final check. After another round of X-rays, they declared me cancer-free, a most welcome Christmas present. I wouldn't die. The weight of impending death lifted off me and I felt light as a feather. I floated out of the hospital and spent the next several days writing to everyone, including Sister Bernarda. Unlike the last time, these letters were a joy to write.

I had been given another chance at life and I was not going to waste it. I decided then and there that I would go back to England to see my sisters and their families, and meet Cale's family. This brush with death made me realize just how precious and how fleeting life is.

Part 3
Home

Chapter Thirty-One
Cornwall and Devon

I stood on the deck of the *Liberté*, Betty at my side, and watched England slowly come into view. At first, I saw only slimmest band of green far away, barely visible above the sea, but gradually it rose up and became larger. Soon I could see Land's End. Cornwall. My home.

We had sailed from New York six days ago, after spending a wonderful 10 days with Marjorie and her family in Washington, D.C. What a treat to leave behind the cold, muddy, barren Saskatchewan prairies of early April and arrive in Washington to find everything green and warm, the cherry trees in full bloom. I was thrilled to finally meet my granddaughter, Linda, although at first she was not thrilled to see this grey-haired old lady. Once she realized I was the one who wrote her letters and sent her presents, she insisted on hugging and being hugged, almost without end. Betty and Marjorie talked a storm all the time we were there, I don't know which one talked more. Poor Henry was shut out of their conversations, giving the two of us time to get to know each other better.

Now, as we stood on the deck of the *Liberté*, Betty was still talking non-stop, this time to some poor gentleman she had cornered, about how this was her first visit to England and she was *so excited*. I was excited, too, but for a different reason. After 40 years, I would see Clive and Dorothy, and meet their families. I would finally meet Cale's family. Perhaps they could tell me why he left England. He never would.

I had tried to persuade Cale to come with me. "Don't you want to see Len and your sisters? Catch up with your nieces and nephews? Relive the past with your old mates?"

He refused. "I left all that when I left England, and I have no need to go back to relive anything with anyone."

I kept watch for Pendennis Castle as we sailed up the Channel. Finally, I saw a gap in the shore and a pile of stone that I decided was the castle.

I nudged Betty. "There! That gap is Carrick Roads, and at the end of it is Feock where I spent my childhood."

Betty gawked into the distance, then shrugged. "If you say so, Mom." She turned and continued chatting with the gentleman.

At length, Plymouth came into view. My childhood memories of that city were hazy, mostly noise and cold and damp and grey. However, today the sky was blue and the weather warm. The harbour appeared to have been rebuilt after the terrible bombing it had received from the Germans.

Clive and Dorothy said they would meet us, but I worried that we wouldn't recognize each other. I needn't have feared. As we walked out of Immigration, I heard, "Yoo-hoo! Mary! Over here!"

There was Clive; I'd forgotten she was half a head taller than me. Dorothy was jumping up and down beside her. Both waved their arms madly. Two men stood beside them.

"Betty, there are your aunts." We pushed our way through the crowds to my sisters. There followed a mad flurry of hugs and greetings.

"How are you?"

"How was the trip?"

"My, you look so young!"

"Betty, at last, we meet. Your mother has written so much about you!"

"Is that your luggage? The car is over there."

Harry and Harold shook my hand. "Finally, we meet the infamous Mary. Welcome to England, or rather, *back* to England."

I smiled. "Thank you. I've heard so much about you from Dorothy and Clive. Now I can see for myself if the stories they've told me are true."

It was their turn to laugh. "Don't believe everything our wives write."

Dorothy embraced me. "We'll be heading back to Strete now, but I just had to come meet you. I couldn't wait a moment longer. We'll have lots of time to talk once you come to our place."

I was sad to see her go but she was right, I would be there in a couple of weeks.

I opened the door of Harry's car to see myself staring at the steering wheel.

"Oh," I stammered. I'd forgotten in England, the driver sits on the passenger's side and the passenger on the driver's side. Harry raised his eyebrows then smiled as I walked around to the correct door.

We drove through the city, Clive and Harry pointing out what had been rebuilt after the war. The exception was Charles Church. It had been bombed into rubble, and the city decided to leave it in ruins as a memorial to all who had died during the war.

The highway to Camborne where Clive and Harry lived was just as narrow and winding and hemmed in with hedgerows as I remembered. Now, however, it was filled with motor cars and trucks and double-decker buses; the horse-drawn conveyances of my youth were long gone.

Betty marvelled at the countryside. Her head swiveled from side to side. She pointed at everything. "Mom, look at all the flowers. Are those primroses? And camelias, oh my heavens. It is so green!"

Clive's home was a modest cottage with a postage stamp-sized bit of grass in the front and a well-kept yard in the rear. Harry hurried through, carrying our suitcases. "I'll take these to your bedroom."

I looked around. The sitting room was small compared to our house. A couple of overstuffed chairs and an equally overstuffed davenport sat either side of a fireplace that contained a coin-operated electric fire. The mantel was filled with framed photographs, a dainty glass vase of primroses, and various items they must have brought with them from Egypt. A bookcase filled with books stood against one wall, and a glass-fronted cabinet filled with dishes and china figurines stood against another. I walked over to examine the cabinet, and turned to Clive.

"I see you have Mother's old silver tea service." Clive had positioned the teapot so the dent was hidden.

She nodded. "Yes, it was all that was worth saving, too, after Mother died. Dorothy certainly didn't want it."

Betty squinted through the glass at the tea set. "Is there a story about it?"

Clive opened the door, took out the teapot and handed it to Betty. "Yes, there is. Father bought it at Mother's urging, she said it was just the thing to celebrate Edward VII's coronation. Of course, we were forbidden from touching it, but one day Dorothy, only seven, decided it would be the perfect thing to serve "tea" to her dolly."

I took up the tale. "Wouldn't you know it? She tripped on the edge of a rug and the pot flew out of her hands, banged onto the floor and bounced against a table leg. Mother was not amused, not so much at the tea spilled on the rug as the dent in her precious tea pot. Dorothy was sent to her room, without tea or dolly. She's hated that tea service ever since."

Harry came back into the room. "Here, let me take your coats."

I took off my coat and immediately shivered. I had forgotten how cold and damp English homes were, even at the end of April.

Betty rubbed her hands together then hugged herself. "It's freezing in here."

I shivered again. "We're spoiled. We're used to central heating."

"Never fear. We'll turn on the electric fire later," Clive said.

Betty raised her eyebrows and whispered to me, "They don't have a furnace?"

I shook my head. "No, and mind your manners."

Clive showed us to our bedroom where we dug sweaters out of our suitcases. Betty went into the sitting room and began quizzing Harry about the Egyptian items. I went into the kitchen where Clive was preparing tea. "Cornish pasties, in your honour, Mary. A classic Cornish meal for the returning Cornish lass."

"I made pasties back home, too, but big long ones. It was quicker to make them big and cut them into pieces rather than making individual ones. My boys ate so much especially when they were growing up."

She paused from rolling out the pastry. "I can't imagine feeding six children. Feeding three was enough of a challenge!"

The bed that night was damp and cold. Betty shuddered as she crawled in beside me.

"Yikes! The ocean is warmer! Mom, we should have packed one of your old bed warmers." Then she giggled. "Maybe they have a brick they can heat up in their electric fire."

The next morning, after finishing breakfast and the washing up, Clive said, "I have to pick up some fruit and veg from the shop for tonight's tea. Come with me. It will be so nice to have company. I used most of our potatoes for last night's pastry. I've become very good at making potato pastry." She picked up her handbag.

Betty started. "You use potatoes to make pastry? I've never heard of that. But don't get me wrong, it was good."

We stopped first at the green grocer's. My mouth dropped when I saw the state of the shop. I looked around in disgust. It certainly wasn't Mr. Jackson's Red and White Store back in Assiniboia; he and his wife kept everything spic and span. Here, the windows were covered with dust and fly specks. The floor had been in need of a good sweeping for a very long time.

Betty whispered, none too softly, "It's filthy. Look at those flies. They're everywhere!"

We had barely walked in when I heard a man yell, "Stop that!"

The shopkeeper, a portly middle-aged man, stomped over to a young lad accompanying his mother and slapped an apple out of the lad's hand.

The lad's mother objected. "He wasn't stealing it!"

The shopkeeper snarled. "He shouldn't be handling the food." He walked back behind the counter.

"Yes?" he snapped at Clive.

I was astonished. No "How are you, Mrs. Wright?" No "Another bracing day, isn't it?" No "How can I help you?" Just a curt "Yes?"

Had shopkeepers been that rude 40 years ago? I couldn't remember. Perhaps they had been and I had forgotten. Clive made her purchases; the fruit and veg weren't rationed but tea was limited to two ounces per week, and sugar to eight ounces per week. As we walked out with our purchases, I asked, "Are all the shopkeepers so rude?"

"He certainly is. I should go to another shop but he's so close."

Next stop was the butcher's shop. Here, my shock wasn't so much the dirt and flies as it was the lack of goods for purchase. The few chops and roasts were so small as to be unrecognizable as such. What a contrast with the large roasts, the many chops, even the ribs and soup bones that we had in such abundance back home.

Clive told the butcher what she wanted: eight ounces of bacon, four chops, four ounces of butter, four ounces of cheese and two eggs.

"Is that all you're buying?" I asked.

Clive nodded. "Yes, that is our ration for the week."

That night I wrote to Maisie, using the Post Office's thin blue Air Letter paper. I had to write small to cram everything in that I wanted to say.

My dear Maisie and all, Apples, oranges, bananas and grapes are plentiful but meat, butter and tea are mean.

Fish, liver, heart, pig's feet, tripe, and hog's pudding are open. There is a canned prepared meat here that is not rationed. Here is a list if you do feel like sending some: butter, tea, canned sausage, canned ham, cottage roll, raisins, currants and peel, the three latter just impossible to get at any price. Apples, oranges, bananas and grapes are plentiful. I imagine Garnet is going full steam ahead with seeding. Love to Margaret, Richard and Garnet. Mother.

But right now, no one was talking about rationing and shortages. Instead, everyone was talking about the new and so very young Queen Elizabeth.

"We were born under a queen and now we will live under a queen again," Clive said one evening. We were in the sitting room drinking tea. Harry was listening to the wireless while reading the *Cornish Guardian* and sipping at his whiskey.

Harry looked over the top of the newspaper at us. "We might still have had a king if that git Edward hadn't gone chasing after a bit of skirt." He put the paper down and picked up his glass of whiskey. He took a sip, then held up the glass to examine the contents. "It was probably all for the better. Can you imagine how England might have fared if we had been ruled by a king sympathetic to those Nazi thugs?"

Clive grimaced. "What a dreadful image. The SS strutting up and down the streets of London. And that madman Hitler in Buckingham Palace."

"As Shakespeare said, all's well that ends well," I said.

* * *

Betty soon became bored listening to two "old ladies" reminisce about the past.

"I'm going to Penzance tomorrow. I want to see where you lived," she declared one morning. "I didn't come to England to listen to you two gabbing all day long."

Clive and I looked at each other, eyebrows raised. "Gabbing? I don't think so, my dear," Clive said. "We're discussing very important events in our lives."

Betty came back at the end of the week, all agog. "What a beautiful city! And Regent Square, oh my goodness, how lovely. You know what I did? I wanted to see inside your house so I walked up to Number 18 and knocked on the door."

"You didn't!" I exclaimed.

"Yes, I did, but no one was home. I was disappointed. So instead, I stood in the middle of the Square, imagining your mother tossing your father out of the house and screaming loud enough for the whole world to hear what a scumbag he was. The Square is such a confined area, I can see why the neighbours could hear every word." With that, she flounced off to her bedroom.

I was beginning to realize how "Canadian" I had become. I was continually getting in on the "wrong" side of the car. I was stiff with terror as we hurtled down the "wrong" side of the highway. I fumbled with shillings and pence, wondering how I had ever managed to get the right change so long ago, and then smiling as I remembered how I had once found Canadian money so confusing. I shivered through chilly days and chillier nights in houses that lacked central heating. When outside, I often wore my coat even though Clive thought it was a "splendid day!" Thank heavens I had packed an extra sweater.

Sometimes it seemed Clive and Harry spoke a foreign language because they called things by different names. What I knew as "hood" and "trunk," Harry called "bonnet" and "boot." Trucks were "lorries," and "asphalt" was "tarmack." Some terms I remembered from my childhood, for example, "supper" was "tea" here.

* * *

My dear Cale, Betty and I took the train to Strete yesterday to spend some time with Dorothy. The railway stations are dreary cold places, even Plymouth, a large station, no heated waiting room, toilets filthy. At the lunch counter you buy whatever you want and carry it back to a small table, if you want it clean, that you must do yourself or use it dirty. No, a traveller waits on the clerk, not the clerk on the traveller. This whole district is outdated, it has not changed one bit in forty years. Love, Mary.

Dorothy and Harold's house was an imposing two-storey brick and stone house with two tall chimneys. A low stone wall ran around three sides of the yard, dividing it from High Street which was also the highway. The front yard was grassed and the back yard had a large vegetable garden and some apple trees. The traffic past the house was continuous: cars, lorries, motorcycles, buses, even bicycles, every hour of the day and night. Fortunately, my bedroom was at the back so I didn't hear much.

Dorothy's house was just as cold as Clive's. It was far more spacious, however. The sitting room was filled with two settees and four easy chairs, along with side tables filled with framed photographs and china figurines, and over all loomed a huge stone fireplace that, as at Clive's, contained an electric fire. The kitchen was Dorothy's domain, a large range set into an alcove, a substantial well-worn table used for both preparing food and eating in the centre of the room, and a tiny refrigerator that couldn't have held more than a pint of milk and a couple of apples. The dining room furniture included a large china cabinet. Everything was polished within an inch of its life. Photographs and paintings hung on the wall, and among them I noticed some of Dorothy's own water colours.

"You do beautiful work. I still have your little drawing of Maude in her nurse's outfit. So does Bessie." I paused. "So sad that she should die so young."

Dorothy stood beside me in silence. "Yes, it was sad."

"I saw some of your other handiwork at Clive's," I teased Dorothy.

She tilted her head. "My other handiwork?" She laughed. "Oh, you mean the dented tea service. Well, Clive is welcome to it. Did she serve tea in it?"

"No. It's only on display. She used her old Brown Betty."

My dear Cale, Betty is in Torquay, for how long I don't know. She took a job as a waitress but it's not to her liking.

She thought it would give her a chance to see the country. She phoned last night to tell me what she thought of the job and she was disgusted. It's a private hotel, the owner a friend of Dorothy's. Everyone tells her it's easy to get work here but she will find out it is not. She enquired about land work but found she couldn't earn enough money to pay for her board. Sun shining, strong wind blowing but not cold. We picked broad beans for dinner, cost 1/10 a lb. Dorothy bought 2 lbs but after shelled there was enough for one person. How are the pigs coming along and have you a new car yet? Love, Mary.

I usually had the days to myself – Dorothy was still teaching and Harold worked in Dartmouth – so from time to time I walked along the roads and trails, looking at the countryside and comparing the fields and equipment to our farm.

The first time I went walking was the day after a hard rain. A few puddles glistened on the otherwise dry tarmac, occasionally reflecting sunlight into my eyes. The sun shone warmly in a brilliant blue sky, warm enough that I almost wished I hadn't worn my coat. The air smelled fresh and sweet. A breeze toyed with my hat.

My dear Cale, Saw some very badly matted hay this morning. It was a good crop. Have seen only one field of clover hay, it was a bumper crop. I saw a weed sprayer working on a field badly infested with dock. A very small boom, but plenty big for the size of the field. It is owned by the Devon County Ag. Committee and rented out. Also combines and drills, the tractors are farmer owned. They must be about the size of our Ford for they draw very small machinery. One to two horses still very common but more tractors in Devon than Cornwall. Love, Mary.

One day, Dorothy said, "Let's go to Torquay to have lunch, maybe do a bit of shopping."

We intended to take the train but as we walked to the station, we saw a passenger boat about to leave. We looked at each other.

"Why not? Let's go. We can always take the train back."

The ticket agent looked askance at us. "There's a gale brewing, ladies. I wouldn't advise taking the boat."

"Nonsense, young man. An adventure is just what we want!" We purchased our tickets and boarded the boat.

The gale hit us as we left the River Dart. The waves hit the boat broadside and rocked it like a cradle. They washed over the sides and thoroughly soaked us. A sailor yelled over the wind, "Ladies, let me help you to one of the cabins. You'll be drier there."

We waved him off. "No, we're enjoying the adventure and we are going to stick it out."

And we did, every inch of the way. It was screams of fun. We laughed and shrieked the entire ride. To top it off, as we approached Torquay, the captain called over the loud speaker, "Ladies, to your left you see a number of vessels including Navy warships and air craft carriers that have all taken shelter in Torquay from the storm."

It was such a rough ride but I would not have missed it for anything. We took the train back to Strete.

My dear Cale, Canada can beat England in curing bacon, it's no wonder they rave over Canadian bacon. There isn't any beef here at all, all lamb and fish, the latter I thoroughly enjoy. I can't understand why there isn't any fresh pork, it's all cured and has an odd taste, not that sweet clear taste we have in our bacon. There is a lot of bacon in the stores but of course rationed. I'd love to live here but the house heating would have to improve greatly. This is a dreadful country for paying out. To go onto the pier to get a tourist boat you must pay a penny. To use a public toilet it costs a penny and so on with everything. How are you making out and are you behaving yourself? I often wish you were here. Tell Bessie she has to come over. She'd love it all but maybe she wouldn't want to go back. Love to all, Mary.

By the end of May, I was getting tired of sight-seeing on my own. It was time to go to Adderbury to visit Cale's brother, Len, and his wife Flo.

Chapter Thirty-Two
Adderbury

My dear Cale, I am at Adderbury now, came up by bus. It was a wonderful trip. This part of England is altogether different to Cornwall. In places a three-lane highway and one continuous stream of traffic. Not nearly so many beautiful flower gardens but broader views. The single fare to Banbury from Cornwall was £1/3/6, have been told about half of rail fare. Len and family all well. Maisie said in her letter yesterday you are getting your teeth out. Your mouth will be sore, and how are you managing for soft foods. Should I come on an earlier boat. That is all up to you, just say and I'll be over right away. Love, Mary.

Len and Flo met me at the Banbury bus depot. I recognized them right away from the photos we had exchanged over the years. Even if I had never seen a photo of Len, I would have recognized those bushy Higham eyebrows. He was taller than Cale and had more meat on his bones, and a very red nose, making me think he perhaps imbibed too freely of his wares.

They greeted me warmly. "Welcome to Oxfordshire!" Flo said as she hugged me. "We'll be home soon. I'll make a pot of tea and you'll soon be right as rain."

I was indeed tired and gladly handed my suitcase over to Len. He strapped it onto a carrier attached to the back of his car. I now knew which side of the car I should enter. As I prepared to climb into the back seat, Flo put her hand on my arm. "I'll get in the back, Mary. You sit up front with Len."

Len wiped a bit of dust off the dashboard, although the car appeared immaculate to me. What a difference compared to our car back home. It was always dusty, cigarette butts in the overflowing ashtray, stains on the upholstery, mud and dirt on the floor.

The trip to Adderbury didn't take more than ten minutes, and Flo kept up a never-ending stream of chatter the entire trip. Len pulled up in front of the Wheatsheaf Inn, a wonderful old stone building on the village green, two storeys high, with two large bow windows flanking a central door.

"Here we are," he said, and we climbed out of the car. Len carried my suitcase inside and put it down just inside the door. "I'll see you in a few minutes."

Flo took off her coat and hat, and motioned me to do the same. "He's going to put the car in the garage. He bought it five years ago, the first car he ever owned. Right chuffed he was, too, when he bought it. I told him he'd have go to the haberdasher's and buy himself a bigger hat. He treats it like a baby, dusting this, polishing that. He was devastated when someone dinged the rear wing. Is Cale like that with his car?"

I shook my head. "No, he checks the oil and tire pressure but that's all. His 'babies,' are his prize-winning Yorkshire hogs. He is as proud of them and all his ribbons as Len is of his car."

Their living quarters were on the right-hand side of the lobby; the pub itself was to the left. Some punters were already there, I could hear the clink of pints, the murmur of conversation, the periodic thwack of a dart hitting the dartboard, and the occasional outburst of laughter. Flo led me through the sitting room, chock-a-block with furniture and all as spotless as Len's car, and up a winding staircase to the bedrooms above.

"Here's your bedroom. I hope you find it comfortable. Make yourself at home, I'll be downstairs in the kitchen making tea. Oh, and the toilet is out back in the little shed."

My bedroom overlooked the village green filled with huge trees. I imagined Cale lying under them, having his afternoon map. I started feeling maudlin, how I wished he was here.

Len turned out to be a very jovial fellow, the epitome of a publican who ran a "tight ship," as he called it. Flo was a charming jolly woman and, I soon learned, a good cook and a meticulous housekeeper intent on keeping the household spic and span.

My dear Cale, Len drove me to Bodicote yesterday. What a dump! Narrow winding streets, thatched roofs, not a flower garden to be seen anywhere. Which Red Lion did you visit? Saw the church, school and your mother's grave, they keep the grave looking lovely. The seat you used to sit on inside the church door has gone, also saw the two seats you occupied during church services, the one in the choir and the one back in the children's section of the church. Flo showed me your old farm. She said it's just as it was when you left England. It looked really nice from the road. The fields were all the green and the hedges very low. Flo and I went to Banbury this morning, Market Day. No more cattle sales on account of the Foot and Mouth outbreak. Love, Mary.

One of the people I wanted to meet was old Bill Taylor who had known Cale's father. I pestered him to "spill the beans" about Cale's childhood antics, but Bill insisted, "Nay, Cale was a model young lad, he was." Then with a twinkle in his eye, he leaned toward me and said, "And if he ain't now, well that must be what Canada's done to him."

The other person I wanted to meet was Sam Greenway, Cale's mate from his days as a runner. When I asked Len about him, he said, "All I know is he was called up for the war, the first one. I don't know if he survived, he never came back here. He wasn't the first lad who never returned from France. Wasn't the last one, either."

He paused, then grinned. "Ah, but you'll love to see this."

He went down into the basement, I heard thumping and banging and scraping, and eventually he came back up, lugging a small cannon! "We found it in an alley all covered with ivy and rust. It took us days to clean it up. Then we had to hide it so our parents wouldn't find it. I don't know what war it was left over from, but we made good use of it, firing it up and down the streets of Bodicote, yes, we did."

He stood over it, sucking on his pipe, "Hmm, maybe Dad didn't leave Bodicote of his own volition, maybe we were run out." And he laughed.

My dear Cale, There are some lovely homes around here but with a small acreage of land. In Cornwell there were lovely homes but surrounded by a big acreage. Maybe further out the estates would be larger here. It's a lovely country, so wide open and all you said of it was true. I have been wondering how you are. Guess your mouth will be sore for a long time. It's really no fun being here and you over there and being sick, not that I am overly kind to you but being away makes a difference. Everybody here says hello to you. Love, Mary.

One day, I walked into Banbury by myself; I'd been imposing on Len and Flo long enough and this would give them a break from catering to me. I walked around town, saw St. Mary's Church that had miraculously survived the bombing, and the famous Banbury Cross of the nursery rhyme "Ride a cock horse to Banbury Cross" standing in the middle of the traffic roundabout but, alas, no fine lady upon a white horse. I purchased some postcards of the Cross to send back to the grandchildren.

I walked to the canal and, on a whim, pulled down the drawbridge and walked over. I stood on the bank and watched the canal boats chug by. They were long and narrow, quite unlike the wide bulky barges I remember from the River Fal, all gaily painted with flowers and designs in bright colours, red, green, blue, magenta and orange. Even the water buckets were painted with flowers. A crazy thought sprang to mind: we could paint our old truck like that, maybe even bolt a gaily painted bucket onto its hood, with some flowers in it. I chuckled. Imagine the heads Cale would turn when he took a load of grain to the elevator at Congress. People would talk for days!

* * *

We were enjoying a quiet evening, Len reading the *Banbury Guardian,* Flo and I chatting over tea, when Len rattled the paper.

"Listen to this. They set the date for the coronation. June 2, next year."

Flo turned to me. "You should have come next year. Then you could see the coronation."

Len guffawed. "Why? Stand twenty deep along the Mall to see what? A 5-second glimpse of a someone going by in a gilded coach? You'd see more in the *London Daily Mirror* the following day."

He turned back to the paper. "Besides, it says here the Duke is wanting the coronation to be televised." He put down his paper and looked at Flo. "Now I suppose you'll be wanting us to buy a telly."

She took up her knitting. "Mr. Matthews next door is talking about buying a telly. Maybe we can go there and see it."

Len snorted, "Harrumph!" and went back to reading the paper.

I felt like the poor cousin listening to Len and Flo wondering if they could buy a telly. We didn't even have electricity. If we did, we couldn't afford a telly. We were lucky to have a radio.

My dear Cale, Len's son Jack and his wife and children are coming to Adderbury tonight. They live a long way from here, 32 miles, so it's not easy for them to get here other than on a Sunday. We had the ham for supper last evening, the one you sent, and really it's a far nicer meat than the cured meat you get here. I saw some roses growing where once were two tiny cottages so I picked them, couldn't resist it. The roses are really grand right now, the trailing roses especially. I just can't feel quite free here although Len and Flo treat me like a Queen, can't do enough for me. Write and say how you are. Love, Mary.

* * *

I so wanted to visit Cale's sisters, Edith and Iris, who lived in Oxford. We'd written to each other for years, but when they heard I was coming to England, they wrote back that I just had to visit.

The first time I asked Len, he shook his head.

"All the way to Oxford? That is quite a distance," he said.

"Nonsense, it's only 20 miles away. We think nothing of driving into Moose Jaw, 60 miles away, for a day of shopping. And back, the same day."

Len raised his eyebrows. "You're taking the mickey. No one drives that far in one day!"

"We do, in Canada. So, 20 miles to Oxford is nothing, no matter what you think. And if we don't go, then I will have to tell Cale that his brother too stingy to take me to visit his sisters. Do you want that?"

Len was silent for a moment. "Let me think about it."

We went to Oxford two days later.

Edith and Iris welcomed me warmly and made me feel at home. Everyone was surprised when Alice and her husband Vic arrived unexpectedly, all the way from Birmingham! Edith served up as grand a meal as she could, given the rationing situation. Then we retired to the parlour to visit, and oh, the stories they told!

"Cale and those other lads were always up to no good. That cannon, for example. How many times did the good citizens of Bodicote hear "Boom!"

"Too many."

"Did Cale ever get caught?"

Edith and Iris looked at one another. "I don't remember, but probably."

"You were in on that, weren't you, Len?"

Len decided it was time to get up and refill his whiskey glass.

"Remember the time they put a paper bag full of fresh horse droppings on Mr. Franklin's threshold and set it on fire?"

"Oh, how could I forget! And when Mr. Franklin came out, he stomped out the fire and got manure all over his shoes."

Everyone laughed.

"Cale got caught that time. You were in on that, too, weren't you, Len?"

Len shook his head. "I don't know what you are talking about."

"Yes, Mr. Franklin caught the two of them by the ears and dragged them off home. Mother gave them a sound scolding, as only she could do."

"And a hiding, once Dad came home."

Everyone paused and sipped their tea. For a moment I heard only the clink of tea cups on saucers.

Edith broke the silence. "Cale said he learned one thing from all this."

"What? Don't play pranks?"

Edith guffawed as she put down her tea cup. "No. He could run."

Everyone laughed.

"He certainly could run."

"Run well enough to bring home prizes."

"Remember that cruet set he won? Mother was so proud of it."

"I was afraid she'd rub the silver right off it, she polished it so much."

Iris asked, "Whatever happened to it? I haven't seen it for donkey's years."

Before anyone could answer, Alice turned to me.

"Mary, come back to Birmingham with us. I'd love to show you around the city and get to know you better." She waggled her eyebrows, exactly like Cale did. "Besides Sophie Tucker is giving a concert, I bet tickets are still available. And you could see the arenas where Cale and his mates raced. He won a couple of races there, you know?"

Sophie Tucker's concert was too much to miss. "I will, but then I want to go to Derby to visit my niece, Anne. She's Dorothy's daughter."

Chapter Thirty-Three
Final Visits

My dear Cale, Birmingham! I wouldn't know just how to describe it if I stayed here a year. I wouldn't see it all. Just around Edgbaston district the destruction by bombing has been dreadful and Alice said this part was only lightly bombed compared to the factory district. Beautiful homes completely demolished. This afternoon we are going to Licky Hills by bus and then this evening we go to the Hippodrome and see Sophie Tucker. Alice doesn't know which sports field you used to come to, there are so many here. Won't be long now before I'll be back home and I'll never go away again without you. I have enjoyed every minute of it but if you had been along it would have been lots better. The drive up to Birmingham was beautiful. England is beautiful, you don't realize it until you see it again. Love to you, Mary.

As we drove through the Edgbaston district where Alice and her husband Vic lived, Alice pointed to buildings still in ruins.

"The bombing was ghastly, Mary. We were in fear of our lives. You'd think there is no sound more terrifying than the air raid siren blaring, but it was nothing compared to the sound of bombs whistling through the air to land God knows where and then one boom after another, and the ground shaking and you know when you finally come up from the shelter another part of the city will be in ruins and on fire and people are injured and dead or dying. . ."

She broke off and rubbed her hand over her face. "It was ghastly," she repeated, softly.

I was sitting in the back seat so she turned to me. "Over 2000 people killed in Birmingham, would you believe? And beautiful Coventry bombed into ruins. I can never forgive those Germans for what they did. Never!"

I patted her shoulder. For once, I didn't know what to say. Telling her I was sorry for everything they endured would sound so trite.

Vic turned his head to me. "And now we have this blasted cold war. Any day now, Russia's going to drop the A-bomb on us. Or so they say. Would you believe that school children have atomic bomb drills? I wish that bomb had never been invented."

The whirlwind tour of Birmingham's sights began with taking the tram up to the Lickey Hills where it seemed I could see all the way to Wales. We visited Warwick Castle built by William the Conqueror and subsequently home to the Earls of Warwick, including the 16th Earl, the "Kingmaker," who made and then unmade Edward IV, thereby unmaking himself.

We took the tram to the Cadbury factory just south of Birmingham. The tour brought back so many childhood memories.

"We almost always had a Cadbury's milk chocolate bar at Christmas, but of course we had to share it among us. Even one little taste was such a treat!" I told Alice and Peggy, her daughter.

Peggy nodded. "Mom said, if we were really good, we might, just might get one in our Christmas stockings."

Stratford-upon-Avon was a disappointment, not the town itself, how could one be disappointed in walking through a beautiful medieval town? No, the disappointment was jostling cheek-by-jowl with hundreds of tourists who found fault with everything about England. I was exhausted by the end. It didn't help that I was wearing new shoes and ended up with blisters on my feet.

My dear Cale, Please note the day, July 2, it is really very warm here. Birmingham had a terrible storm yesterday, wheat, barley and oats are looking really bad, patches in some fields look like burn outs. It is still thundering and to look at the skies it looks to me like another storm. Glad the strawberries are good, are they the ones you set out last spring? The time is getting short for sailing date, can count it in days now. It's not quite fair my having all this grand time and you staying at home. You would love visiting Edith. Say hello to everyone and with lots of love, Mary.

* * *

I caught the bus to Derby to visit Anne who lived in a lovely house right on the edge of the moors. She had lost her first husband, an RAF pilot shot down in Germany only a month after they were married in 1944, but now she was happily remarried and had two beautiful and well-behaved children. She was a delightful and vivacious young woman, just as John had described her. Anne asked about him, and was pleased to hear he was married with three children.

We went to Kinder Scout, the highest point of the Pennines near Derby. It was a long climb and we stopped several times to rest. I was winded when we got to the top but not so out of breath I couldn't gasp out, "What a view! You can see all of England from up here."

Anne encompassed the view with a sweep of her arm.

"Maybe not all of England, Aunt Mary, but certainly Derbyshire, Yorkshire, Lancashire and Staffordshire. I've even seen the Welsh hills from up here, but it has to be a very clear day."

The drive back to Derby was hampered by flocks of sheep that seemed to think they owned the road. They straggled across it, or along its length, or even lay on it chewing their cud, completely oblivious to the cars wanting to proceed, and very put out that they had to get up to let us pass.

Anne snarled as she sounded the horn. "Off the bloody tarmac, you sods!"

I was shocked at her language but amused by the sheeps' disregard. I thought it added to the charm of this country, and I said so. Anne laughed. "Dear Aunt Mary, if you had to deal with these beasts every day you wouldn't think it so charming, as you put it."

My visit was over all too soon. Anne took me to the Manchester bus station where she handed my bags to the bus attendant. She turned and gave me a hug.

"I am so glad to have met you. Please give my love to John, I remember our jaunts around Cornwall like they were yesterday."

I might complain about the dirt and the lack of food and service in shops and restaurants but I could not complain about the bus service. It seemed no matter where you wanted to go, there was a bus going there, if you had the time. Ten hours after leaving Manchester, I was back in Dorothy's house in Strete, ready for a cup of tea and bed.

We had planned a quiet week together but then Betty arrived from Babbacombe, full of vim and vinegar, all excited about going to France. "I can't wait to see it. Paris is supposed to be so beautiful!"

My dear Cale, There are three Canadian boats (H.M.C.S) in harbour at Dartmouth, Betty and I were watching them sail into the harbour from Dorothy's garden but then didn't know they were Canadian. The town is lousy with Canadian sailors now, and will be until Monday morning early. Betty was terribly excited when we discovered where the boats were from. She is leaving for France about September 8. England's customs and ways will never change. Betty hasn't been warm since she has been here. We have potatoes but once a week here and that is on Sundays. No fruit, no breakfast cereals, no bacon, no eggs for breakfasts, so you can guess what we have for that meal. I have decided the English cook and cooking is rotten. I do like the bread and butter tho', jam's 1/- a lb jar, but you hardly see it. I would like to stay here but when I think of the unheated houses, it makes me think I'd be warmer in Canada. Also the children, I couldn't go so far from them. You don't know what you have missed and your not being here with me, when I tell you something interesting you won't be able to contradict me, and that will spoil the fun. I'm feeling excited now I am packing up to go home. Love Mary.

The day after Betty left, Dorothy and I went to Dartmouth to visit Mother's grave where Maude was also buried. A magnificent stone cross on a stepped plinth marked where they lay. We laid some roses then stood there in silence, holding hands. After a moment, Dorothy turned to me.

"Mother was glad to go, she hadn't been in good health that last year."

She chuckled. "Mother was one stubborn lady. She never forgave Dad, and it took her forever to forgive you and Amelia for abandoning her, as she saw it. But . . ." and she sighed. "Well, in the end she did."

I spent one last week with Clive and Harry. I was tired of sight-seeing, so we didn't go anywhere except to the shops, the same dirty shops with the same rude shopkeepers of three months ago. One difference now – the shops were beginning to stock and sell coronation souvenirs, cups and saucers, glasses, plates, tea caddies, biscuit tins, tea pots, trays, even tea towels.

"How insulting to use the queen's face to dry dishes," Clive muttered.

I bought two cup-and-saucer sets and two glasses to take home, and the shopkeeper, polite and considerate, for once, wrapped them well in newspaper before putting them in a box.

"This should see them home safely," he said, and wished me a safe voyage.

The day of leave-taking finally came. Clive and Harry took me to the station to return to Strete. We hugged each other, we cried, we promised to write faithfully.

Clive said, "Come again soon, with Cale this time. Maybe John can fly you over."

"I may have to hog-tie Cale to get him away but I will do my best."

My last week with Dorothy was the same. We didn't go anywhere. We sat and talked, about our childhood, about our families, and sometimes about nothing at all. Sometimes we just sat in the garden without talking, drinking tea, admiring Dorothy's flowers and listening to the birds sing. We knew the time was upon us when I would leave. The question of would I ever return hung over both of us, like a cloud.

Chapter Thirty-Four
Home

I took the bus to Liverpool where I would board the *Empress of Canada*. How appropriate, seeing as how I was returning to Canada. Was it really 40 years ago I left for Canada? However, this time it was from a different port and under different circumstances. And this time I wouldn't be sea sick. Thank heavens for those pills. I'd be able to enjoy the voyage.

I stared out the bus window at the passing landscape without really seeing it. Too many thoughts raced through my head. It was a long bus ride, ten hours, so I had a lot of time to think.

I couldn't believe this country. It was so beautiful, so green, so flourishing. Flowers bloomed with so little tending. Some times I thought I could live here but then I remembered our children and grandchildren in Canada, and I knew I had to go back.

At the same time, England seemed so backwards compared to Canada. It wasn't the country of my childhood, but then I was only a child with no knowledge of the world. I didn't remember filthy shops or rude shopkeepers or abysmal service. I didn't remember so little food in the shops. How could the country that once ruled the world, that once had an empire on which the sun never set, have fallen on such desperate times? Was it really all a result of the war?

The worst of it was, everyone seemed to accept all that without question. They seem to think that nothing would change. That nothing *could* change. Better to sit with what we have than take a chance on the unknown, seemed to be their philosophy. Perhaps this was the result of surviving the terror and destruction of two world wars, of not knowing what the outcome would be. It was so very different from Canada.

I had longed to return to England, to my home, but instead I discovered that England was no longer my home. I belonged in Canada. I had become Canadian not only in name but also in outlook. Perhaps Cale was right when he said that England held nothing for him. It seemed to hold nothing for me other than my sisters and their families. And roses.

I boarded the *Empress of Canada* the mid-afternoon of July 22. The attendant carried my bags to my room, C-22, first class this time and no squabbling crying children to mind. I unpacked and then went on deck as we pulled away from the quay and sailed into the Irish Sea. Once again, like 40 years ago, I stood and watched England fade into the distance. When it disappeared over the horizon, I turned my face to the west.

I was going back to Canada. To Assiniboia and to Cale. To the children and grandchildren.

I was going home.

Historical Notes and Acknowledgements

There's more to one's life than dates and places. A person has character that can be discerned only by the way in which that person meets and overcomes challenges, successes, failures, and worries. This story, which is partly fact and partly fiction, is my attempt to put flesh on the skeleton of dates and places that genealogical research and archival documents tell, to get to know Mary Louisa Higham, née Appleton, the grandmother I never really knew.

Grandma Higham passed away at the end of September, 1955, shortly before my eighth birthday, so she is only a hazy figure in my memory. Fortunately, my mother, aunts and uncles all have (or had) vivid memories of her and her character. I am grateful to all of them – Aunt Marjorie, Uncle Bob, Uncle John, Maisie (my mother), Aunt Betty and Uncle George – for being so willing to share. Uncles John and George, in particular, suffered my many questions with graciousness and the typical Higham humour. Uncle John's book about his service as a World War II Bomber Command pilot was invaluable. Through some amazing stroke of luck, my mother found and kept the letters that Mary wrote when she returned to England in 1952; she also found and saved a few other, older letters. I owe a deep debt of gratitude to them all, both for the help they given and for being such wonderful relatives.

My cousins shared stories, photographs and documents. Linda Chaney (Aunt Marjorie's daughter) gave me letters and other documents her mother had saved; she also sent me a photograph of the amethyst pendant she inherited from Great Aunt Maude via her mother Marjorie. Aunt Betty's children – Louise Vajdek, Barbara Spencer, David Brooks and the late Fred Brooks – also shared their family resources. David Higham (Uncle George's younger son) video-taped Aunt Marjorie and Aunt Betty in the 1990s. What a joy to hear their voices again. Kathy Knox, Uncle Bob's daughter, obtained her parents' marriage certificate, thereby determining when and where her parents were married.

Marjorie Hamilton, Great Aunt Bessie's granddaughter, provided photographs including one of Great Aunt Amelia in Australia (Sidney?) probably taken in the 1950s. It's the only photograph I have seen of her, and she definitely looks like an Appleton.

Courtesy of Ancestry's far-flung web, I found two second cousins in England: Janet Hammond, the granddaughter of George Appleton (Mary's only brother), living in St. Ives, Cornwall; and Kim Sparling, the granddaughter of Mary (née Higham) Dale, one of Caleb's younger sisters, living in Upavon, Pewsey, Wiltshire. Both shared photographs, stories and interesting tidbits about my grandparents, their siblings and their lives. Thanks to Kim's photographs, I have seen Len and Flo standing in front of the Wheatsheaf Inn (it is now only a residence), Len's car (a Morris 8, so identified by members of the Glossop Vehicle Enthusiasts Club) of which he was so proud, and the farm at Keystown that Caleb rented for a year or so about 1917. Kim also replaced my Canadian terms with correct English ones.

After listening to all these stories, I have come to one conclusion – being a rebel is encoded in both the Higham and Appleton genomes. Consider the evidence: George David flouted his father by returning to England from New Zealand. Mary defied her parents by leaving for Canada, and then bilked her father out of the fare to bring Bessie to Canada (that is a true story!). Dorothy married in secret and then lived as a "spinster" until she and Harold Kerswell could be publicly married. John Edwin abandoned his wife and child to live in Canada. All our respective aunts, uncles and parents are well-known to be jokesters, pranksters and, yes, even curmudgeons, and those characteristics reside in many of my cousins, some more so than others. I am not saying which ones.

I have not been able to go to England while writing this story, but courtesy of Google Maps, I have (virtually) "walked" the streets of Feock, Regent Square in Penzance, Coinagehall Road in Helston (Mr. Oxenham's draper's shop is still a draper's shop, and the Angel Inn still exists), Strete and Cambourne, all in Cornwall; and Bodicote, Banbury and Adderbury in Oxfordshire. I've seen Park Brawse in Landewednack where Great Grandfather Dr. George Appleton lived, and peered into what is left of Grange Farm (only the great stone barn, now a residence).

The inspiration to write Grandma Higham's story arose from a course with the macabre title of *Raising the Dead: Harvesting Historical Fiction from Your Family Tree*, offered by the Alexandra Writing Centre, Calgary, AB. My thanks to Carolyn Pogue, the instructor, for encouraging me to write Grandma Higham's story.

This story is based on fact, but I have had to fill in the gaps with a lot of suppositions, assumptions, and best guesses. For example, no one knows how Mary and Caleb met; however, according to their wedding certificate they both lived at Belbeck, and they remained life-long friends with Will and Emeline Grigg, so why couldn't they have worked for the same farm family? As for the letters, most of them are figments of my imagination, but the following are excerpts from existing letters: Maude's two letters to Mary, and Dorothy's letter to Marjorie in Chapter 22; Mary's letter to Marjorie just before she married in Chapter 29; Sister Bernardo's letter in Chapter 30; and all of Mary's letters to Maisie and Cale in Chapters 31 to 33.

Bibliography

On-line Sources

Ancestry.ca

Cornishman; *Cornish Telegraph*; *Cornubian and Redruth Times*; *Banbury Advertiser*; *Banbury Guardian*; Find My Past, https://search.findmypast.com/search/british-newspapers

Regina Leader, 1914. Newspapers.com, https://www.newspapers.com/paper/the-leader-post/11033/

Henderson's Directory for Regina: 1913, 1914, 1915; http://peel.library.ualberta.ca/index.htm

Henderson's Directory for Moose Jaw, 1914, 1915. http://peel.library.ualberta.ca/index.htm

The Strathmore Standard, 1914. http://peel.library.ualberta.ca/newspapers/SMS/

Keystown Saskatchewan. 2011. https://www.youtube.com/watch?v=JKcJxLcxUm4

Boharm, Saskatchewan. 2011. https://www.youtube.com/watch?v=-58XE6GVCeE

The Official Guide of the Railways and Steam Navigation Lines of the United States, Porto [sic] Rico, Canada, Mexico and Cuba. 1906. The American Association of General Passenger and Ticket Agents. https://babel.hathitrust.org/cgi/pt?id=mdp.39015076287336&view=1up&seq=7

Minutes of the Committee of Council on Education; Correspondence, Financial Statements, etc. 1852-53. London, Her Majesty's Stationery Office. https://books.google.ca/books?id=9C0GAAAAQAAJ&pg=PA580&lpg=PA580&dq=Cornwall+Central+School,+truro+cornwall&source=bl&ots=nuFz7TslZJ&sig=093Ac1JvtNQpfTidxISlGw409Zs&hl=en&sa=X&ved=0ahUKEwj15tK

GoMTOAhVP3GMKHc0gCwYQ6AEINjAE#v=onepage&q=Cornwall%20Central%20School%2C%20truro%20cornwall&f=false

Books:

Caron History Book Committee (editors). 1982. *From Buffalo Trails to Blacktop: A history of the R.N. of Caron #162*

Rita S. Kranides. 1979. *The Victorian Spinster and Colonial Emigration: Contested Subjects*. St. Marten's Press. New York.

D. Blake McDouball. 2009. *I heard a Meadowlark*. Edmonton, AB

John Higham. nd. *A Memoir*. Self-published.

Limerick Historical Society. 1982. *Prairie Trails and Pioneer Tales: R.M. of Stonehenge #73*

Bill McKee and Georgeen Klasen. 1983. *Trail of Iron: The CPR and the Birth of the West, 1880 - 1930*. Glenbow Alberta Institute, Douglas & McIntyre Ltd.

Angelina Parker. 1876. *A Glossary of Words Used in Oxfordshire [with]*. Oxford University.

Pense Historical Society. 1987. *Pense Community 1882 to 1982*.

A.G. Street. 1932. *Farmer's Glory*. Faber and Faber

Joan Thirsk (editor). 2000. *The Agrarian History of England and Wales, Vol. 7, 1850 – 1914, Part 1*. Cambridge University Press.

Tuxford Heritage Committee (editors). 1977. *Heritage of the Wheatlands*.

Phyllis (Ray) Zado (editor). 1980. *Furrows and Faith*. Lake Johnson – Sutton Historical Society.

Margaret G. Hanna is a farmer's daughter, born and raised in Saskatchewan, and is still a Saskatchewanian at heart. After a long and distinguished career as an archaeologist and curator at the Royal Saskatchewan Museum, Regina, she married and moved to Airdrie, Alberta. She now uses her research skills to explore family and prairie history. She is a member of the Writers' Guild of Alberta, Women Writing the West, Alexandria Writers' Centre and the Airdrie Writers' Group.

Hanna is the author of the acclaimed *"Our Bull's Loose in Town!" Tales from the Homestead*, the story of her paternal grandparents. Follow her on *A Prairie Perspective* at www.margaretghanna.wordpress.com.

www.ingramcontent.com/pod-product-compliance
Lightning Source LLC
Chambersburg PA
CBHW051419290426
44109CB00016B/1363